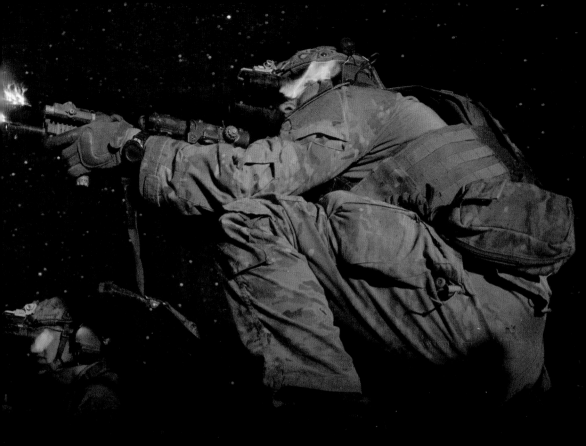

US SPECIAL OPS

THE HISTORY, WEAPONS, AND MISSIONS OF ELITE MILITARY FORCES

Quarto is the authority on a wide range of topics.

Quarto educates, entertains and enriches the lives of our readers—enthusiasts and lovers of hands-on living.

www.quartoknows.com

© 2016 Quarto Publishing Group USA Inc.
Text © 2016 Fred Pushies

First published in 2016 by Voyageur Press, an imprint of Quarto Publishing Group USA Inc., 400 First Avenue North, Suite 400, Minneapolis, MN 55401 USA. Telephone: (612) 344-8100 Fax: (612) 344-8692

quartoknows.com
Visit our blogs at quartoknows.com

Voyageur Press titles are also available at discounts in bulk quantity for industrial or sales-promotional use. For details contact the Special Sales Manager at Quarto Publishing Group USA Inc., 400 First Avenue North, Suite 400, Minneapolis, MN 55401 USA.

10 9 8 7 6 5 4 3 2 1

ISBN: 978-0-7603-4986-1

Library of Congress Cataloging-in-Publication Data

Names: Pushies, Fred J., 1952- author.
Title: US special ops : the history, weapons, and missions of elite military
   forces / Fred Pushies.
Description: Minneapolis, MN : Voyageur Press, [2016] | Includes index.
Identifiers: LCCN 2015043307 | ISBN 9780760349861 (sc)
Subjects: LCSH: Special operations (Military science)--United States. |
   Special forces (Military science)--United States.
Classification: LCC UA34.S64 P8722 2016 | DDC 356/.160973--dc23
LC record available at http://lccn.loc.gov/2015043307

Acquiring Editor: Dennis Pernu
Project Manager: Madeleine Vasaly
Art Director: James Kegley
Cover Designer: Korab Design
Layout: Simon Larkin

On the front cover: Navy SEALs demonstrate winter warfare capabilities at Mammoth Lakes, California, in 2014. *US Navy photo by Visual Information Specialist Chris Desmond*

On the back cover: A US Army Special Forces soldier scans the horizon in Shah Wali Kot District, Kandahar Province, Afghanistan, during a clearing operation in 2011. *US Army photo by Staff Sgt. Jeremy D. Crisp*

On the frontis: A MARSOC Marine navigates through the woods, armed with an M4A1 Carbine. *US Marine Corps photo by Lance Cpl. Thomas W. Provost*

On the title pages: US Army Rangers assigned to 2nd Battalion, 75th Ranger Regiment, fire at an enemy bunker during training at Camp Roberts, California, in 2014. *US Army photo by Spc. Steven Hitchcock*

Printed in China

Contents

Dedication

To the Warriors—from the beginning to the upcoming.

Acknowledgments

First, I thank the Almighty God, author of liberty and freedom. Also: Victor Di Cosola, president/CEO, and Charles Lasky, director of operations, Tactical Night Vision Company; Mark Wiggins, Col. Arthur D. Simons Center for the Study of Interagency Cooperation and MHW Public Relations and Communications; Darren Proctor and Dan Foukes; David Gardiner, *Stars and Stripes*; Angela Harrell, Heckler and Koch; Caroline Simms, NRA Museum; Dan Dudley, Rogers' Rangers Inc; Pam Pagac in memory of Joe Pagac, paramarine; Travis Haley and Jon Chang, Haley Strategic Partners; Claudio Castro and Deirdre Brinlee, S. O. Tech; John Bailey, EOTech; Alan Baribeau, Naval Sea Systems Command; Kevin Rowlee, SAFE Boats International; Charles Pinck, OSS Society; Bill Becker, 801st/492nd Bombardment Group, "the Carpetbaggers"; Robert E. Passanisi, Merrill's Marauders Association; Roxanne Merritt, curator, John F. Kennedy Special Warfare Museum; Robert "Bob" Stoner, GMCM (SW) (Ret.); James Gray; Gene Mappin, HA(L)-5; Ruth McSween, curator, National Navy SEAL Museum and Memorial; Kristina DeMilt, FN America; Andrew E. Woods, McCormick Research Center; Edward Lynch; Allan Bierlein, Force Recon Association; Erasmo "Doc" Riojas; Al O'Canas; Lance Strahl and Todd Seigmund, Accuracy International; Dennis Pernu, Voyageur Press; and my family for their support.

Preface

When they hear the term "special forces," many people think of the various elite units of the US military, including the Navy SEALs, the Army Rangers, and the Green Berets. In fact, in this context "special forces" refers exclusively to the US Army Special Forces, historically known as the Green Berets. The broader collection of various army, navy, marine, and air force commandos (Rangers, SEALs, Green Berets, and so on) is defined as Special Operations Forces (SOF), which comes under the command and control of the US Special Operations Command (SOCOM).

This book presents details about SOF operators and their equipment, tactics, techniques, and procedures. Before going any further, remember: when a man stands apart from his compatriots in combat, it's not because of the weapon he carries, the knife he has slung on his belt, or any high-tech gadget or gizmo in his tactical vest or pack—these are mere tools in his hands. What sets a member of the US Special Operations Forces apart is the fire in their gut, the tenacity of their spirit, and the certainty instilled into their warrior soul, mission after mission. They are successful because they *do* sweat the small stuff. Taken as individuals, each is the best of the best; as part of a team, they are unrelenting and invincible.

Today, more than ever, the words of Gen. Douglas MacArthur apply to SOF units:

> Your mission remains fixed, determined, inviolable—it is to win our wars. Everything else in your professional career is but a corollary to this vital dedication. All other public purposes, all other public projects, all other public needs, great or small, will find others for their accomplishment; but you are the ones who are trained to fight; yours is the profession of arms—the will to win, the sure knowledge that in war there is no substitute for victory.

Whether you consider the army's Special Forces, Rangers, and Night Stalkers; the navy's SEALs; the marines of MARSOC; or the Air Force's Special Operations Squadrons and Special Tactics Squadrons, US Special Operations Forces are the tip of the spear of America's military—they are the first in and the last out. Once, when there was a need for saber rattling, the call went out to "Send in the marines!" Today, you don't have to send in the Special Operations Forces—most likely, they're already there!

A Note about the NRA Museums

Since 1935, the NRA Museums collection has become one of the world's finest dedicated to firearms. Now housed in three locations, the NRA Museums offer a glimpse into the firearms that built our nation, helped forge our freedom, and captured our imagination.

The National Firearms Museum, located at the NRA Headquarters in Fairfax, Virginia, details and examines the nearly seven-hundred-year history of firearms with a special emphasis on firearms, freedom, and the American experience. The National Sporting Arms Museum, at the Bass Pro Shops in Springfield, Missouri, explores and exhibits the historical development of hunting arms in America from the earliest explorers to the modern day, with a focus on hunting, conservation, and freedom. The Frank Brownell Museum of the Southwest, at the NRA Whittington Center in Raton, New Mexico, is a jewel-box museum with two hundred guns, recounting the region's history from the earliest Native American inhabitants through early Spanish exploration, the Civil War, and the Old West.

For more information on the NRA Museums and hours, visit www.nramuseum.org.

Major Robert Rogers

Robert Rogers (November 7, 1731–May 18, 1795) was an American colonial frontiersman and skilled woodsman. During the French and Indian War, Rogers assembled and commanded Rogers's Rangers, a band of mountain men skilled in fieldcraft, wilderness skills, and shooting. Rogers trained his Rangers to be a rapidly deployable light infantry force for reconnaissance and direct raids against the enemy.

The Rangers fought for the British, using the techniques and tactics of the American Indians. They conducted long-range reconnaissance patrols across difficult terrain in poor weather conditions that would have hampered local militias in special operations raids against distant French targets. Major Rogers did not invent unconventional warfare, but he was able to exploit tactics and establish them in Ranger doctrine; his "Rules for Ranging" comprise twenty-eight tenets for commanding such units.

A simplified set of the rules is still taught to US Army Rangers, who today claim Rogers as their founder. Rogers's "Standing Orders" are still quoted on the first page of the US Army *Ranger Handbook*. The first rule? "Don't forget nothing."

MAJOR ROBERT ROGERS,
Commander in Chief of the INDIANS in the Back Settlements of AMERICA.
Published as the Act directs Oct'r 1776, by The' Hunt

"Brown Bess" Carbine

While they were winning fame during the French and Indian War, the primary weapon of choice for Rogers's Rangers was the "Brown Bess."

The Long Land Pattern musket was the British infantryman's basic arm from about 1740 until the 1830s. A challenge to carry through the woods, the 1742 Long Pattern 1st Model musket was often cut down several inches, resulting in a Brown Bess carbine. The musket had a flintlock action and weighed 10.5 pounds. It fired a .75-caliber ball with an effective firing range of 50 to 100 yards.

Jäger Rifle

The standard rifle of Rogers's Rangers was the Brown Bess, but some in the band carried the German Jäger rifle, a flintlock, muzzle-loading musket with an average length of 45 inches. It weighed 9 pounds and was fitted with a 30-inch barrel. In most cases, individual Rangers used Jägers as their personal weapon, which meant each had a unique character. A trigger guard for improved grip or a raised cheek rest to help aim might be found on some examples of this rifle. The Jäger was an accurate rifle, though it took longer to load than the Brown Bess.

Tomahawk

The hatchet was a useful tool for fieldcraft and chopping wood. In the hands of Rogers's Rangers, this general purpose tool turned into a lethal weapon. Taking a lesson from American Indians, Rogers's men carried tomahawks along with their muskets. The wooden handle of the "hawk," as it was called, averaged 18 inches. One end of the head had a hardened spike, while the other had a chopping blade that was to be kept honed at all times.

The hawk was a formidable weapon. It could be thrown with deadly precision and, in hand-to-hand combat, gave the Ranger an extended reach. This weapon could be used to slash at the enemy's torso, neck, or extremities, while the sharpened point could be used to puncture a skull and the pommel (handle end) could be modified to deliver a fatal blow. The crook of the hatchet could be used to hook and restrain an attacker's arm.

The tomahawk was hands-down an integral weapon in Rogers's Rangers' mobile arsenal. In fact, tactical tomahawks have found their way into the kits of many special-ops soldiers today.

General Francis Marion, the "Swamp Fox"

Born and raised in South Carolina, Francis Marion fought the Cherokee in 1760 as a lieutenant in the state's militia. During the Cherokee War, Marion learned Cherokee fighting techniques, including the tactic of initiating surprise attacks and then quickly fading away.

During the Revolutionary War, Marion received a commission as captain in the Continental Army and took up arms in the fight for freedom. He brought guerrilla war tactics against the British, establishing his position in the Special Forces lineage. When Charleston fell to the British, General Marion escaped capture and headed into the South Carolina swamps, where he established a base camp and, with 150 men, formed what would become known as Marion's Brigade. As the war progressed, the brigade employed unconventional warfare tactics against the British, ambushing troops, attacking supply lines, and performing hit-and-run raids. Try as they might, the British could not follow these guerrillas into the swamp, earning Marion his famous nickname.

Flintlock Pistol

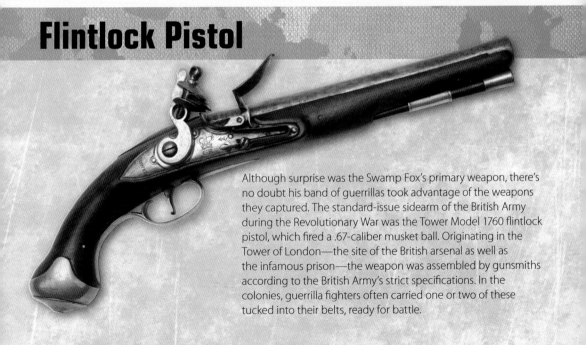

Although surprise was the Swamp Fox's primary weapon, there's no doubt his band of guerrillas took advantage of the weapons they captured. The standard-issue sidearm of the British Army during the Revolutionary War was the Tower Model 1760 flintlock pistol, which fired a .67-caliber musket ball. Originating in the Tower of London—the site of the British arsenal as well as the infamous prison—the weapon was assembled by gunsmiths according to the British Army's strict specifications. In the colonies, guerrilla fighters often carried one or two of these tucked into their belts, ready for battle.

Colonel John Singleton Mosby, "the Gray Ghost"

Mosby's Rangers were one of the most celebrated units to practice unconventional warfare during the American Civil War. Under the command of Colonel John Singleton Mosby of Virginia, these Confederate guerillas operated behind the Union lines just south of the Potomac. Colonel Mosby began with a three-man scout element in 1862; by 1865, his Rangers had evolved into a force of eight guerilla companies.

A firm believer in reconnaissance, aggressive action, and surprise attacks, Colonel Mosby and his Rangers cut off Union communications and supply lines, sabotaged railroads, and raided base camps behind the enemy lines. His stealth and uncanny ability to avoid capture earned the colonel his nickname. Mosby's Rangers were well trained and well disciplined, setting a standard for future unconventional forces to follow.

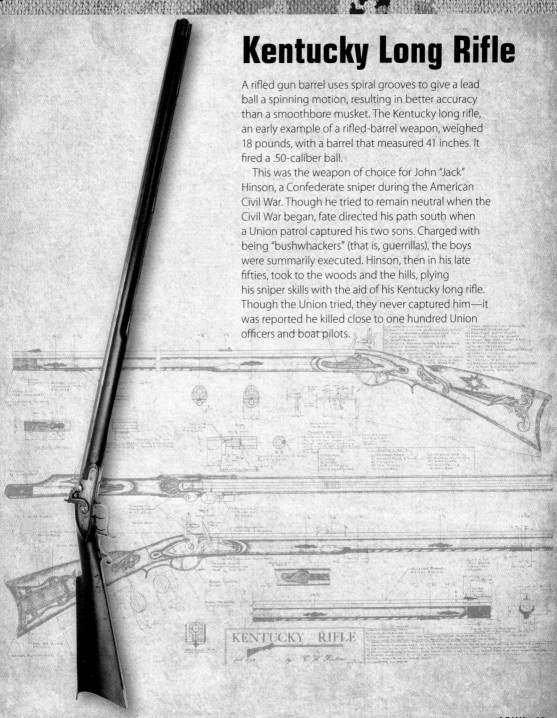

Kentucky Long Rifle

A rifled gun barrel uses spiral grooves to give a lead ball a spinning motion, resulting in better accuracy than a smoothbore musket. The Kentucky long rifle, an early example of a rifled-barrel weapon, weighed 18 pounds, with a barrel that measured 41 inches. It fired a .50-caliber ball.

This was the weapon of choice for John "Jack" Hinson, a Confederate sniper during the American Civil War. Though he tried to remain neutral when the Civil War began, fate directed his path south when a Union patrol captured his two sons. Charged with being "bushwhackers" (that is, guerrillas), the boys were summarily executed. Hinson, then in his late fifties, took to the woods and the hills, plying his sniper skills with the aid of his Kentucky long rifle. Though the Union tried, they never captured him—it was reported he killed close to one hundred Union officers and boat pilots.

KENTUCKY RIFLE

Sharps Carbine

The Sharps carbine was a large-bore, single-shot gun firing a .52-caliber projectile. Known for its long-range accuracy, it was a favorite among both Union and Confederate cavalry units; prior to the Civil War, close to two thousand Sharps were purchased for Georgia troops. During the war, most of the Sharps used by Confederate soldiers had been captured in battle.

The Sharps employed a falling-block action in conjunction with a percussion cap. The carbine's primer feed was unique: each time the trigger was pulled and the hammer fell, a new primer fed from a stack, which made the gun easier to fire on the move. It weighed 9.5 pounds and had a range of 500 to 1,000 yards.

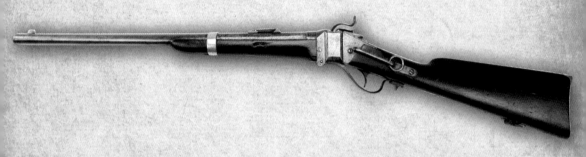

Army Model 1860 Pistol

There's a saying that "God created all men, but Sam Colt made them equal." In 1836, Colt patented a firearm with a revolving cylinder capable of holding five or six bullets. The resulting Colt Army Model 1860 was the major sidearm for Union troops during the Civil War. It weighed 2 pounds and carried six .44-caliber paper-wrapped cartridges in its cylinder; the bullet could be either a round lead ball or a conical projectile. The percussion cap contained fulminate of mercury, which provided a substantial explosion on impact. When ignited by a copper percussion cap, the round fired at a rate of approximately 900 feet per second.

Colonel William Darby

With America's entrance into World War II, the term "Army Rangers" became part of military history. Major General Lucian K. Truscott Jr. submitted the idea for an American unit similar to the British commandos to Gen. George Marshall. General Truscott and Maj. Gen. Russell P. Hartle, who commanded US Army forces in Northern Ireland, received a reply from the War Department authorizing the formation of the special unit.

Hartle chose his aide-de-camp, Capt. William O. Darby, to recruit, select, and organize the newly formed unit. Captain Darby, a West Point graduate, was considered intelligent and enthusiastic, and he had gained the confidence of his superiors and the loyalty of his men. Promoted to major, he began by interviewing volunteers from the 1st Armored Division, the 34th Infantry Division, and other units stationed in Northern Ireland. He had completed selection for his unit in June 1942, a few weeks after receiving his assignment.

While General Truscott liked the term "commando," he felt the term was British and believed the new unit should adopt a name from American history. In keeping with the United States' own legacy of unconventional warfare roles, the group chose the name that had been used by Major Rogers during the Revolutionary War (see page 8)—thus, we have the US Army Rangers.

Darby's Rangers

Activated on June 19, 1942, the 1st US Army Ranger Battalion served under the command of Major Darby. The unit became known as Darby's Rangers, harking back to its Revolutionary War namesake, Rogers's Rangers.

Darby and his Rangers spent three months at the Commando Training Centre at Achnacarry, Scotland, where, under the tutelage of combat-seasoned British commandos, they learned the basics of unconventional warfare. Out of the six hundred men who began the training, five hundred finished. The men fought throughout Western Europe during World War II, but they achieved their greatest recognition on D-Day, when they scaled the cliffs of Pointe du Hoc as part of the Allied invasion of Normandy.

Brigadier General Frank Merrill

At the start of World War II, Maj. Frank Merrill, West Point class of 1929, served on the staff of Gen. Douglas MacArthur. In November 1943, he gained the rank of brigadier general, becoming the youngest US Army general since the Civil War. In the same year, Merrill was appointed to take command of a new all-volunteer US Army unit that would perform long-range patrols and missions behind Japanese lines. Operating under Gen. Joseph Stilwell, Merrill personally oversaw the training and deployment of the three battalions, officially named the 5307th Composite Unit (Provisional). (The term "Provisional" meant that the unit was drawn together for special missions and would disband afterward.) The 5307th was thus one of America's first Special Missions Units (SMU).

General Joseph Stilwell

While commander of Fort Benning, Georgia, Gen. Joseph Stilwell's harsh performance evaluations during a field training exercise won him the nickname "Vinegar Joe." A sign reportedly hanging in his office gave insight into his character: it featured the mock-Latin phrase *Illegitimi non carborundum*, meaning "Don't let the bastards grind you down!"

This attitude carried over into his leadership style. A 1904 graduate of West Point, General Stilwell was a no-nonsense commander with very little use for vain or ceremonial displays. He was a soldier; his trademark was a well-worn US Army campaign hat and sterile uniform sans rank or insignia. In lieu of a sidearm, his preference was to carry a Model 1903 Springfield rifle.

General Stilwell's claim to fame was his activity in the China-Burma-India theater during World War II, where he served under acting Vice Adm. Lord Louis Mountbatten. One of the units in his command was the 5037th Composite Unit (Provisional) commanded by Brig. Gen. Merrill. Stilwell ordered Merrill's men to conduct long-range missions behind enemy lines.

Stilwell and Maj. Gen. Curtis E. LeMay at a B-29 base in China, 1944

Merrill's Marauders

While Darby's Rangers and the 1st Special Service Force, better known as the Devil's Brigade (see page 20), were conducting their operations in the Europe, another group of men was drafting a chapter in the journal of unconventional warfare in the Pacific. Here, the 5307th Composite Unit (Provisional), under the leadership of Brigadier General Merrill, brought the war to the Japanese in the jungles of Burma.

Organized in 1943, this unit of three thousand volunteers was tasked with the mission of long-range infiltration behind the Japanese lines, with the objective of destroying the enemy's "jugular" (i.e., their communications and supply lines). Furthermore, the men were to harass and attack the Japanese at will. This unit became known as Merrill's Marauders.

One of the Marauders' greatest undertakings was the seizure of the Myitkyina Airfield in present-day Myanmar. Merrill and his men infiltrated through the hot, humid, insect- and disease-ridden jungle—and that was the easy part. These unconventional warriors were constantly outnumbered by the enemy, and support was almost nonexistent. The actions of Merrill's Marauders are legendary and inspirational even by today's standards.

M1 Garand

Gen. George S. Patton called the M1 Garand rifle "the greatest battle implement ever devised." From the hedgerows of Normandy to the beaches of the Pacific islands, the M1 was the standard-issue rifle for US infantryman during World War II. It was 43 inches long and weighed in at 9.5 pounds. Air-cooled, gas-operated, and semiautomatic, the M1 was chambered for the .30-06 Springfield rifle cartridge and had a range of 500 yards, with a rate of fire of forty to fifty rounds per minute. Eight of these rounds were loaded into a clip (yes, a clip . . . not a magazine). Loading the M1, the soldier pulled back the bolt, inserted the clip, and released the bolt. Occasionally, the rifleman would experience a malady called "M1 thumb," which occurred when the shooter didn't get his thumb out of the way of the bolt before it slammed home, leaving a telltale mark.

M1 Carbine

The M1 Carbine was a .30-caliber infantry rifle that provided a lightweight alternative to the heavier M1 Garand. It provided the soldier with a defensive weapon with more stopping power than a pistol and more accuracy than a submachine gun. The carbine was normally issued to officers and armor and artillery crews. Loaded with a fifteen-round magazine, it weighed close to 6 pounds. Later versions were fitted with a folding stock to give paratroopers a lighter and more compact infantry weapon.

During World War II, every branch of the US military used the M1 carbine. Afterward, the carbine went into battle with American armed forces in Korea and again during the Vietnam War, predominantly with US Army Special Forces advisors.

Fairbairn–Sykes Fighting Knife

The Fairbairn–Sykes fighting knife, a double-edged fighting knife similar to a dagger, was the creation of William Fairbairn and Eric Sykes and manufactured by Wilkinson Sword. Though strongly associated with the British commandos (it was often called the "commando knife"), it was also popular with Office of Strategic Services (OSS) operators and Marine Raiders. The overall length of the Fairbairn–Sykes knife was 11.5 inches. Designed exclusively for surprise attack, its trim 7-inch blade would easily penetrate an enemy's ribcage while the handle provided a secure grip.

Colonel Robert T. Frederick of the Devil's Brigade (1st Special Service Force) is credited with a similar weapon, the V-42 stiletto, itself a derivation of the Fairbairn–Sykes design. The V-42 was manufactured by W. R. Case and Sons Cutlery in the mid-1940s.

1st Special Service Force, "the Devil's Brigade"

Established at Fort William Henry Harrison, Montana, on July 9, 1942, as a unit specially trained to fight in winter conditions, the 1st Special Service Force (1st SSF) featured three battalion-size units of unconventional-warfare troops comprising both American and Canadian soldiers under the command of Col. Robert T. Frederick.

The 1st Special Service Force saw combat against the Japanese in the Aleutian Islands and against the Germans in Italy and France. Allegedly, the unit got its nickname in Europe: the story goes that the captured diary of a German officer contained a description of *die schwarzen Teufeln*—"the black devils." Soldiers of the 1st SSF came to be known as members of the Devil's Brigade.

Colonel Robert T. Frederick

The 1st Special Service Force (1st SSF) sought out soldiers from various units; in some cases, commanders eagerly "volunteered" some of their more troublesome soldiers and sent them out to Montana. If men arrived less than highly motivated, Col. Robert Frederick saw they were weeded out; in fact, one could argue Frederick was responsible for instituting the first Special Forces Assessment and Selection (SFAS). According to Gordon Sims, president of the 1st Special Service Force Association, "Many people think the American soldiers were roughnecks and yardbirds. The truth was, some of these men were more at home in the field then in garrison. What regular army commanders saw as troublesome actually turned out to be some of the best operators."

Frederick formulated a training schedule for his men that stressed physical conditioning, hand-to-hand combat, weapons training, demolitions, infantry tactics, and mountain work. The soldiers of the 1st SSF were also airborne trained and schooled in skiing and winter operations. Their specialty was close-quarter combat against numerically superior forces.

Alamo Scouts

This unit of highly skilled soldiers was created by Lt. Gen. Walter Krueger, commander of the US Sixth Army. Those who volunteered for assignment to this force went through six weeks of arduous training and field exercises encompassing land navigation, hand-to-hand combat, weapons, communications, survival, small-boat operations, and advance patrol techniques. Graduates of the training were selected to become Alamo Scouts and formed into small teams, each usually consisting of one officer and six or seven enlisted men.

These teams infiltrated numerous Japanese-held islands throughout the South Pacific, inserting from PT boats and rubber rafts. While their primary mission was originally reconnaissance, one of their foremost achievements took place when a group of Scouts led US Rangers and Filipino guerrillas in an attack on a Japanese prison camp at Cabanatuan, freeing all 511 Allied prisoners. Never numbering more than seventy men, the Alamo Scouts conducted more than a hundred missions without the loss of a single soldier.

Colonel Aaron Bank

Colonel Bank is known as the "father of the US Army Special Forces," being the founder and first commander of this unconventional fighting force. Born November 23, 1902, he traveled extensively in Europe prior to the outbreak of World War II, becoming fluent in German and French. He enlisted in the army in 1942 and, after completing Officer Candidate School (OCS), became a member of the OSS's Special Operations (SO) Branch. During the war, he led a Jedburgh team (see page 169) in parachuting into France to work with the Maquis, the guerilla fighters of the French Resistance.

Bank was also chosen to be the commanding officer for Operation Iron Cross, whose mission was to snatch Adolph Hitler from his "Eagle's Nest" retreat in the Bavarian Alps. The men were kitted out with German uniforms and weapons, and all the training was conducted in German. In the end, the mission was aborted; Bank and his men got the word as they were headed across the runway to a waiting C-47 transport.

After the war, Bank still saw a need for an OSS SO type of unit—men to fight the enemy behind their own lines. In June 1952, this concept was realized and he became the first commander of the US Army Special Forces as the unit was activated.

US Army Special Forces

On June 19, 1952, the 10th Special Forces Group (Airborne) was activated at Fort Bragg, North Carolina; it became the nucleus of the Special Warfare Center, later renamed the John F. Kennedy Special Warfare Center and School. In 1953, the group was split, with half of the unit sent to Bad Tölz, Germany. The remaining half would form the 77th Special Forces Group, which remained at Fort Bragg and was activated on September 25, 1953.

The army had created the US Special Forces for the purpose of waging unconventional warfare; units would operate behind enemy lines in the event of a Soviet invasion of Europe. As this fledgling unit was coming to its own, it attracted many World War II veterans from the OSS, Rangers, and paratrooper forces, as well as many foreign nationals.

The primary operational component of Special Forces is the Special Forces Operational Detachment A, also known as an "A Detachment," "A-Team," or "ODA." The team consists of twelve Special Forces soldiers—two officers and ten sergeants—all of whom are cross-trained in weapons, demolitions, medical, communications, and operations and intelligence. The A-Team is almost unlimited in its capabilities to operate in hostile or denied areas and can infiltrate and exfiltrate their area of operations by air, land, or sea (see pages 305–306).

The Siege of Plei Me

During the Vietnam War, Special Forces A-Teams fought the Communist insurgency from camps scattered throughout South Vietnam. Their primary mission was to advise and assist in the training of paramilitary forces recruited in that area, and the Special Forces training program generally concentrated on strike-force troops. The teams were "officially" there as advisors to the Vietnamese special forces; these in turn commanded the Civilian Irregular Defense Group (CIDG), which was composed of local indigenous personnel. From 1961 to 1965, over eighty CIDG camps were established, many built from the ground up right in the middle of Viet Cong (VC) territory.

One of these camps, Plei Me, was 215 miles north of Saigon in the central highlands, less than 20 miles from border of Cambodia. Shortly after midnight on October 19, 1965, Plei Me was attacked by a company of North Vietnamese Army (NVA) regulars. At the time of the attack, the camp was defended by ten Americans, fourteen South Vietnamese, and approximately three hundred Montagnards. Constant airstrikes, resupply sorties, and reinforcements kept the camp from falling. The attack on this isolated Special Force outpost of freedom would initiate a change in America's involvement in the war in Southeast Asia.

The Green Berets, Yarborough, and JFK

President Theodore Roosevelt's foreign policy was to "speak softly, and carry a big stick." Half a century after his presidency—on October 12, 1961, as the United States plunged headlong into the Cold War—President John F. Kennedy visited Fort Bragg, North Carolina, the home of the airborne forces, to get a look at America's "big stick." At the pointed end of that stick were some soldiers wearing funny green hats, who displayed their capabilities, weapons, and techniques for the president. These men, commanded by Brig. Gen. William P. Yarborough, were from the US Army Special Warfare Center, home of the US Army Special Forces.

President Kennedy affirmed his unfailing support for the Special Forces in an official White House memorandum to the army, dated April 11, 1962. This memo stated in part that the unit's singular headgear, which had also been worn by the British Commandos in World War II, was "again becoming a symbol of excellence, a badge of courage, a mark of distinction in the fight for freedom." He authorized the hats to be the official headgear for all US Army Special Forces members, and these unconventional warriors were known thereafter as the Green Berets.

Special Forces Aviation Company

An integral component of the US Army Special Warfare units was the Special Forces Aviation Company. In 1965, the Green Berets were given their own dedicated air assets, providing exclusive service to their missions. The 7th Special Force Group (Airborne) had a full-strength aviation company, and the 3rd and 6th Groups each had a reduced-strength aviation company.

The aviation company offered an assortment of aircraft earmarked for Special Forces missions. For example, the CV-2B Caribou was a versatile twin-engine, short-takeoff-and-lading (STOL) plane capable of inserting men and equipment into a unimproved landing field. The U-10 Helio Courier was a light single-engine plane used for reconnaissance, resupply, and psychological operations. The UH-1B Iroquois helicopter provided a swift means of recon, insertions, and extractions of SF teams. The UH-1B was also used for supply and support missions in areas inaccessible to fixed-wing aircraft and was armed with machine guns as well as 2.75-inch folding-fin aerial rockets.

MOH: Captain Roger Donlon

Roger Donlon, a member of the 7th Special Forces Group (Airborne), was deployed to the Republic of South Vietnam in the spring of 1964. He was in command of a twelve-man Special Forces A-Team (A-726) assigned to Camp Nam Dong, a few miles from the border of Laos. In addition to the Green Berets, Nam Dong was also home at the time to three hundred South Vietnamese irregulars and sixty Nung soldiers.

In the early hours of July 6, 1964, an enemy mortar round exploded on the roof of the mess hall. Captain Donlon, having just entered the building alter making his rounds of the camp, was knocked to the ground. In concert with the mortar attack, three Viet Cong (VC) sappers attempted to breach the camp's main gate. Captain Donlon immediately killed them, but another mortar round hit, knocking him down again. Then a third round came into the camp, severely wounding the young officer in the stomach and arm. He tore a piece from his jungle fatigues, stuffed the material into his stomach wound, and kept fighting. Braving enemy fire, he ran from position to position resupplying his men with ammunition. The battle raged on until daybreak of the next day, and it was later discovered that approximately nine hundred VC had attempted to enter the camp. Captain Donlon was the first Special Forces soldier to be awarded the Medal of Honor for his actions in the Vietnam War.

M16

As America's involvement in Southeast Asia increased during the Cold War, some saw the need for a newer weapon. Most combat veterans liked the heavier 7.62-millimeter rounds of the M14, but an argument ran that a lighter weapon would allow the solder to carry more ammunition. Enter the Armalite rifle (AR-15), designed by Eugene Stoner. In the summer of 1961, air force Gen. Curtis LeMay viewed a demonstration of the AR-15 and liked what he saw, leading to eighty thousand AR-15s being ordered for the US Air Force.

The AR-15 would soon evolve into the M16, and, as Special Forces teams headed off to Vietnam, they took the new plastic rifle with them. This would eventually replace the M14 as the US military's standard-issue assault rifle. A lightweight, 5.56-millimeter, air-cooled weapon with direct-impingement gas system operation and a rotating bolt, the M16 is made of a combination of steel, aluminum alloy, composite plastics, and polymer materials. In the weapon's early deployment, there were many malfunctions due to the military providing ball powder instead of the Improved Military Rifle (IMR) powder made for the M16. After this problem was worked out, the "little black rifle" would serve throughout the war; it remains the main battle rifle for the US military.

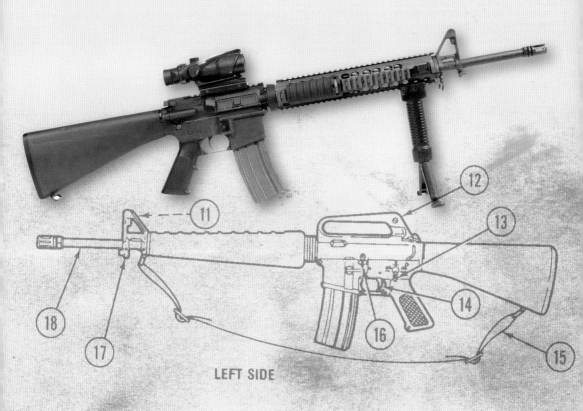

LEFT SIDE

Special Operations Group (SOG)

In February 1964, the commander of the Military Advisory Group, Vietnam (MACV), Gen. Paul D. Harkins, authorized the creation of the SOG. Officially, the acronym stood for Studies and Observation Group; unofficially, and more accurately, it stood for Special Operations Group. While SOG did engage members of the other services—Navy SEALs, Air Commandos, and even Marine Corps Force Reconnaissance— the majority of personnel came from the 5th Special Forces Group (Airborne).

The purpose of SOG was to conduct covert missions on "the other side of the fence." This meant insertion of teams into North Vietnam, Laos (codename Prairie Fire), and Cambodia (codename Daniel Boone). SOG missions could include, but were not limited to, guerrilla warfare, direct action, sabotage, psychological operations, E&E (escape and evade) nets, and other operations that are still classified.

SOG was broken down into three operational areas: Command and Control North (CCN), with Forward Operating Bases (FOBs) located in the area of Hue and operated in North Vietnam and Laos; Command and Control Central (CCC), with FOBs in Kontum, operating in Laos and northeastern Cambodia; and Command and Control South (CCS), with FOBs in Ban Me Thuot and Quan Loi, operating in Cambodia.

Swedish K Submachine Gun

While its official name was the Carl Gustaf M/45 submachine gun (SMG), in US service the 9×19 millimeter Parabellum/NATO submachine gun was simply known as the "Swedish K." Developed in 1944–1945 and manufactured at the Carl Gustafs Stads Gevärsfaktori factory in Eskilstuna, Sweden, the gun drew from and improved upon the designs of several German, British, and Soviet submachine guns.

The SMG had a blowback system with a cyclic rate of six hundred rounds per minute and weighed 9 pounds fully loaded. Its overall length was 32 inches, and, with the stock folded, it went down to 22 inches. Most M/45s were "sterile," meaning they were devoid of any markings. They could take a thirty-six-round, double-stack magazine, one of the benefits that made them popular with Navy SEALs, SOG teams, and CIA operatives.

Colt Automatic Rifle 15 (CAR-15)

"CAR-15" was a generic term used for shortened versions of the M16 assault rifle. Officially, the army called it the XM177, while the air force knew it as the GAU-5/A. In both incarnations, this submachine gun was a modified version of the standard-issue M16 assault rifle. Like the M16, it was a gas-operated weapon with select fire for semi- or full-automatic fire. It used the same 5.56-millimeter ammunition as the larger M16, with one difference: it was fielded with the coveted thirty-round magazine. The CAR-15 had a shortened 11.5-inch barrel with a new fiberglass handguard to better dissipate the heat, a telescopic stock, and several flash suppressors. The only difference between the XM177 and the GAU-5/A was the lack of the forward bolt assist on the latter. Once introduced on the battlefield, the compact XM177 soon reached the hands of SOG teams, long-range recon patrol troopers (LRRPs), and other elite units. The GAU-5/A was used by Combat Control Teams (CTT).

Colonel Arthur "Bull" Simons

After attending the ROTC at the University of Missouri, Arthur David Simons was commissioned as a second lieutenant in 1941. In 1943, then holding the rank of captain, Simons joined the ranks of the 6th Ranger Battalion, where he served as a company commander and battalion executive officer. He was no stranger to the perils of special operations—during World War II, he took part in several landings in the Pacific. He received the Silver Star for his actions in the famous Cabanatuan Raid, where he contributed to the rescue of more than five hundred prisoners of war.

Simons is perhaps best remembered for his role in the 1970 Son Tay Raid (see page 34), also known as Operation Ivory Coast, for which he was selected as ground commander in the effort to rescue American prisoners of war. The target, Son Tay prison, lay in North Vietnam, 23 miles west of Hanoi. Due to faulty intelligence, the mission failed to recover any prisoners, but it did force the North Vietnamese (NVA) to relocate POWs to a few centralized Hanoi compounds, ultimately resulting in their better treatment. Simons received the Distinguished Service Cross for his leadership on the mission.

Son Tay Raid

The raid on the Son Tay prison camp began at approximately 0215 Hanoi time on November 21, 1970. An air force C-130 flare ship illuminated the area, and an HH-53 helicopter (see page 229) began firing on the guard towers with its twin Gatling guns. The raiders then had less than thirty minutes to land and complete their mission before North Vietnamese reinforcements would arrive to engage with them. The first glitch occurred when Colonel Simons's helicopter mistakenly set down at another site—instead of landing just outside the prison compound, the support group was 400 meters away at what was referred to as a secondary school on the maps. This building was actually a barracks housing Chinese and Soviet advisors and a large number of NVA troops. The raiders took this force under fire and prevented them from reinforcing the prison.

Colonel Simons and the support group reloaded the HH-53 and moved to the prison compound. Nine minutes into the raid, Simons was outside the prison wall; he and his group augmented the assault and security elements, eliminating approximately sixty guards. The second glitch of the raid came when they realized the camp was empty.

The Son Tay raid ended after twenty-seven minutes. Colonel Simons had not lost a single man, and, although there were no prisoners to rescue, the mission's planning and execution were flawless.

Major Dick Meadows

For an example of a "soldier's soldier," look no further than Richard J. "Dick" Meadows. Born in Covington, Virginia, he enlisted in the US Army at the age of fifteen; by the age of twenty, he was the youngest master sergeant in the army. Meadows spent the next three decades operating with the Special Forces or Rangers, fighting in Korea and working with SOG to run covert ops for the CIA in Vietnam. By the end of his tour, he received the direct commission as a captain. Captain Meadows would serve as the team leader for the initial assault team in the Son Tay raid.

Meadows served briefly as an exchange officer with the British Special Air Service (SAS), and, in the mid-1970s, he drew upon this experience when he participated in the formation of Delta Force (see page 38). Although he retired in 1977, he was reactivated as the man behind the scenes in Operation Eagle Claw, the attempt to end the Iran hostage crisis (see page 39). Major Meadows performed reconnaissance in Tehran, Iran, as well as securing a building and vehicles for the Delta assault force. Unfortunately, the force never reached the US embassy.

Major Meadows died in July 1995, but this legendary warrior remains an icon in the chronicles of special operations.

Special Mission Units (SMUs)

The US Department of Defense (DoD) has acknowledged the formation and maintenance of select SMUs, organized, trained, and equipped to conduct a range of specific and highly classified missions. These SMUs are routinely under the direct supervision of the highest command levels, usually the National Command Authority (NCA). They are specially manned, equipped, and trained to deal with an assortment of international threats identified by the Joint Special Operations Command (JSOC) at Fort Bragg, North Carolina.

SMUs are generally understood to include the army's Combat Applications Group (CAG) and the Naval Special Warfare Development Group (DEVGRU); the army's 75th Ranger Regiment (see page 67) and the 160th Special Operations Aviation Regiment (page 78) can also be assigned as needed to augment these groups. The tactics, techniques, procedures, equipment, and personnel of the SMUs remain classified. These units are trained to execute a variety of special operations missions, covertly or clandestinely, while maintaining absolute minimum individual and organizational visibility during day-to-day operations.

Colonel Charles Beckwith

If Aaron Bank (see page 23) is the father of Special Forces, then Charles "Chargin' Charlie" Beckwith is the father of Delta Force. From its beginnings, Delta was heavily influenced by the British Special Air Service (SAS), a philosophical result of Colonel Beckwith's yearlong exchange tour with that unit (1962–1963). From his time with these elite among the elite in the world of special-operations units, Beckwith formulated the concept of a US military elite counterterrorist unit.

In 1977, as a direct response to numerous well-publicized terrorist incidents, Colonel Beckwith helped forge his concept into reality. He had seen the results of the British unit's selection process and sought to mirror its success rate with Delta. Most of the unit's operatives come from US Ranger battalions and Special Forces groups, but candidates are drawn from all branches of the military. Even a few Air Commandos and marines now call "the Unit" their home.

Delta Force

Delta Force is officially designated as the 1st Special Forces Operational Detachment-DELTA. For many years, its cover name was the Combat Applications Group (CAG). Eventually this designation was thrown out with the adoption of the new unclassified designation for Delta Force squadrons: Army Compartmented Elements (ACE). Still, its members usually just call it "the Unit."

Delta Force is organized into three operating squadrons (A, B, and C), all of which are subdivided into small groups known as troops. As is the case with the SAS, the troops specialize in High-Altitude Low-Opening (HALO) parachuting (see page 49), scuba, or other skill groups. These troops can each be further divided into smaller units as needed to fit mission requirements. Delta also maintains support units, which handle selection and training, logistics, finance, and the unit's medical requirements. Within this grouping, a vital (if little known) technical unit operates covert eavesdropping equipment for use in hostage rescues and similar situations.

Operation Eagle Claw

In November 1979, a group of radical Iranian "students" captured the US embassy in Tehran, Iran, prompting the US Air Force to rush to regenerate its special-operations capabilities. By December 1979, a rescue force was chosen, and training commenced. Training exercises were conducted through March 1980, and on April 16, the Joint Chiefs of Staff (JCS) approved the mission. On April 19, rescue forces consisting of assets from the US Army, Navy, Air Force, and Marines assets began to deploy to Southwest Asia. Delta Force was tasked with the assault on the embassy and the rescue of the American hostages.

On April 24, 1980, after six months of failed negotiations, the National Command Authorities (NCA) ordered the execution of Operation Eagle Claw to free the US hostages held in Iran. Under cover of darkness, eight RH-53D helicopters departed the USS *Nimitz* aircraft carrier on station in the Arabian Sea; at the same time, six C-130s left Masirah Island, Oman. Both sets of aircraft set off for a prearranged site 600 miles into the desert, code designation Desert One.

Ultimately, the mission would end in disaster. A few hours in, two helicopters aborted due to mechanical failure; an unexpected *haboob* (a desert dust storm) caused the remaining helicopters to arrive late, while yet another suffered an unfixable hydraulic leak at the Desert One site. Without enough air assets to complete, the mission was aborted. Then, during a movement to refuel the helicopters, one of the RH-53s collided with a C-130, setting both aircraft ablaze and killing eight servicemen. Subsequent evaluation of the mission would lead to the formation of the US Special Operations Command (SOCOM).

Operation Eagle Claw: Helos

The failure of the 1980 attempt to rescue American hostages from the Iranian embassy (see page 39) was largely due to the performance of the helicopters used in the operation. A few hours into the mission, two of the helicopters had to abort due to mechanical failure. The balance of the helicopters ran into a *haboob*, an intense sandstorm, which blinded the pilots and wreaked havoc on the helicopters. The effects of the dust cloud caused the remaining helicopters to arrive at the rendezvous site late. Another of the helicopters suffered a hydraulic leak that its crew determined was unfixable at the Desert One site. This determination resulted in only five operational helicopters, one fewer than mission planners had ascertained to be the minimum required for the mission to continue. With only five craft available, then, the mission was aborted.

Considering the aircraft and equipment of the day, Operation Eagle Claw was a monumental undertaking; nevertheless, it failed. Turning failure into success, however, this debacle in the desert was the catalyst in the creation of a new aircraft, the V-22 Osprey.

Rubber Duck

"Rubber duck" is the term Special Operations Forces (SOF) troops use to describe any mission requiring a Zodiac raft. Further, there are several types of rubber duck missions. In a "soft duck," the fully inflated Zodiac raft is deployed from the rear cargo ramp of a helicopter. The raft is slid out of the helicopter and the SOF team follows right behind. Once in the water, the team jumps in, fires up the outboard engine, and heads out on the mission. A "hard duck" employs a craft with a metal bottom that is delivered in the same manner as a soft duck.

Yet another method of deployment is the K duck (the K stands for kangaroo). The inflated Zodiac raft is slung underneath a Pave Hawk and is mission ready upon hitting the water.

Rounding out the alphabet ducks is the T duck (T for tether). In this case, the raft is totally deflated, rolled up, and secured inside the helicopter. Once deployed, the team will inflate the raft, load up, and begin its mission.

Finally, there is deployment from an MC-130 Combat Talon, called the RAMZ drop (Rigging Alternate Method-Zodiac). The Zodiac is fully deflated and secured to a disposable pallet; parachutes are then attached to the harness. Moments after the loadmaster releases the package, the SOF troops parachute in after it.

Operation Just Cause: Acid Gambit

During Operation Just Cause—the US invasion of Panama—in 1989, the 160th Special Operations Aviation Group (Airborne), SOAG (A), participated in a daring raid: the rescue of American civilian Kurt Muse. Initial planning for the rescue, named Operation Acid Gambit, began at Delta's complex at Fort Bragg. As the mission drew closer, the Delta operators moved down to Eglin Air Force Base, Florida, where a full-size mockup of the prison that held Muse had been built.

   On December 20, 1989, using four MH-6 "Little Bird" light attack helicopters (see page 88), the Delta assault team landed on the prison roof and performed a dynamic (forced) entry by placing explosive charges on the doors. The team then worked its way into the bowels of the prison, eliminating any hostile threats as they went. Once Muse had been located, the door of his cell was blown open using a small explosive charge, the team brought him to the roof, and the waiting helicopter whisked him away to safety. In support of this mission, a team of Delta snipers armed with .50-caliber sniper rifles was positioned in the vicinity, with the purpose of neutralizing any threat from outside guards. Working in conjunction with the SOAG (A) helicopters were two AC-130H Spectre gunships from the 1st Special Operation Wing from Hurlburt Field, Florida.

Operation Desert Storm: The Great Scud Hunt

In February 1991, a Joint Special Operations Task Force (JSOTF) arrived in Saudi Arabia. Comprised of approximately four hundred men, including the 160th SOAR (A) (see page 78) and Delta Force (page 38), the JSOTF worked alongside the SAS in western Iraq. As A-10 Warthog jets scoured the desert below and F-15 Eagles and other coalition aircraft streaked across the skies, Delta operators dashed through the desert sand—all in search of the elusive Transporter Erector Launcher (TEL), scuds, and their command and control elements. The SAS operated in the southern area known as "Scud Alley," while Delta teams would be assigned to the north, in the area between the Tigris and Euphrates Rivers known as "Scud Boulevard."

Inserted by MH-47 Chinook helicopters of the 160th SOAR (A), the Delta teams unloaded their Fast Attack Vehicles (FAV) and began their mission. As well armed as the FAVs were, laser-aiming designators and radios represented the most lethal weapons Delta carried. If soldiers located a missile, they could "light up" the target and signal an attack aircraft to drop a smart bomb, which would then lock on to the laser and destroy the target.

Special Forces Hide Site

A hide site can be as simple as crook in a mountainside, blanketed with netting and vegetation to camouflage a reconnaissance or sniper team. It can also be elaborate enough to conceal a pair of Ground Mobility Vehicles (GMVs) and make them look like just another sand dune in a desert. The latter variant, called a Mission Support Site (MSS), serves more as a base of operations than as a simple storage place. The hide site provides a base from which to stage high-frequency/ultra-high-frequency (HF/UHF) or satellite communications, either using a remote communication site or broadcasting directly from the hide site.

An example of a basic hide site is a hole approximately 9 feet square and 5 feet deep, dug into the desert. Up from the hole comes the center stand, an umbrella-like device, and into this go the conduit arms that stretch over the hole. The hole is covered with plastic and burlap, then topped off with sand, making the hide site blend in with the terrain. The whole assembly averages over 100 pounds and can be broken down and distributed among the team to be carried in their rucksacks.

Operation Desert Storm: Special Reconnaissance

On February 23, 1991, Chief Warrant Officer 2 John "Bulldog" Balwanz and Operational Detachment A-525 (ODA-525) were loaded onto two MH-60 Black Hawk helicopters. Their mission was to shadow and report on the movements of the Iraqi Republican Guard. With the mission-essential equipment packed, their rucksacks weighed 175 pounds per man.

They inserted 150 miles into Iraq and began preparing their hide site. Their location, a rock-hard earthen canal, was unlike the soft sand in which they'd practiced. The men worked diligently to construct rudimentary concealment. At first light, they heard children playing nearby—a little girl looked into the makeshift hide site and saw the Green Berets. Startled, the children ran away. The hide site was now compromised: the villagers became curious, and then a roving Iraqi patrol happened into the area. Approximately 150 soldiers poured from the vehicles and initiated a firefight.

The SF team needed to exfiltrate, and fast. Making contact with a USAF F-16 fighter flying over their position, they arranged for Close Air Support (CAS) and extraction. A total of sixteen sorties were flown, many close to 200 meters—"danger close"—in support of ODA-525. As daylight faded, so did the fighting. Two MH-60s came in and the team hustled aboard. The helicopters lifted into the night sky and headed back to base.

MOH: Master Sergeant Gary Gordon

On October 3, 1993, Master Sgt. Gary Gordon, 1st Special Forces Operational Detachment-Delta (1SFOD-D)—Delta Force—was serving with Task Force Ranger in Mogadishu, Somalia. His sniper team had been providing precision fire from their helicopter during Operation Gothic Serpent when he learned that another helicopter, an MH-60L Black Hawk codenamed Super Six-Four and piloted by Chief Warrant Officer Michael Durant, had crashed. Gordon and a teammate, SFC Randall Shughart, volunteered to secure the crash site. Their request was denied twice, but on their third attempt permission was granted. Ground fire was so intense that Gordon and Shughart had to be inserted 100 meters south of the downed Black Hawk.

Master Sergeant Gordon, armed with a CAR-15 (see page 32) and a sidearm, led his teammate though the winding slums of "the Mog" to the helicopter, where they pulled the crew from the wreckage. Fighting from a precarious position, Master Sergeant Gordon continued to engage the approaching Somali horde—using his pistol after he exhausted his rifle's ammunition—until he was fatally wounded. For his extraordinary heroism and devotion to duty, he was posthumously awarded the Medal of Honor.

SINE PARI

MOH: Sergeant First Class Randall Shughart

The second man on the ground with Master Sergeant Gordon that fateful October day was SFC Shughart, another Delta sniper. Shughart had also volunteered to join his team leader in support of Chief Warrant Officer Durant's downed helicopter. Inserted a 100 yards from the crash site, the two Delta snipers maneuvered to MH-60L Black Hawk Super Six-Four.

Equipped with only his M14 rifle and a pistol, Sergeant First Class Shughart fought his way through a maze of shanties and shacks with Gordon to reach the critically injured crew members. Shughart pulled the pilot and the other crewmembers from the aircraft, establishing a perimeter that placed him and his fellow sniper in the most vulnerable position. He used his M14 and sidearm to kill an undetermined number of attackers while traveling the perimeter, protecting the downed crew.

When Gordon was killed, Sergeant First Class Shughart retrieved his teammate's weapon and passed it off to Durant. He then continued to fight as the Somalis drew closer. Eventually, with his ammunition depleted, his position was overrun and he was fatally wounded.

Airborne Training

The common bond between all SOF units is they are airborne qualified—it is a rite of passage into the Special Operations Forces. The three-week training is conducted at the US Army Airborne School at Fort Benning, Georgia, broken into weeklong phases: Ground, Tower, and Jump.

During Ground Week, trainees learn how to execute a flawless Parachute Landing Fall (PLF) to land safely within the Landing Zone (LZ). The PLF consists of five points of contact, designed to absorb the shock of landing and distribute it across the body: (1) balls of the feet, (2) side of the calf, (3) side of the thigh, (4) buttocks, and (5) side of of the back (or the "lats" muscles). Training also includes the proper way to exit an aircraft.

During Tower Week, trainees jump from a 12-foot-high elevated platform as an apparatus provides the downward motion and oscillation simulating that of an actual parachute jump. During this second week of training, the student gets to ride the "tower," which is designed to give the student practice in controlling their parachute during 250-foot descent and executing a PLF upon landing.

Finally, during Jump Week, trainees perform five parachute jumps. Upon graduation, they are awarded the coveted Sliver Wings and are considered airborne qualified.

High Altitude Low Opening (HALO)

There are times when, for political reasons or due to strategic or tactical considerations, a team can't just drop into an enemy's backyard and must instead be inserted clandestinely from afar, outside the target nation's territorial airspace or boundaries. For such an insertion, one choice is HALO.

HALO infiltrations are normally conducted under the cover of darkness or at twilight to lessen the chance of observation by hostile forces. Using the Ram Air Parachute System (RAPS), operators deploy their parachutes at a designated altitude, assemble in the air, and land together in the arranged drop zone (DZ) to begin their mission. This type of drop can be conducted even in adverse weather conditions. Flying at an altitude of 25,000 to 43,000 feet mean sea level (MSL), the jump aircraft—such as an MC-130 Combat Talon (see page 238)—will appear as a legitimate aircraft on an enemy's radar screen, perhaps as just another commercial airliner traversing the globe.

High Altitude High Opening (HAHO)

The alternative to HALO is the advanced infiltration technique of HAHO. The difference between the two is that in HAHO, as soon as the team jumps off, they immediately deploy their parachutes and use them to glide into a denied area. For this type of jump, parachutists also use GPS units and altimeters. In order to maintain formation integrity, each jumper wears a helmet-mounted strobe, either normal or infrared, and the team wears the appropriate night-vision goggles. Additionally, each member of the team remains tuned to an interteam radio for command and control of the insertion as well as formation on the DZ. There are times when, due to the presence of enemy air defenses, HAHO is the best means to infiltrate a team into a hostile area; it also increases the survivability of the support aircraft.

Special Forces Crest

The distinctive Special Forces crest is black and silver, emblazoned with the Special Forces motto: *De oppresso liber*. This Latin phrase translates to "To free the oppressed." The two crossed arrows symbolize the Special Forces' role in unconventional warfare, while the upturned fighting knife reflects the attributes of a Special Forces soldier, straight and true. Both arrows and knife were silent weapons used by the American Indians, thus providing a further link to the warrior spirit of this great nation. The crossed arrows are also symbolic of the insignia worn by the Indian Scouts and, later, the 1st Special Service Force (see page 20) during World War II.

Special Forces Arrowhead Insignia

The Special Forces shoulder insignia was authorized for wear in 1955. The arrowhead shape represents the craft and stealth of the American Indian warriors who inspired the 1st Special Service Force and reflects the skills of the Green Berets. The upturned dagger represents the Fairbairn–Sykes knife used by British Commandos in World War II (see page 20), a version of which was also used by members of the Office of Strategic Services (OSS). The three bolts of lightning bisecting the dagger evoke the unconventional nature of Special Forces operations and represent their ability to strike or infiltrate rapidly by air, sea, or land.

Worn above the shoulder insignia are the Airborne and Special Forces tabs. The airborne tab is authorized within the army in three colors, which coordinate with those used in the shoulder sleeve insignia.

Special Forces Groups

The 1st Special Forces Group (Airborne) is headquartered at Joint Base Lewis–McChord, Washington, with its 1st Battalion forward deployed at Torii Station, Okinawa. The 1SFG (A) is orientated toward Southeast Asia.

The 3rd Special Forces Group is headquartered at Fort Bragg, North Carolina, and is oriented toward all of sub-Saharan Africa with the exception of the Eastern Horn of Africa.

The 5th Special Forces Group is headquartered at Fort Campbell, Kentucky, and is oriented toward the Middle East, Persian Gulf, Central Asia, and the Horn of Africa (HOA).

The 7th Special Forces Group relocated in 2011 from Fort Bragg, North Carolina, to its current headquarters at Eglin Air Force Base, Florida. The 7SFG (A) is oriented toward the Western Hemisphere: South America, Central America, and the Caribbean.

The 10th Special Forces Group is headquartered at Fort Carson, Colorado, and its 1st Battalion is forward-deployed in the Panzer Kaserne (Panzer Barracks) in Böblingen near the city of Stuttgart, Germany.

The 19th Special Forces Group, National Guard Special Forces Groups, is headquartered in Draper, Utah.

The 20th Special Forces Group, National Guard Special Forces Groups, is headquartered in Birmingham, Alabama.

Special Forces Assessment and Selection (SFAS)

Becoming a member of the US Army Special Forces begins at the Rowe Training Facility, located near Fort Bragg, North Carolina, at Camp MacKall. The forty-day Special Forces Assessment and Selection (SFAS) program is conducted by the 1st Battalion, 1st SWTG (A). The purpose of SFAS is to identify those soldiers who have the determination to continue on to Special Forces Qualification Course. The SF cadre has the opportunity to assess each soldier's capabilities by testing his physical, emotional, and mental stamina. Any male soldier may volunteer for SFAS. While a typical class contains a number of volunteers from the Rangers, many are soldiers with varying Military Occupational Specialties (MOSs).

Special Forces Qualification Course (SFQC)

Each branch of service that produces special operations personnel has its own unique training. This specialized, physically demanding training focuses on the military skills used by Special Forces and encourages teamwork, unit cohesiveness, and esprit de corps. For the US Air Force Special Tactics Teams (STTs), this is accomplished with Indoctrination and the Pipeline, while US Navy SEALs are trained via Basic Underwater Demolition/SEAL (BUD/S) and "Hell Week." US Army soldiers undergo the Special Forces Qualification Course, or "Q Course."

Before participating in the Q Course, all Special Forces trainees must complete the Army Airborne School. The Q Course consists of five phases (II through VI), together lasting approximately forty-five weeks. Each phase is designed to foster expertise in the following areas: small-unit tactics, advanced Special Forces tactics, survival skills, language and cultural training, unconventional warfare, survival, escape, resistance and evasion, and advanced combat survival tactics.

The SFQC teaches and develops necessary skills, including Foreign Internal Defense (FID) and Direct Action (DA) missions, as part of a small operations team (ODA). Duties at other levels involve command, control, and support functions. Frequently, duties require regional orientation, which includes foreign language training and in-country experience. Unconventional tactics are one emphasis for Special Forces training, but trainees also develop an understanding of different national and regional landscapes through waterborne, desert, jungle, mountain, or arctic operations.

Robin Sage

The Robin Sage exercise is the culmination of a Special Forces soldier's training. The student ODA (see page 56) in this course infiltrates an area, humping a "ruck" through some of the roughest terrain in the Uwharrie National Forest of the fictional country of Pineland (otherwise known as North Carolina).

After a day or two, depending on the scenario and how good the team is, they will make contact with a guerrilla force. Carrying an 80- or 100-pound rucksack through the woods is nothing compared to the task ahead: meeting the Guerrilla Chief. The G Chief is played by an experienced SF soldier, usually a senior noncommissioned office (NCO), or possibly a retired SF soldier brought in to test the mettle of those seeking to join the ranks. These people know their business and will not spare the fledgling team or their detachment commander any hardship.

In the US Navy SEALs' BUD/S Hell Week, sleep deprivation is a given; the exercise is 90 percent physical. Robin Sage, which lasts two weeks, allows participants a few more hours of sleep, and, while physically demanding, it is a thinking man's game. Upon successful completion of this course, the solider will be awarded the sought-after green beret.

Operational Detachments–Alpha (ODA)

Also known as "A-Teams," Operational Detachments–Alpha remain the essence of the US Army Special Forces. An ODA will typically comprise twelve men: two officers and ten NCOs specializing in operations/intelligence, weapons, medical, engineering, and communications. Each soldier on the team is also cross-trained in each other's skills.

This is where "the rucksack meets the ground," where missions are carried out. No matter how you get to this point—HALO, scuba, GMV, Zodiac, or helicopter—here is where the planning is put into action. The ODA is specifically designed to organize, train, advise, direct, and support indigenous military or paramilitary forces in Unconventional Warfare (UW) and FID operations, capable of training a force up to a battalion in size.

A Special Forces unit is unlike its conventional equivalent, which deploys with its full chain of command, staff officers, support, and logistics units; in such a unit, infantry squads are not sent on a mission with the instruction, "By the way, sergeant, it's all yours." This is exactly how an ODA deploys. Often, the SF team is the only US military presence conducting an operation within a country.

ODA: Commanding Officer

The commanding officer (CO) of the Special Forces ODA is a captain. The CO may also command or advise indigenous combat troops up to a battalion in size. He is proficient in those tasks that support the detachment's mission essential task list (METL), with knowledge of a broad spectrum of common and special operations tasks. Not only must the SF captain know the skills that will make him mission capable during independent special operations, he must also be able to operate in concert with conventional forces in large-scale operations. As the team leader, he is accountable for everything that happens on that team, right or wrong. He is tasked with mission planning, working with the team specialist to establish the best possible strategy for mission success.

Captain "Steve" of the 5th SFG (A) summed up the team leader's roles and responsibilities this way: "He is responsible for the men and their equipment, and makes sure that everything happens the way it is supposed to happen." The US Army Special Forces allows and expects its solders to think "outside the box"; this is one of the characteristics that makes such units "special."

A Special Forces ODA commander meets with village elders and members of the Afghan National Army Corps in Afghanistan

ODA: Executive Officer

The executive officer (XO) of the ODA is the detachment technician, a warrant officer. He serves as second-in-command, ensuring that the detachment commander's decisions are implemented. His tasks also include administrative and logistical portions of area studies, briefbacks and operational plans (OPLANs), and operational orders (OPORDs). He will assist in the recruitment of indigenous troops and the subsequent training of these combat forces up to and including a battalion size. In the event the mission requires the ODA to run a "split-team op," the XO commands one of these teams.

An ODA executive officer shakes hands with a shop owner in Uruzgan province, Afghanistan

An operations/intelligence sergeant with local children in Helmand province, Afghanistan

ODA: Operations/Intelligence Sergeant

The next man on the team is the operations/intelligence sergeant, or "team sergeant," who is the senior NCO on the detachment. A master sergeant, he advises the ODA commander on all training and operational matters. His job also entails providing the team with tactical and technical guidance and support. He will prepare the operations and training portion of the area studies, briefbacks and OPLANs, and OPORDs. In the absence of the warrant officer, the team sergeant will serve as executive officer.

Directing the ODA's intelligence training, collections, analysis, and dissemination is the assistant operations and intelligence sergeant, a sergeant first class. As the name implies, he assists the operations sergeant in preparing area studies, briefbacks, and other documentation. He is responsible for field interrogation of enemy prisoners, briefs and debriefs SF and indigenous patrols, and filling in for the operations sergeant when necessary.

The operations/intelligence sergeant comes from the ranks of Special Forces, having served on an ODA for some time and attending the Advanced Non-Commissioned Officers Course (ANCOC) at the NCO Academy, John F. Kennedy Special Warfare Center, at Fort Bragg.

ODA: Weapons Sergeants

Next on the team are the two weapons sergeants (18B40) and (18B30), a sergeant first class and a staff sergeant, respectively. They are responsible for the employment of weapons using conventional and unconventional tactics and techniques. They train indigenous troops as well as other team members in the use of small arms (pistols, rifles, assault weapons); crew-served weapons (machine guns, mortars); antiaircraft weapons (stingers); and antitank weapons (LAW, AT-4). They may assist the operations sergeant, and they can organize, train, advise, and command up to a company-size indigenous force.

The weapons sergeants also have a working knowledge of legacy and foreign (Russian, North Korean, and Chinese) weapons. They know how to operate and maintain enemy weapons, and they must also share their expertise in Foreign Internal Defense missions that may take place in developing countries. Training for the Special Forces weapons sergeant consists of forty-three weeks of formal classroom training and practice exercises.

ODA: Medical Sergeants

Two medical sergeants, a sergeant first class and a sergeant, provide emergency, routine, and long-term medical treatment for the ODA and associated allied or indigenous forces. They train, advise, and direct detachment members and indigenous soldiers in emergency medicine and preventive medical care; they will establish a medical facility in the event of a prolonged mission, and they are also trained in veterinary care. ODA medical sergeants receive their training at the US Army Joint Special Operations Medical Training Center (JSOMTC) and are considered physician substitutes, but they are also fully trained in SF skills and are recognized as combatants. Like the other team members, they are capable of training and commanding up to a company-size force. Special Forces medical sergeants are considered to be the finest first-response and trauma medical technicians in the world.

Though they are primarily trained with an emphasis on trauma medicine, they also have a working knowledge of dentistry, veterinary care, public sanitation, water quality, and optometry. Training for the Special Forces medical sergeants consists of sixty weeks of formal classroom training and practice exercises.

ODA: Engineer Sergeants

Two engineer sergeants—a sergeant first class and a staff sergeant—supervise, lead, plan, perform, and instruct all aspects of combat engineering and light construction. They can build a school or church for a local village, and they also know the best place to blow up a bridge, dam, or refinery. They are knowledgeable in demolitions and improvised munitions and can plan and perform sabotage operations. Like the weapons and medical sergeants, they can organize, train, advise, and command an indigenous force up to a company in size. Special Forces engineer sergeants are specialists across a wide range of disciplines, from field fortifications to topographic survey techniques.

Training for the Special Forces engineer sergeant consists of forty-four weeks of formal classroom training and practice exercises.

ODA: Communications Sergeants

Two communications sergeants, a sergeant first class and a staff sergeant, advise the detachment commander on communications matters. They install, operate, and maintain FM, AM, High Frequency (HF), Very High Frequency (VHF), and Super High Frequency (SHF) radio communications in voice, CW, and burst radio nets. They prepare the communications portion of briefbacks, OPLANs, and OPORDs, and train ODA members and indigenous personnel in the use and maintenance of communications equipment. They can advise, train, and command indigenous forces up to a company in size.

Special Forces communications sergeants can operate every kind of communications gear, from encrypted satellite communications systems to old-style, high-frequency Morse key systems. Their training consists of sixty weeks of formal classroom training and practice exercises.

Language Training

Language skills are imperative to the successful achievement of many Special Forces missions when operating with indigenous personnel. After completing Phase III of the Qualification course, soldiers attend functional language training at the Special Operations Academic Facility (SOAF) at Fort Bragg, North Carolina. The language course the solider attends will correlate directly with the SF group in which they will operate.

During this twenty-four-week phase (Phase V), candidates will perfect their skills in the language to which they have been assigned. Languages include French, Indonesian (Bahasa), Spanish, Arabic, Chinese (Mandarin), Czech, Dari, Hungarian, Korean, Pashto, Persian (Farsi), Polish, Russian, Tagalog, Thai, Turkish, and Urdu.

Special Forces Creed

I am an American Special Forces Soldier!
I will do all that my nation requires of
me. I am a volunteer, knowing well
the hazards of my profession.

I serve with the memory of those who
have gone before me. I pledge to
uphold the honor and integrity of
their legacy in all that I am—in all that
I do.

I am a warrior. I will teach and fight
whenever and wherever my nation
requires. I will strive always to excel in
every art and artifice of war.

I know that I will be called upon to
perform tasks in isolation, far from
familiar faces and voices. With the
help and guidance of my faith, I will
conquer my fears and succeed.

I will keep my mind and body clean,
alert and strong. I will maintain
my arms and equipment in an
immaculate state befitting a Special
Forces Soldier, for this is my debt to
those who depend upon me.

I will not fail those with whom I serve. I
will not bring shame upon myself or
Special Forces.

I will never leave a fallen comrade. I will
never surrender though I am the last.
If I am taken, I pray that I have the
strength to defy my enemy.

I am a member of my Nation's chosen
soldiery, I serve quietly, not seeking
recognition or accolades. My goal is
to succeed in my mission—and live to
succeed again.

De Oppresso Liber

Ranger Training

US Army Ranger training is broken into three phases. The first is conducted at Camp Rogers and Camp William O. Darby at Fort Benning, Georgia, and is designed to assess and develop the military skills, physical and mental endurance, stamina, and confidence a soldier must have to successfully accomplish combat missions.

The second phase takes place at Camp Merrill in the mountains of Dahlonega, Georgia. During the Mountain Phase, students receive instruction in military mountaineering techniques as well as methods of employing a squad and platoon for combat patrol operations in a mountainous environment.

The third phase is conducted at Camp James E. Rudder, Eglin Air Force Base, Florida. This final phase emphasizes continued development of the students' combat skills. The Ranger student must be capable of operating effectively under conditions of extreme mental and physical stress. During the course, they prove they can overcome apparently overwhelming mental and physical hardships. They master the skills needed to plan and execute small unit operations day and night, low-altitude mountaineering, and infiltration and exfiltration techniques via land, air, and sea. Upon successful completion of training, they are awarded and authorized to wear the Ranger tab.

Ranger Creed

Recognizing that I volunteered as a ranger, fully knowing the hazards of my chosen profession, I will always endeavor to uphold the prestige, honor, and high esprit de corps of my ranger regiment.

Acknowledging the fact that a ranger is a more elite soldier, who arrives at the cutting edge of battle by land, sea, or air, I accept the fact that as a ranger, my country expects me to move further, faster, and fight harder than any other soldier.

Never shall I fail my comrades. I will always keep myself mentally alert, physically strong, and morally straight, and I will shoulder more than my share of the task, whatever it may be, one hundred percent and then some.

Gallantly will I show the world that I am a specially selected and well trained soldier. My courtesy to superior officers, neatness of dress, and care of equipment shall set the example for others to follow.

Energetically will I meet the enemies of my country. I shall defeat them on the field of battle for I am better trained and will fight with all my might. Surrender is not a ranger word. I will never leave a fallen comrade to fall into the hands of the enemy and under no circumstances will I ever embarrass my country.

Readily will I display the intestinal fortitude required to fight on to the ranger objective and complete the mission, though I be the lone survivor.

75th Ranger Regiment (Airborne)

The 75th Ranger Regiment is the army's premier light-infantry rapid assault force assigned to the US Special Operations Command (SOCOM). The unit's primary mission—in fact, its only mission—revolves around Direct Action (DA) operations. Its members' specialty is airfield seizure, though they are also more than capable of conducting raids, recovery of personnel (combat search and rescue, CSAR), and special-equipment and other light-infantry operations. They may be inserted and extracted by land, sea, or air. Ranger units focus on mission-essential tasks that include movement to contact, ambush, reconnaissance, airborne and air assaults, and hasty defense.

The regiment maintains a constant state of readiness, and each of the Ranger battalions can deploy anywhere in the world with limited notice. On any given day, one battalion is on Ready Reaction Force (RRF) 1 with the requirement to be wheels up within eighteen hours of notification. Additionally, one rifle company with battalion command and control can deploy in nine hours.

Headquartered at Fort Benning, Georgia, the 75th Ranger Regiment's mission is to plan and conduct special missions in support of US policy and objectives. The regiment's three battalions are located at Hunter Army Airfield, Georgia (1st Battalion); Fort Lewis, Washington (2nd Battalion); and Fort Benning, Georgia (3rd Battalion).

75th Ranger Recon Companies

The Ranger Reconnaissance Company (RRC), formerly known as the Ranger Recon Detachment (RRD), provides worldwide reconnaissance and operation preparation of the 75th Ranger Regiment and other special operations units. The 75th Regimental Special Troops Battalion (RSTB) was officially activated on October 16, 2007, in response to the war on terror and the changing nature of Ranger operations.

The RRC is part of the RSTB and conducts command, control, communications, computer, intelligence, surveillance, and reconnaissance functions in support of the 75th Ranger Regiment and other Special Operations Task Forces missions. The unit has three primary responsibilities: active reconnaissance, surveillance, and direct action.

After the attacks on September 11, 2001, the RRD saw extensive use in combat operations. The RRC has made four combat parachute jumps into Afghanistan in support of Operation Enduring Freedom, twice to establish an airhead for follow-on forces and twice to emplace tactical equipment. The Ranger Reconnaissance Company (RRC) provides reconnaissance and preps environments for operation in order to enable the execution of Joint Special Operations anywhere in the world.

75th Ranger Crest

In August 1944, the 5307th Composite Unit was consolidated with the 475th Infantry. On June 21, 1954, the 475th was redesignated the 75th Infantry. It is from the redesignation of Merrill's Marauders into the 75th Infantry Regiment that today's 75th Ranger Regiment traces its current unit designation.

The colors blue, white, red, and green in the Ranger crest represent four of the original six combat teams of the 5307th Composite Unit (Provisional), which were each identified by a color code word. The unit's close cooperation with the Chinese forces in the China-Burma-India theater is represented by the sun symbol, which is drawn from the Chinese Nationalist flag. The five-point white star came from a star used by the Burmese. The lightning bolt symbolizes the strike characteristics of the unit's behind-the-lines activities. The crest is affixed to a flash depicting the Ranger battalion, which are worn together on a tan beret.

In 2001, after much debate and many challenges, the Ranger regiments transitioned from a black beret to a tan one. The color was chosen as a reminder of the numerous beach assaults in the European theater and the jungle fighting in the Pacific theater during World War II. It also represented the khaki uniforms won by the Rangers in Korea and Vietnam.

M203 Grenade Launcher

The M203 grenade launcher provides an operator with additional firepower, giving them both point and area engagement capability. The most commonly used ammunition is the M406 40-millimeter projectile, which includes a High Explosive Dual Purpose (HEDP) cartridge, has a deadly radius of 5 meters, and is used as an antipersonnel and anti-light-armor weapon.

The receiver of the M203 is made of high-strength forged aluminum alloy, providing extreme ruggedness while keeping the launcher lightweight. Included in the receiver is a complete self-cocking firing mechanism, including striker, trigger, and positive safety lever. The barrel is also made of high-strength aluminum alloy and measures just 9 inches, allowing for excellent balance and handling. It slides forward in the receiver to accept a round of ammunition, then slides backward to automatically lock in the closed position, ready to fire.

Vertical Handgrip ("The Broom Handle")

A forward handgrip attaches quickly and easily to firearms using a Rail Integration/Accessory System (RIS/RAS), allowing users more precise control of a carbine during firing, including added support and control for full auto and rapid firing. It also allows for quicker handling when additional components are attached to the weapon, can be used as a monopod in a supporting position, and allows the operator to hold the weapon, even if it overheats.

One versatile handgrip favored by many of the troops is the Grip Pod system, which combines an innovative vertical foregrip with a strong and stable integrated bipod in a 7-ounce package. With the simple push of a button, the Grip Pod's legs deploy instantly. Soldiers in Afghanistan have commented, "If it's light, it's right"; for them, the Grip Pod fits the bill: "If we are in an ambush, we are tired, breathing heavy, humping all our gear. With the push of a button we have a bipod and a steady platform to shoot from."

M900 Lighted Grip

Another model of vertical grip popular among many Special Forces troops is the SureFire M900, a vertical foregrip with an integral weapon light. The M900 attaches to the underside of the quad rail, thus providing the operator additional weapon control and a blazing prefocused beam of incandescent white light.

The weapon light features four types of switches: two momentary-on pressure pads, one on each side of the grip for ambidextrous operation, which activate the main light; a rotary constant-on switch for the main light; a system-disable switch to shut down the entire unit; and a momentary-on thumb switch that controls two low-output LEDs. These LEDs are available in red, white, and blue and are ideal for low-signature navigation, while the white light is bright enough to temporarily blind the night-adapted vision of an enemy combatant. The MN10 lamp assembly is rated at 125 lumens for sixty minutes. The M900A is powered by three lithium batteries, which fit into the grip.

Ranger GMV-R

Similar to the other SOF GMVs (see page 90), the GMV-R used by the 75th Ranger Regiment (Airborne) includes 15-gallon auxiliary fuel tanks to achieve longer distances, storage racks for ammo, an air compressor, an electric winch, reinforcement of the rear floor, rollover bars, rear bench seats, electronic rack mounting for communications equipment, recovery strap kits, jacks, skid plates, spare tire carriers, side rails, and an assortment of weapon mounts.

Add-on armor provides 360-degree protection for the vehicle. Additionally, there is a cupola for the gunner, and the GMV can be fitted with smoke-grenade launchers positioned in the rear and front. These tubes launch smoke canisters that airburst above and around the vehicle, creating an instant smokescreen, which is very useful when breaking contact.

Operation Enduring Freedom: Objective Rhino

America's official answer to the heinous attacks on September 11, 2001, came on the night of October 19, 2001. Near Kandahar, Afghanistan, a company-sized element of approximately two hundred Rangers from the 3rd Battalion, 75th Ranger Regiment, departed in four loaded US Air Force Special Operations Command (AFSOC) MC-130 Combat Talon aircraft and headed toward a desert landing strip south of the city, code named Objective Rhino.

Prior to the Rangers' airdrop, US air power targeted several targets on and around the objective—first with bombs dropped from B-2 stealth bombers and then with fire from orbiting AC-130 gunships. These airstrikes resulted in a number of enemy KIAs as well as others fleeing the area. Following the airstrikes, the MC-130s flew over the drop zone at 800 feet. In zero illumination, the Rangers jumped into the blackness of the Afghanistan night.

This was the bread and butter of Ranger missions: a direct-action raid. The Rangers' several tasks that night included seizing the landing strip, closing with and destroying any Taliban forces, gathering intelligence, assessing the suitability of the landing strip for future operations, establishing a Forward Aerial Refuel/Rearm Point (FARP) for helicopters involved in a nearby operation at Objective Gecko, and then destroying any weapons and utilities. The raid was a success, and forces established a base at the airstrip, which would become Camp Rhino.

Operation Enduring Freedom: Combat Control Team—First There

Following the September 11 attacks, the US military shifted into high gear, and the special operations units went into overdrive. Master Sergeant Bart Decker, a combat controller with the 23rd Special Tactics Squadron, along with a handful of other AFSOC Special Tactics Squadron team members, would be among the first combat controllers inserted into Afghanistan.

On November 2, 2001, Master Sergeant Decker grabbed his gear and loaded aboard an MH-47E helicopter for his insertion into the country. For the mission, the Combat Control Team (CCT) "went native," wearing neutral Battle Dress Uniforms (BDUs), longer hair, and beards. The combat controllers were each armed with an M4A1 carbine, a Beretta M9, a 9-millimeter pistol, and a pair of radios (an AN/PRC-117F and an AN/PRC-148 MBITR). The radio would be the most lethal weapon carried—for every enemy killed with the M4A1, the CCT would kill 168 using their comm gear by calling in Close Air Support (CAS).

The Afghan Northern Alliance provided the SF team and combat controllers with horses, which became the standard mode of travel. Though the horse was an old-fashioned means of transportation, it was the only way to traverse the mountain paths.

Mark 12 Special-Purpose Receiver

Special operations personnel deployed in support of Operation Enduring Freedom wanted a weapon that could reach farther than the M4A1 carbine but was still short enough to conduct patrol and Close Quarter Battle (CQB) missions. The Mark 12 Special Purpose Receiver (SPR) was designed by Naval Surface Warfare Center Crane Division (NSWC Crane) for SOCOM units as an add-on upper for the M4/M16 series of weapons. It subsequently evolved into a complete standalone weapon, and the nomenclature was modified to Mark 12 Special Purpose Rifle (SPR) Mod 0 and Mod 1. The SPR is chambered in 5.56×45-millimeter NATO, using the same twenty- to thirty-round magazines as the M4 and M16. The primary differences between the Mod 0 and Mod 1 are the rail systems, handguards, and flip-up Back-Up Iron Sight (BUIS). The Mark 12 is designed to provide SOF units with a modified, designated-marksman version of the M4/M16. The 18-inch, match-grade, stainless-steel barrel is free floating for improved accuracy. The rifle was used in Iraq by Army Special Forces, Rangers, SEALs, and Marines in Afghanistan and again in Operation Iraqi Freedom.

AN/PEQ-1C Laser Acquisition Marker (SOFLAM)

When it absolutely, positively has to be destroyed, you put an SOF team on the ground and a fast mover with a smart bomb in the air—the result will be one smoking bomb crater. The SOFLAM is lighter and smaller than other laser markers in service with the US military. It provides the STT with the capability to locate and designate critical enemy targets for destruction using laser-guided ordnance. It can be used in daylight or, with attached night-vision optics, at night.

The SOFLAM uses a Pulse Repetition Frequency (PRF)—the number of pulses per second transmitted by a laser—that can be set to NATO STANAG Band I or II or is programmable. STANAG represents the standards and agreements set forth by NATO for the process, procedures, terms, and conditions under which mutual government quality assurance of defense products is to be performed by the appropriate national authority of one NATO member nation, at the request of another NATO member nation or organization.

160th Special Operations Aviation Command (Airborne) (SOAC)

The 160th SOAC (A) is Special Operations Command for everything in army special operations aviation, responsible for the organization, manning, training, and equipping of SOAC units. The units under SOAC (A) include the 160th SOAR (A), the "Night Stalkers"; the USASOC Flight Company, which provides fixed- and rotary-wing training support to USASOC; and the Special Operations Training Battalion, the old "Green Platoon."

The Technology Applications Program Office furnishes the 160th SOAR (A) with highly modified and/or unique aircraft and facilitates modernization; manages the life cycles of the Army Special Operations Aviation fleet; and oversees the US Special Operations Command Rotary Wing Aviation Night Vision Device and Advanced Aircraft Survivability Equipment Programs.

The Systems Integration Management Office equips USASOAC with state-of-the-art rotary-wing aircraft and mission systems and works to maintain and improve them.

The new SOAC insignia is a Fairbairn–Sykes dagger centered between red wings. Beneath is the Latin phrase *Volare Optimos*, which translates as "To Fly the Best."

160th Special Operations Aviation Regiment (Airborne) (SOAR)

After the failure of Operation Eagle Claw (see page 39), the army formed a special aviation unit, attracting some of the branch's best aviators to immediately begin a concentrated training program in low-level flying and night operations. The unit became a standalone battalion on October 16, 1981. Designated the 160th Aviation Battalion, it was commonly known as Task Force 160 because of the constant attachment and detachment of units to prepare for a wide variety of missions. Its focus on night operations resulted in the nickname "Night Stalkers."

Supporting the SOCOM special-operations forces with aviation assets, the 160th SOAR (A) includes MH-6M light recon/insertion helicopters, AH-6 light armed helicopters, MH-60 Black Hawk utility helicopters, MH-60L Direct Action Penetrators (DAPs), armed CAS helicopters, and MH-47 Chinook medium-lift helicopters.

The 160th SOAR (A) has participated in Operations Urgent Fury, Prime Chance, Just Cause, Desert Storm, Gothic Serpent (leading to the Battle of Mogadishu), Enduring Freedom, Iraqi Freedom, and New Dawn. Today, 160th SOAR has almost three thousand soldiers and more than two hundred aircraft.

Special Operations Aviation Training Battalion (SOATB)

The Special Operations Aviation Training Battalion (SOATB) is located at Fort Campbell, Kentucky. A Company is HQs and combat skills, B Company is the flight company, and D Company handles field maintenance. SOATB conducts basic army special operations aviation individual training and provides education for aircrews and support personnel with basic and advanced qualifications for duty with the 160th Special Operations Aviation Regiment (Airborne).

"Green Platoon" is a five-week program and the first step for any soldier to become a "Night Stalker." The cadre of A Company provides training in the basic combat skills of land navigation, first response, weapons, and combatives (hand-to-hand), with an emphasis on teamwork. With all the high-tech avionics, aircrews are still required to master land navigation with a lensatic compass and map. They get time in the Allison Aquatics Training Facility, where they experience and are trained in the dunker and emergency breathing. Here they will also receive flight training: mission planning, mission briefing, advanced skills in specific aircraft qualifications, environmental operations, aerial operations, and combat mission flight simulators. Those who graduate will be awarded the maroon beret and the crest of the 160th SOAR (A), at which point they become Night Stalkers.

160th SOAR (A) "Night Stalker" Creed

Service in the 160th is a calling only a few will answer for the mission is constantly demanding and hard. And when the impossible has been accomplished the only reward is another mission that no one else will try. As a member of the Night Stalkers I am a tested volunteer seeking only to safeguard the honor and prestige of my country, by serving the elite Special Operations Soldiers of the United States. I pledge to maintain my body, mind and equipment in a constant state of readiness for I am a member of the fastest deployable Task Force in the world, ready to move at a moment's notice anytime, anywhere, arriving time on target plus or minus 30 seconds.

I guard my unit's mission with secrecy, for my only true ally is the night and the element of surprise. My manner is that of the Special Operations Quiet Professional, secrecy is a way of life. In battle, I eagerly meet the enemy for I volunteered to be up front where the fighting is hard. I fear no foe's ability, nor underestimate his will to fight.

The mission and my precious cargo are my concern. I will never surrender. I will never leave a fallen comrade to fall into the hands of the enemy, and under no circumstances will I ever embarrass my country.

Gallantly will I show the world and the elite forces I support that a Night Stalker is a specially selected and well trained soldier.

I serve with the memory and pride of those who have gone before me for they loved to fight, fought to win and would rather die than quit.

Night Stalkers Don't Quit!

Operation Urgent Fury: Task Force 160

The men of Task Force 160 (see page 73) did not have to wait long to spread their wings and put their exhaustive training into practice. Their baptism by fire took place in the air over the small Caribbean island of Grenada. Slightly over two years after the formation of TF160, on October 19, 1983, members of the Revolutionary Military Council (RMC) of the People's Revolutionary Army (PRA) assassinated Grenada Prime Minister Maurice Bishop along with several of his aides. The brutal coup of this stalwart Communist and the insertion of an even more violent Marxist regime sparked mounting unease over the Communist involvement in the region. The US response was a joint military operation, as a vast assortment of army, navy, and marine forces were tasked with various missions for invasion of the island. The special operations element in the invasion force was Task Force 123, also known as "the JSOC/Rangers Task Force," under the command of Maj. Gen. Richard A. Scholtes. This element included two reduced-strength infantry battalions of the 75th Ranger Regiment, as well as operators from SEAL Team 6 and Delta Force. Air support came from the 16th Special Operations Squadron and TF160, which provided the insertion/extraction platform.

Aircrew Survival Egress Knife (ASEK)

The Aircrew Survival Egress Knife (ASEK) was designed and manufactured by the Ontario Knife Company as a survival knife for US Army aircrews, placed into service in 2003 as part of the army's Air Warrior equipment system. It can be used for cutting as well as hammering, and the saw teeth are capable of ripping through aircraft fuselage and the acrylic windows of a cockpit. Attached to the sheath is a pouch containing a strap cutter for cutting seat belts and a diamond-impregnated sharpening disk. The scabbard is designed to fit on the pilot's vests, load-bearing equipment, or web belt, or it can be worn on the calf. The older standard USAF model 499 survival knife, also from Ontario, is still used by some aircrews.

MH-60

The Sikorsky UH-60 Black Hawk utility helicopter was introduced into the US Army inventory in the 1980s as a replacement for the UH-1 "Huey." It was not long until the 160th gravitated to this new aircraft, adapting it to their missions; thus, the MH-60 variant was born. The MH-60 is a version of the UH-60 that has been specially modified for special-operations missions. Among the modifications are Aerial Refueling (AR) capability, a sophisticated collection of Aircraft Survivability Equipment (ASE), and improved navigation systems, allowing the helicopter to operate in the harshest environments and adverse weather conditions. The 160th SOAR (A) operates three Black Hawk variants: the MH-60K, the MH-60L, and the MH-60L DAP.

The primary use of the MH-60 is to conduct overt or covert infiltration, exfiltration, and resupply of SOF over a broad range of environmental conditions and mission profiles. Secondary missions include external load, CSAR, and MEDEVAC operations. The MH-60 features a Fast Rope Insertion/Extraction System (FRIES) capable of supporting 1,500 pounds per side and of operating from fixed-base facilities, austere remote sites, or oceangoing vessels.

Tech Specs

Length: 64 ft. 10 in.
Height: 17 ft. 2 in.
Rotor Diameter: 53 ft. 8 in.
Maximum Speed: 222 mph
Cruise Speed: 138 mph
Range: 450 nm
Crew: 4
Payload: 10 personnel with internal tanks
Armament: 7.62mm M-134 miniguns (2×)

MH-60K

The MH-60K is a hybrid derivative of the field-proven UH-60A Black Hawk extensively modified and developed for special-operation missions. Like the MH-60L, its improvements include AR capability, an advanced suite of ASE, and improved navigation systems, including multimode radar to further improve pinpoint navigation in all environments and under the harshest conditions.

The helicopter is powered by twin General Electric T700-GE-701C turboshaft engines rated at 1,700 shaft horsepower each. It features a gearbox with improved durability and can be refueled in midair in a variety of tank configurations. It has a digital automatic flight control computer with coupled automatic approach/depart/hover functions.

A specifically designed airframe and landing gear contribute to a high degree of battlefield survivability, as do ballistic-hardened flight controls; redundant electrical and hydraulic systems; a self-sealing, crash-resistant fuel system; and energy-absorbing landing gear and crew seats. With fully integrated cockpit and avionics, it is capable of precise navigation day or night, in all kinds of weather conditions.

Tech Specs

Length: 64 ft. 10 in.
Height: 16 ft. 10 in.
Rotor Diameter: 53 ft. 8 in.
Maximum Speed: 222 mph
Cruise Speed: 138 mph
Range: 450 nm
Crew: 4
Payload: 10 personnel with internal tanks
Armament: 7.62mm M134 miniguns (2×)

MH-60L Direct Action Penetrator DAP

The MH-60L's DAP variant is modified to accept a wide assortment of weapons systems. Its primary mission is armed escort and fire support, conducting CAS by means of precision-guided ordnance to support the infiltration or exfiltration of small units.

An integrated fire-control system used in concert with the pilot's Heads-Up Display (HUD) makes the DAP a highly accurate and effective weapons-delivery platform in any combat environment. It is capable of mounting two M134 miniguns; two chain guns; two nineteen-shot, 2.75-inch rocket pods; and sixteen Hellfire air-to-ground and Stinger air-to-air in a wide range of combinations. The standard configuration of the DAP is one rocket pod, one 30-millimeter cannon, and two miniguns; this can be changed based on mission, enemy, troops, terrain, and time (METT-T).

The MH-60L DAP can perform both the assault and close air support. Time to reconfigure the aircraft from the armed to the utility configuration or back again is minimal. The M134 miniguns remain with the aircraft regardless of the mission.

Tech Specs

Length: 64 ft. 10 in.
Height: 16 ft. 10 in.
Rotor Diameter: 53 ft. 8 in.
Maximum Speed: 222 mph
Cruise Speed: 138 mph
Range: 450 nm
Crew: 4
Armament: 7.62mm M134 miniguns (2×), M230 30mm chain gun, 70mm Hydra rockets, AGM-114 Hellfire air-to-ground missiles

MH-47G

The MH-47G is the newest aircraft coming on line with the 160th SOAR (A). This modernization program is planned as an improvement on the MH-47D and MH-47E Chinooks currently in service with the regiment, and upgrades will include aircraft remanufacturing, vibration reduction, and installation of more powerful Honeywell T55-GA-714A engines. Improved avionics will feature integrated digital mission management systems and a digital map.

In addition, the MH-47G will employ a dual-embedded Global Positioning System (GPS)/Inertial Navigation Unit (INU), together known as EGI. A second EGI is being incorporated to provide enhanced navigation accuracy and a more reliable, redundant navigator. This second unit will replace the aging Aircraft Heading Reference System (AHRS). All of the regiment's helicopters will also have the capability of receiving and displaying Near-Real-Time Intelligence Data (NRTID) to provide the crew and SOF with up-to-the-minute situational awareness.

Tech Specs
Length: 99 ft.
Height: 18 ft. 8 in.
Maximum Speed: 195 mph
Cruise Speed: 132 mph
Rotor Diameter: 60 ft.
Unrefueled Range: 525 nm
Crew: 6
Armament: M134 and M240 7.62mm machine guns (up to 3)

Delta Queen

The Delta Queen is a method for retrieval and extraction of the team. Upon mission completion, the team returns to its Zodiac inflatable craft and goes "feet wet," meaning in the water. The team then meets up with an MH-47 Chinook, whose pilot brings his aircraft to a hover and then settles it down, closer and closer to the water's surface. He will continue his descent until the aircraft actually rests on the water.

With its rear cargo ramp lowered, the MH-47 will actually begin to take on water. Wave after wave begins to cascade over the ramp, and soon the flight engineers are standing in water over the tops of their boots. As the Zodiac begins to line up with the rear of the chopper, a crewmember holds a red-filtered light to signal the team. The exfiltrating team guns the boat's engine, ducks their heads, and aims for the ramp and the now-flooded fuselage. With a splash and a thud, the team is aboard, and the helicopter crew begins to raise the ramp slightly. The pilot lifts the behemoth aircraft from the surface, creating a small version of Niagara Falls as the water pours from the rear of the helicopter. The extraction complete, the Night Stalkers and the Special Forces team proceed to Return To Base (RTB).

MH-6M Little Bird

The MH-6 is a single-engine, light utility helicopter similar to the Vietnam-era OH-6 "Loach." Based on the Hughes 500 Defender series, the MH-6J currently manufactured by MD Helicopters has been modified with outboard platforms on each side of the aircraft. This configuration, referred to as the external personnel system, can accommodate a total of six external and two internal seating positions.

The *Little Bird* is capable of conducting covert infiltration, exfiltration, and combat assaults over varying terrain and weather conditions. It is also used for reconnaissance missions and for command and control. The helicopter can be self-deployed with refuel support at ground or surface vessel locations every 270 nautical miles. Its compact size allows for rapid deployment in any air force transport—a C-141 is capable of transporting up to six MH-6s, and a C-130 up to three. The C-5A/B Galaxy and C-17 Globemaster can also transport the Little Birds, with a rapid upload/offload capability.

Tech Specs

Length: 32 ft.
Height: 8 ft. 11 in.
Rotor Diameter: 27 ft. 6 in.
Speed: 143 mph
Range: 230 nm
Crew: 2
Payload: 6 personnel

AH-6J

This aircraft is a single-turbine-engine, dual-flight-control, light attack helicopter normally flown by two pilots. It is primarily employed in close air support of ground troops, target-destruction raids, and armed escort of other aircraft. Its communications equipment is capable of secure operations, including UHF, VHF, satellite (SATCOM), and navigation systems include GPS and Tactical Air Navigation (TACAN), which is a line-of-sight, beacon-type system that provides slant-range, bearing, and identification data to other TACAN-equipped aircraft in determining the aircraft's position.

The normal aircraft weapons configuration consists of two 7.62-millimeter miniguns and two seven-shot, 2.75-inch rocket pods. The helicopter can support a wide range of other weaponry, including the M134 7.62-millimeter minigun, a six-barrel, air-cooled, link-fed, electrically driven Gatling gun. For some mission profiles, a GAU-19 .50-caliber machine gun or Mark 19 40-millimeter automatic grenade launcher may be substituted for the miniguns.

Tech Specs
Length: 32 ft.
Height: 8 ft. 11 in.
Rotor Diameter: 27 ft. 6 in.
Speed: 143 mph
Range: 230 nm
Crew: 2
Armament: 12.7mm GAU-19 or 7.62mm M134 miniguns (2×), M260 or MJ-12 rocket pods (2×), anti-tank guided missile, AGM-114 Hellfire air-to-ground missiles (2×)

Ranger Special Operations Vehicle (RSOV)

Each US Army Ranger battalion possesses twelve Ranger Special Operations Vehicles (RSOVs), which are ideal for their mission of airfield seizure. The vehicles, based on the Land Rover Defender Model 110, provide the Rangers with a multipurpose tactical transportation and weapons platform capable of moving the soldiers and their equipment through an assortment of environments.

Tech Specs
Length: 14 ft. 6 in.
Height: 6 ft. 4 in.
Width: 5 ft. 11 in.
Weight: 7,734 pounds (fully loaded)
Range: 200 mi.
Powerplant: 4-cylinder turbocharged diesel

Ground Mobility Vehicle: Special Tactics Squadron

The Ground Mobility Vehicle (GMV) is constructed on a steel frame with boxed frame rails and five crossmembers constructed from high-grade alloy steel. Once the substructure is assembled, electrocoating (e-coating) is applied to provide additional corrosion protection. The aluminum body reduces weight and provides resistance to corrosion. Aluminum body panels are riveted and bonded together with technologically advanced adhesives to provide additional strength. The body's design allows for flexing to accommodate off-road stresses. With 16 inches of ground clearance, the GMV is an exceptional off-road vehicle.

Fully loaded M1165 utility trucks can scale road grades as steep as 60 percent and negotiate side slopes of up to 40 percent. The GMV is capable of traversing hard-bottom water crossings up to 30 inches deep without a deep-water fording kit and up to 60 inches with the kit installed. The engine is equipped for deep-water fording and has a specially sealed dipstick, dipstick tube, and vented crankcase depression regulator (CDR) valve.

Ground Mobility Vehicle: Gun Truck

The workhorse GMV of the US Special Operations Forces is the 1.5-ton M1165 4×4 vehicle. This tactical vehicle is designed for use over all types of roads, as well as cross-country terrain, and in all weather conditions. The vehicle has four driving wheels powered by a 6.5-liter turbocharged, liquid-cooled V-8 diesel engine that develops 190 horsepower at 3,400 rpm. It features four-wheel hydraulic disc brakes and a mechanical parking brake as well as power steering. The truck is equipped with a pintle hook for towing, while tie-downs and lifting eyes are provided for air, rail, or sea shipment.

The M1165 is an expanded-capacity vehicle capable of transporting a four-man crew, weapons, and mission-essential equipment. It is equipped with a reinforced frame; crossmembers; lifting shackles; heavy-duty, variable-rate rear springs; shock absorbers; reinforced control arms; military 37×12.5 low-profile, run-flat radial tires; and a transfer case and differential with a modified gear ratio to accommodate higher payloads. The suspension uses an independent coil-spring-type system.

Ground Resupply Vehicle (GRSV)

When Special Forces teams venture out beyond the support of their Forward Operating Base (FOB), they rely on the GRSV. This unique truck, referred to as the "mother ship" or "war pig," is from the US Army's M1078 Family Of Medium Tactical Vehicles (FMTV). The GRSV is a highly modified version of the Stewart and Stevenson M1078 2.5-ton cargo truck.

As they do with many other special operations vehicles, Special Forces soldiers put their own mission-specific updates to the truck. Stripped down to the basics, the first thing to go was the removal of the enclosed cab. Then, mounts were added to accommodate an assortment of weapons, from M240B 7.62-millimeter to M2 .50-caliber machine guns. Radio equipment was enhanced to include SATCOM communications.

The GRSV's cargo bed has a payload capacity of 5,000 pounds and can be filled with spare tires, fuel, water, ammunition, and other mission-specific equipment. The truck is powered by a Caterpillar 3126 heavy-duty six-cylinder, electronically controlled, turbocharged fuel-injection engine. With a 58-gallon fuel tank, this full-time, all-wheel-drive vehicle has a range of 400-plus miles. It can travel at speeds in excess of 50 miles per hour and is easily air transportable.

Mark 19 Grenade Launcher

The Mark 19 Mod 3 automatic grenade launcher fires 40-millimeter cartridges, sending a volley of M430A1 High Explosive Dual Purpose (HEDP) grenades to its target with a press of the trigger. It has proven effective in destroying light armored vehicles, protecting convoys, and even defending against hovering rotary aircraft. The Mark 19 can send round downrange out to 2,000 meters, providing SOF units with a means to deliver massive direct or indirect fire on the enemy. The 40-millimeter grenade will penetrate 75-millimeter rolled homogenous armor at a maximum range of 2,050 meters. Dismounted personnel within a radius of 15 meters from impact will be hit by blast and fragmentation. The weapon weighs 77.6 pounds and is 43.1 inches in length.

Mark 47 Mod 0 Advanced Lightweight Grenade Launcher (ALGL)

Mark 47 Mod 0 weapon system is produced by General Dynamics, with Raytheon responsible for the Lightweight Video System (LVS) fire control. The Striker 40 ALGL is a 40-millimeter grenade launcher equipped with an integrated fire-control system capable of firing programmable airbursting ammunition as well as conventional high-velocity ammunition.

The Striker 40 ALGL is recoil operated and fires from the closed-bolt position. Compared to the Mark 19, it is much lighter and more compact and has a greater effective range and increased accuracy. The standard Mark 47 is mounted on a tripod, but it has also been installed on ATV light reconnaissance vehicles and can be installed on light armored vehicles as main or secondary armament. It weighs 39.6 pounds and is 36.6 inches in length.

Mine-Resistant Ambush Protected (MRAP) RG-31 Charger

When US Special Operations Forces first conducted operations in Afghanistan in support of Operation Enduring Freedom (see page 73), they did so in standard GMVs. As the exposure to improvised explosive devices (IEDs) became greater, however, they needed a vehicle that would provide better protection.

The Mine Resistant Ambush Protected (MRAP) RG-31 Charger auxiliary utility vehicle provides SOF units with a highly mobile vehicle that offers protection, ease of handling, crew comfort, and lethal offensive capability in the form of an integrated remote weapon station. The RG-31, manufactured by BAE Land Systems, uses a V-shaped monocoque welded-steel hull and high suspension, providing the crew superior protection against land mines, IEDs, and ambushes. Primary access into the vehicle is through a wide rear door, and eight roof hatches guarantee ease of access and egress.

The Charger is powered by a 125- or 154-kilowatt diesel engine, all-wheel drivetrain, and effective suspension system, providing for exceptional on- and off-road mobility. The DoD has stated that the casualty rate for MRAPs is 6 percent, making it the US military's most survivable vehicle; the rate for the more heavily armored HMMWV (Humvee), on the other hand, is 22 percent.

Mine-Resistant Ambush Protected (MRAP) RG-33

The BAE Land Systems RG-33 is a larger (6×6) category II vehicle in the MRAP family, providing protection for SOF operators against enemy ambushes using IEDs and other explosive ordnance. As with the RG-31, it is capable of employing an integrated remote weapon station, such as the CROWS (see page 96).

The SOCOM variant of the RG-33 is a 4×4 vehicle with two additional seats and rear-door access. It features a monocoque armored V-hull for maximized interior space, seats and footrests suspended from the ceiling, run-flat tires, and an optional armored glass turret (Gunner Protection Kit, or GPK) for maximized visibility and protection. The hull does not extend under the engine like those of some other armored vehicles; instead, the engine compartment is a separate monocoque structure that bolts on to rest of the hull.

The RG33 series is in the medium weight class, providing survivability, advanced mobility, and mission flexibility.

Tech Specs
Length: 265 in. (4×4)/338 in. (6×6)
Width: 96 in.
Maximum Speed: 68 mph (4×4)/ 67 mph (6×6)
Crew: 8 (4×4)/14 (6×6)

Common Remotely Operated Weapon Station (CROWS)

Manufactured by Kongsberg Defence and Aerospace, the Common Remotely Operated Weapon Station can be mounted atop MRAP vehicles so that the crew can acquire and engage the enemy with accurate fire from the protection of the armored crew compartment. The CROWS uses a stabilized mount containing a sensor suite and fire-control software, which allows on-the-move target acquisition and first-burst target engagement in both day and night environments. The suite includes a daytime video camera, thermal camera, and laser range finder.

The weapon system is designed to attach to any tactical vehicle and supports the Mark 19 grenade machine gun, M240B machine gun, M249 Squad Automatic Weapon (SAW), and M2 .50-caliber Browning heavy machine gun. Future systems may include the integration of the Javelin missile.

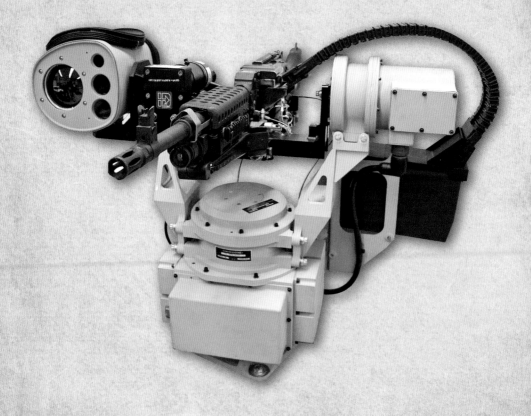

MOH: Staff Sergeant Robert J. Miller, 3rd SFG (A)

Staff Sergeant Robert J. Miller was a weapons sergeant with ODA-3312 in Afghanistan. While conducting a combat reconnaissance patrol through the Gowardesh Valley on January 25, 2008, Staff Sergeant Miller and a team of US and Afghan National Army (ANA) soldiers engaged a force of insurgents. Miller engaged the enemy with the Mark 19 40-millimeter grenade launcher on his GMV and at the same time provided intel on the enemy's positions to his command, enabling them to provide accurate Close Air Support (CAS).

Staff Sergeant Miller continued to lead his squad forward. At this time, the squad was ambushed by a large insurgent force. With little to no cover, the patrol was exposed to enemy rocket-propelled grenades and automatic weapons fire. Miller was on point and now cut off from any support. Less than 20 meters from the enemy, disregarding his own safety, he ordered his men back to cover. He then charged across exposed ground and overwhelming fire to close in on the insurgents, providing cover for his team. Wounded in the upper torso, Staff Sergeant Miller continued to engage the enemy. Though he was drawing fire from over one hundred insurgents, he drove on until his teammates had reach cover and safety.

Using the fire-and-maneuver tactic, he killed ten insurgents and wounded several others. His heroic actions saved his team and the fifteen ANA solders. However, it came with a high cost, as Staff Sergeant Miller was mortally wounded by enemy fire. For these acts of valor, he was awarded the Medal of Honor posthumously.

Survival, Evasion, Resistance, and Escape (SERE)

Special-operations forces are deployed around the world. They may conduct activity in the desert or on the side of a mountain; conditions can range from the extreme heat of the jungle to the frigid cold of subarctic regions. Most often, the team works together and draws strength from each other. There may be times, however, when operators find themselves alone with little or no personal equipment. Due to the nature of SOF missions, it is likely that a soldier will operate behind enemy lines, and he may be captured. Because of this, all SOF members attend the Survival, Evasion, Resistance, and Escape (SERE) School.

The keyword for the course is
SURVIVAL:
Size up the situation (the surroundings, your physical condition, equipment)
Undue haste makes waste
Remember where you are
Vanquish fear and panic
Improvise
Value living
Act like the natives
Live by your wits (or, for the new students, Learn basic skills)

General Henry Hugh Shelton

Henry Hugh Shelton, born January 2, 1942, in Tarboro, North Carolina, graduated from North Carolina State University and was commissioned as a second lieutenant. Other alma maters in his biography include Auburn University and Harvard. As he rose through the ranks, his military education would include the Air Command and Staff College and the National War College.

On his second tour in country in the Republic of South Vietnam, he would serve as a member of Detachment B-52, better known as Project Delta. During his tour of duty he also served as the commanding officer of an A-Team, Detachment A-104, 5th Special Forces Group (Airborne).

On July, 17, 1997, General Shelton became the commander of the US Special Operations Command at MacDill Air Force Base, Florida. The one-time A-Team commander was now in command of all US special-operations forces. General Shelton established a reputation for placing the welfare of his troops ahead of any politics, and it was not uncommon to see the general strap on a parachute and take his place in the chalk waiting to board an aircraft.

He served as the Chairman of the Joint Chiefs of Staff from October 1997 until his retirement in September 2001. General Shelton is the only chairman to date who has worn both the Ranger and Special Forces tabs.

Mark 18 Close Quarter Battle Receiver (CQBR)

The CQBR is a replacement upper receiver for the M4A1 carbine (see page 138) developed by the US Navy. The 10.3-inch-long CQBR replaces the 16-inch M4 1:7 twist barrel; this shorter barrel makes it easier to use in and around vehicles and in confined spaces. With the stock retracted, the overall length of the weapon is 26.75 inches. The Mark 18 is well suited for CQB as well as Personal Security Details (PSD). It is outfitted with a Special Operations Peculiar Modification (SOPMOD) stock from Lewis Machine and Tool, which also enhances the check weld for the shooter, though some operators may prefer to use one of various commercial stocks. The weapon is fitted with a Knight's Armament Company (KAC) M4QD flash suppressor, which facilitates the use of the KAC Quick Detach Sound Suppressor (QDSS). The standard handguard is the KAC Rail Interface System (RIS), which allows the shooter to attach tactical accessories as the mission dictates. Under SOCOM Block II, the handguards have been modified to the Daniel Defense rail system. The Mark 18 remains chambered in 5.56-millimeter.

SCAR-L Mark 16 Mod 0 Assault Rifle

The Special Operations Forces Combat Assault Rifle (SCAR) is a modular assault rifle designed from the ground up with input from US Special Operations Forces. Designed by FN Herstal (FNH), headquartered in Herstal, Belgium, the SCAR is manufactured at the FN manufacturing plant in Columbia, South Carolina. The SCAR system includes the Mark 16 Mod 0 chambered in 5.56-millimeter. The SCAR weapons employ a short-stroke gas piston system, eliminating the gas direct system of the M16/M4 family. This provides a more reliable weapon that does not heat up the rail system. The butt features a folding, telescoping stock as well as an adjustment allowing the operator to set the proper eye alignment to the assortment of SOPMOD optics. The SCAR-L was to replace the Mark 18 CQBR (10-inch SOPMOD upper), the standard M4A1 carbine, and the Mark 12 Special Purpose Rifle (SPR). However, in August 2010, SOCOM announced the cancellation of any further acquisitions of the Mark 16 version of the SCAR.

M26 Modular Accessory Shotgun System (MASS)

The M26 is a departure from the Mossberg 500 and Remington 870 shotguns in use before it. The 500 and 870 are tube fed and weigh in around 8 pounds; the M26 attaches to the bottom of an M4 carbine and uses a magazine, adding 3.5 pounds to the weapon. With the addition of a stock and pistol grip, the M26 can also be used as a standalone weapon weighing 5.5 pounds. To address the concern that lightweight means more recoil, the M26 features a hydraulic recoil buffer in the buttstock, which reduces the felt recoil. The flexibility of the five-round magazine allows the shooter to swap between breaching round and 12-gauge antipersonnel buckshot. The shooter can change a magazine faster than it takes to reload the traditional shotgun tube.

Glock 19

Love them or hate them, Glocks are considered by some as the most versatile handgun. Manufactured by Glock GmbH in Deutsch-Wagram, Austria, this polymer-framed handgun was introduced in the early 1980s. It was scorned by some law enforcement and counterterrorism specialists as a "plastic" gun that would elude airport metal detectors. In reality, it was hardly invisible.

The first Glock, a short-recoil-operated, locked-breech semiautomatic pistol, was considered revolutionary at the time of its introduction. Today it is favored by law enforcement, and even FBI G-men holster the 9-millimeter wonder. The pistol features a modular back strap to accommodate a variety of shooters. The fourth-generation version also incorporates an accessory rail fore of the trigger guard for lights and laser sights.

The Glock 19 is chambered for a 9×19-millimeter Parabellum round, which feeds from a fifteen-round magazine.

M9 Pistol

Since 1985, the M9 has seen service as the standard-issue sidearm for US troops in both conventional and special operations units—from Operation Urgent Fury in Grenada to the Global War on Terrorism. Along with the standardization of the 9-millimeter round, the M9 brought the armed forces a larger-capacity magazine. The M9 holds fifteen rounds, compared to the Colt 1911's seven or eight. Although the 9-millimeter ammunition is lighter and smaller, the US military determined that this was adequate for line troops. This tradeoff also allowed the troops to engage more rounds in a firefight before needing to reload. The original M9 was viewed with some apprehension among operators in the special operations community when the usage of overpressure (+P) ammunition reportedly caused stress fractures in the weapon's slides. Beretta addressed this problem, however, and today's M9 has an average life of 72,250 rounds. The slide is open for nearly the entire length of the barrel, which facilitates the ejection of spent shells and virtually eliminates stoppages. The open-slide configuration also allows the pistol to be loaded manually. It is worth noting that the only two units that did not switch over to the M9 were US Marine Force Recon and Delta Force.

M1014 Shotgun

The M1014 tactical shotgun, or M4 Super 90, was originally designed in 1998 by Benelli for the US Marine Corps. The M4 was the first gas-operated shotgun produced by the manufacturer and uses a unique Auto-Regulating Gas-Operated (ARGO) system. The short-stroke design uses two self-cleaning, stainless-steel pistons located just ahead of the chamber to function opposite the rotating bolt, eliminating the need for the complex mechanisms found on other gas-actuated automatics.

The M1014 has collapsible stock with a pistol grip. The 12-gauge shotgun weighs 8.42 pounds; its overall length is 34.8 inches, with an 18.5-inch barrel, and its effective range is 55 yards. It has a Picatinny (MIL-STD-1913) rail for mounting optics, a laser, and lights.

M72 Light Anti-Armor Weapon (LAW)

Introduced in the 1960s, the M72 is still found on the battlefield today. It weighs a mere 2 pounds and is a fire-and-discard weapon. The firing tube, firing mechanism, carrying case, and 66-millimeter rocket are all self-contained in a pair of waterproof tubes. When prepared to fire, the shooter unlatches the endcaps of the container and extends the inner tube; this allows the sighting mechanism to pop up, ready for use. The front sight features a reticle in 25-meter increments, and the rear functions as a peep sight.

The M72 fires a 66-millimeter High-Explosive Antitank (HEAT) warhead. Once fired, the rocket engines ignite and six folding fins spring out to stabilize its flight to the target. The rocket has a maximum effective range of 200 meters.

AT4 Antitank Weapon

The M136 AT4 is the army's principal light antitank weapon, providing precision delivery of an 84-millimeter HEAT warhead with negligible recoil. It is a man-portable, self-contained antiarmor weapon consisting of a free-flight, fin-stabilized, rocket-type cartridge packed in an expendable, one-piece, fiberglass-wrapped tube. Unlike the M72 LAW, the AT4 launcher does not need to be extended before firing. When the warhead makes impact with the target, the nose cone crushes, causing the impact sensor to activate the internal fuse. Upon ignition, the piezoelectric fuse element triggers the detonator, initiating the main charge and sending the warhead body into a directional gas jet, which is capable of penetrating over 17 inches of armor plate. The aftereffects include "spalling," the projecting of fragments, and incendiary effects, which generate blinding light and obliterate the interior of the target.

M3 Carl Gustaf Rifle

Officially known as the Multi-Role Anti-Armor Anti-Personnel Weapon System, or MAAWS, this breech-loaded, shoulder-fired recoilless rifle is known as the M3 Carl Gustaf by SOF units. Similar to the AT-4 in its design as a shoulder-fired, antitank weapon, the chief distinction is that the M3 Carl Gustaf can be used more than once. It has been in service with SOCOM since 1991.

Once a gunner has fired the 84-millimeter High-Explosive (HE) or High Explosive Dual Purpose (HEDP) round, the weapon is reloaded and is ready to fire again. The purpose of the M3 is to engage lightly armored vehicles out to 700 meters and soft targets out to 1,000 meters. The blast radius from an HE round is approximately 50 to 75 meters.

The gun can be fired from a standing, kneeling, sitting, or prone position. A built-in, detachable bipod helps the shooter raise the weapon off the ground while shooting from a prone position. The current M3 weighs approximately 22 pounds, with each round of ammunition weighing less than 10 pounds.

M224 60mm Lightweight Company Mortar System (LWCMS)

The General Dynamics M224 60-millimeter LWCMS is a man-portable, lightweight, smoothbore, muzzle-loaded mortar with high angle and rate of fire. It is ideally suited for use by airborne, air assault, mountain, and special operations forces. The M224 can be drop fired (conventional mode) or trigger fired (conventional or handheld mode). A lightweight auxiliary baseplate is used when firing the mortar in the handheld mode. Standard 60-millimeter mortar ammunition includes HE, smoke, illumination (visible and infrared), and practice. The mortar has a range of 231 feet, out to 2.17 miles. It is 40 inches long and weighs 46.5 pounds.

Breaching Shotgun

For mechanical breaching of a door or window frame, "door kickers" may use a cut-down version of the Remington 870 shotgun. The 870P is a breaching gun with an 11.5-inch barrel that fires a 12-gauge round. It can use a standard shotgun shell, buckshot, or a special breaching round made specifically for breaching doors.

Standing back approximately 6 inches, the shooter fires a round at the door, aiming at the hinges or an area between the door and the doorjamb. The round is designed to destroy the target and disperse the powder harmlessly.

Snipers

The primary mission of the sniper in combat is to support combat operations by delivering precision fire on selected targets from concealed positions. The sniper's secondary mission is to gather information for intelligence purposes.

A selected volunteer, the special-operations sniper is specially trained in advanced marksmanship and fieldcraft skills. He can support special operations missions and is able to engage selected targets at ranges and under conditions that are not possible for the regular rifleman. A sniper should be comfortable in the woods, have an interest in weapons, and be a competent shooter; often, a sniper will have previous experience as a hunter. Additionally, he possesses an attention to detail, perseverance, physical stamina, and, above all, patience.

Operating in two-man teams, snipers and spotters will work up range cards representing key locations and distances, then enter this information into their Data On Personal Equipment (DOPE). SOF snipers are trained to Level 1 category, which means that an SOF sniper can drop an enemy at extreme close range. Their missions range from removing specific targets to overwatch force protection.

AN/PVS-10 Sniper Night Sight

The AN/PVS-10 Sniper Night Sight (SNS) is a lightweight, weapon-mounted, self-contained, image-intensified passive device designed for use by the sniper in both day and night operations. The sight provides the shooter with 8.5 times magnification as well as a variable-gain image intensifier that can be adjusted by the user depending on ambient light levels. The PVS-10 includes a black-line reticle for day use and can be illuminated for night use when required. The system enables the shooter to accurately acquire and engage targets using M24 SWS (see page 284) or M110 Semi-Automatic Sniper System (SASS) at night to a range of 600 meters and during daylight to a range of 800 meters. A day/night lever enables the sniper to switch between day and night modes of operation. The sight is powered by two AA batteries with an operational time of twenty-four hours per set of batteries.

M2010 Enhanced Sniper Rifle

The M2010 Enhanced Sniper Rifle (ESR) was developed by the US Army Program Executive Office Soldier (PEO Soldier) as a replacement for the M24 SWS (see page 284). The ESR has been rechambered to fire .300 Winchester Magnum ammunition; it has a hammer-forged, free-floating 24-inch barrel with a 1:10 twist. It is a bolt-action, five-round, magazine-fed system that provides precision fire on targets at ranges 50 percent farther than previous 7.62-millimeter sniper systems. The M2010 is equipped with the Remington Arms Chassis System (RACS) with a right-folding stock, allowing the shooter to adjust the length of pull and cheek height. The chassis features a monolithic Picatinny accessory rail and accessory cable routing channels. The M2010 is fielded with a Leupold Mark 4 6.5–20×50 Long-Range/Tactical (LR/T) riflescope that includes a first-focal-plane Horus Vision H58 grid system reticle for ranging and targeting and an AN/PVS-30 clip-on sniper night sight. Also included in the kit is an Advanced Armament Corporation fast-attach suppressor, which reduces the sound of the weapon by 32 decibels.

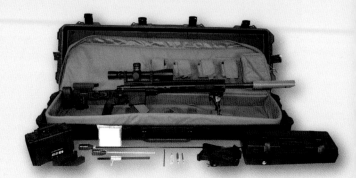

M110 Semi-Automatic Sniper System (SASS)

The M110 is a semiautomatic sniper rifle chambered for the 7.62×51-millimeter NATO round, developed and manufactured by Knight's Armament Company. The M110 was intended to replace the M24 Sniper Weapon System (SWS) used by the US Army (see page 284), but both are in use today. The M110 SASS is capable of delivering precision fire to enemy targets out to 800 meters. The weapon is shorter and lighter than traditional sniper rifles, which enhances the mobility of SOF and allows for rapid follow-up shots. The complete system includes a Leupold 3.5–10×40-millimeter variable-power daytime optic and a Harris swivel bipod. The rifle has ambidextrous controls to accommodate both right- and left-handed shooters. As configured with scope and twenty-round magazine, the rifle weighs 15.3 pounds and is 40.5 inches in length. It is similar to the SR-25 Mark 11 Mod 0 sniper rifle, differing significantly in buttstock and rail system design.

SCAR Mark 20 Sniper Support Rifle (SSR)

With the acceptance and success of the SCAR Mark 17 Mod 0 by SOF units down range (see page 203), FN Herstal has now developed the SCAR Sniper Support Rifle (SSR). Designated the Mark 20 SSR, it is designed for long-range, precision-fire applications while also providing the ability for close-in engagements. Based on the Mark 17 SCAR platform, the SSR is capable of sub-minute-of-angle accuracy out to 1,000 yards and beyond. The Mark 20 features an extended receiver rail and Picatinny accessory rails at the three, six, nine, and twelve o'clock positions for mounting lights, lasers, and night-vision and thermal devices with standard or sniper optics.

Like the SCAR-H (see page 203), it is chambered for 7.62×51-millimeter NATO ammunition from a ten- or twenty-round magazine. The 20-inch, hammer-forged barrel is chrome lined and free floating. Unlike that of the Mark 17, the stock on the Mark 20 SSR does not fold. It features an adjustable cheek piece and length of pull to accommodate the SOF shooter.

Though common among sniper rifles, the Mark 20 SSR is not light, weighing in at 10.69 pounds empty with a length of 42.5 inches with the stock fully extended.

AX338 Sniper Rifle

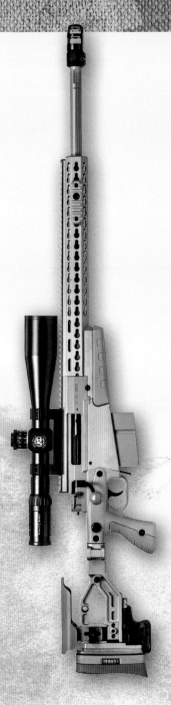

Accuracy International (AX) of Portsmouth, England, is well known throughout the special operations community worldwide as a premier manufacturer of precision sniper rifles. The AX338 is chambered in .338 Lapua Magnum, designed and engineered specifically for this caliber, and uses a ten-round, double-stack magazine.

The combat-proven, polymer-and-alloy, ergonomic and functional folding chassis—don't call it a stock—provides the rigidity, strength, and durability necessary to provide a stable, rugged platform for the barreled action in all weather and in any environment. The butt pad is fitted with either a bolt-on pad, including 10- and 20-millimeter spacers, or with an optional quick-adjust butt pad, with which the user can customize the length of pull. A butt spike enables the user to observe the target area for extended periods with minimal fatigue, and the cheek piece adjusts left, right, up, and down to accommodate night-vision equipment or telescopic sights with large objective lenses. The fore end is a combination of Picatinny and KeyMod rails for attaching optics, lasers, lights, and other accessories.

The weapon weighs 14.6 pounds empty and without a scope. The overall length is 48.2 inches, which can be trimmed down to 38 inches with the buttstock folded. The barrel measures 27 inches, including the muzzle break.

Claymore

The M18A1 antipersonnel mine, more commonly known as the claymore, is primarily employed as a defensive weapon, but it can also be used as an offensive weapon. The M18A1 can be deployed as a booby trap or as a pursuit-deterrence device. Additionally, the claymore can be sighted directionally to provide fragmentation over a specific target area and can be command-detonated.

The claymore consists of a curved, rectangular, plastic case that contains a layer of composition C-3 explosive, packed with seven hundred steel balls. The front face containing the steel balls is designed to produce an arc-shaped spray, which can be aimed at a predetermined target area. It comes in a bandoleer that includes the M18A1 mine, an M57 firing device, an M40 test set, and an electrical blasting-cap assembly.

C-4

The M112 block demolition charge consists of 1.25 pounds of composition C-4 shaped into a rectangular block and packaged in a peelable, olive-drab, Mylar-film container with pressure-sensitive adhesive tape on one surface, allowing the charge to be attached to any relatively flat, clean, dry surface. C-4 is white and has a unique lemony citrus smell. The M112 block demolition charge is used primarily for cutting and breaching all types of demolition work. Because of its moldability, the charge is perfect for cutting irregularly shaped targets, such as steel beams.

Breaching Charges

Explosive breaching covers a diverse selection of explosives and techniques. Explosives such as flexible linear charges, detonation cords ("det cords"), and C-4 are all to be found in this demolition specialist's repertoire. A common technique used is the silhouette charge: using a cardboard silhouette with one to three wraps of det cord around the perimeter does a good job of cutting through a door. Replace the det cord with the proper amount of C-4 and the silhouette will blow out a substantial passageway through a cinder block wall. Assorted initiators are also employed for instant detonation. Explosive breaching is extremely useful for dynamic entry, when seeking to focus the bad guys' attention on the noise, light, and pieces of shrapnel zooming toward them from the door; this split-second distraction provides the entry team enough time to neutralize an enemy in the room.

Blasting Caps

A blasting cap is a small, sensitive, primary explosive device generally used to detonate a larger, more powerful and less sensitive secondary explosive, such as TNT, dynamite, or plastic explosive. The M7 is a nonelectric blasting cap assembly consisting of an aluminum-alloy cup that contains an ignition charge of lead styphnate, an intermediate charge of lead azide, and a base charge of Research Department Explosive (RDX). When initiated by a timed blast fuse, the ignition charge detonates the intermediate charge, which then detonates the base charge, initiating the explosive charge.

The M6 is an electric blasting cap used to initiate high explosives with a blasting machine or other electric power to detonate military explosives. Like that of the M7, the assembly of the M6 is an aluminum-alloy cup; however, in this case, it contains potassium chlorate and lead salt with a base charge of RDX. Two 12-foot lead wires, connected by a bridge wire in the ignition charge, extend through a rubber (or rubber and sulfur) plug assembly in the open end of the cup.

M2 Selectable Lightweight Attack Munition (SLAM)

The M2 weighs a mere 2.2 pounds and is small enough to fit in the pocket of a BDU. The warhead can penetrate targets of 40-millimeter rolled homogeneous armor out to 25 feet. Its four operating modes include bottom attack (magnetic influence fuse), in which it senses the magnetic signature of a vehicle as it passes over the M2, detonating upward; side attack (passive infrared), in which detonation occurs upon sensing a passing vehicle's infrared signature; time demolition of a target in increments of fifteen, thirty, forty-five, or sixty minutes; and operator-initiated command detonation, using standard army blasting caps of the new Time-Delay Firing Device (TDFD).

M84 Stun Hand Grenade

The M84 was developed by the US Army to provide a non-lethal, non-fragmentation diversionary stun grenade. Also known as a flashbang, the stun grenade is used to confuse, disorient, or momentarily distract potential threats in a dynamic-entry situation. The M84 is easily identified by its two hexagonal endcaps on a perforated tube as well as its round and triangular safety rings. When deployed, it creates an extremely loud bang of 175 decibels and a blinding flash of more than 1 million candlepower. Any individual in range is subject to flash blindness, deafness, disorientation, confusion, and loss of coordination and balance. This allows the entry team a split second to enter and clear the room of any hostiles. The stun grenade is used when minimum force is necessary in missions such as hostage rescue or capture of high-value targets (HVTs).

Fast Rope Insertion/Extraction System (FRIES)

The Fast Rope Insertion/Extraction System offers a method for inserting an assault force on the ground in seconds. It begins with small woven ropes made of wool, which are braided into a larger rope, rolled into a deployment bag, and secured to a helicopter. Depending on the model of chopper, it can be placed just outside on the hoist mechanism of the side door or attached to a bracket off the back ramp. Once over the insertion point, the rope is deployed; even as it is hitting the ground, ODA members jump onto the woolen line and slide down, as easily as a fireman goes down a pole. Once the team is safely on the ground, the flight engineer or gunner (depending on the type of helicopter) pulls the safety pin, and the rope falls to the ground.

Such a system is useful for the rapid deployment of SOF personnel; an entire ODA can be inserted within 12 to 15 seconds. The most accepted way of getting a force on the ground expeditiously, FRIES is distinct from rappelling in that, once the trooper hits the ground, he is free of the rope and can begin his mission.

Special Procedure, Insertion, and Extraction System (SPIES)

The follow-up to FRIES is the extraction method, originally known as the Special Procedure, Insertion, and Extraction System (SPIES); the army has since combined both methods into one term. While fast roping gets ODA members down quickly, there are times when speedy extraction is just as important. For extraction, a single rope is lowered from the hovering helicopter. Attached to this rope are rings, woven and secured into the rope at approximately 5-foot intervals, with as many as eight rings per rope. Wearing a special harness, each SOF operator attaches himself to the rope by clipping a snap link to a ring at the top of the harness. Once all team members are secured, a signal is given to the helicopter, the soldiers become "airborne" in reverse, and they are extracted out harm's way.

This method, tried and tested, allows the team to maintain covering fire with their weapons as they extract. Once the unit has been whisked out of enemy range and a Landing Zone (LZ) can be located, the helicopter pilot brings the troops to ground again. They disconnect from the rope and board the chopper, which completes the extraction.

Rappelling

Originating when the first Special Forces soldiers operated in the mountains of Bavaria, near Bad Tölz, Germany, this old mountaineering technique has served SF troops well, and is a still in the inventory of unit skills employed today. Whether a team is working in mountainous terrain or in an urban environment, rappelling is a valuable skill. When traversing a steep hill while carrying an 80- to 100-pound rucksack, it may be the best way down the contour.

SOF teams will train in this procedure with full combat gear, or will practice rappelling while carrying a casualty. Attaching a regular military assault line through carabiners or a specially designed rappelling device known as a "figure eight," a team easily negotiates down the side of a mountain or a building.

Close Quarters Battle (CQB)

The principles of CQB are surprise, speed, and violence of action. The key to a successful assault is surprise. In a dynamic entry, the team, also called the "stack," may begin the attack with a flashbang grenade—the deafening sound, smoke, and extreme bright light disorient any hostiles in the room, providing the team with extra seconds that can give them the edge to engage and neutralize the enemy (see page 113). Speed provides a measure of security to the assaulting force, as these split seconds offer an advantage to the attacker. Violence of action neutralizes the enemy, eliminating the least chance of them inflicting casualties. SOF units practice these tactics and techniques religiously. There is a saying that "amateurs practice till they get it right; professionals practice until they can't get it wrong."

Cultural Support Teams

On January 24, 2013, the policy barring women from combat roles ended. Shortly thereafter, SOCOM began introducing women into Special Forces and Ranger units as Cultural Support Teams (CSTs). The CSTs are composed entirely of female soldiers who support army special operations teams' contact with the indigenous female populations in their areas of operations (AO). Reminiscent of the Vietnam-era Green Berets, the CSTs endeavor to win the hearts and minds of area women and children. They provide a means of contact in situations in which the interaction between female civilians and male soldiers would be culturally inappropriate. CSTs directly support activities ranging from medical civic action programs and humanitarian assistance to searches and seizures and civil military operations.

CST soldiers begin their training with a nine-day assessment and selection course at Fort Bragg, North Carolina. The candidates go through physical, mental, and intellectual evaluations designed to determine whether they have the ability to maintain their composure, apply logic, communicate clearly, and solve problems in demanding environments downrange.

If they complete this assessment period, they attend the cultural support training course for six weeks. The course focuses on human behavior, Islamic and Afghan cultures, women and their role in Afghanistan, and tribalism, concluding with a field training exercise. Following graduation, each soldier is attached to an army special operations unit overseas for approximately nine months.

MREs

During the American Civil War, soldiers consumed a biscuit-like staple made from flour, water, and sometimes salt. Once baked, it would harden to an almost inedible substance, leading to its familiar name: hardtack. "Good eating" was some hardtack and salted pork. As GIs headed off to Europe and the Pacific in World War II, they satiated their hunger with K-rations, which offered more of a meal. Later in the war, and through to Vietnam, C-rations became standard, consisting of several cans of food and accessories, including cigarettes.

Today's operators dine on the Meal, Ready to Eat (MRE)—variously called "meals rejected by everyone," "meals rejected by the enemy," "meals rarely enjoyed," and so on. If you are within walking distance of any type of real food, the MRE is often less than palatable. However, if you are in the boonies, miles away from any food source and hungry, MREs are not so bad. The military's culinary specialists are constantly on the hunt for ways to tantalize warriors' taste buds, and menu items appear and disappear as part of this ongoing process. One interesting fact: unlike its predecessors, today's MRE no longer contains cigarettes. While a soldier can be sent off to deal with insurgents, IEDs, hostile environments, and the like, the US military has determined that cigarettes are too hazardous to their health.

Individual First Aid Kit (IFAK)

An IFAK, or Blow Out Kit (BOK), provides an operator with basic medical supplies. A medic may not be able to reach a wounded individual in the heat of battle, and the IFAK allows soldiers to carry their own medical supplies to dress their own wounds or those of a teammate. The kit is intended to treat the three leading causes of preventable death from battlefield wounds: hemorrhaging, tension pneumothorax (collapsed lung), and airway obstruction. The treatment of such wounds provides operators a greater chance of survival, allowing them to be stabilized and medevaced for surgical treatment.

The Viper Flat IFAK by S. O. Tech was designed for and issued by SOCOM. The operator deploys this quick-access IFAK, which carries the essential medical supplies, by pulling the handles from either side. Trim enough to give the operator several options for locating, as determined by personal choice or team Standard Operating Procedure (SOP), the kit has Pouch Attachment Ladder System (PALS) webbing on the pouch, while the internal carrier has sufficient room for the necessary medical supplies.

Mark VI Patrol Boat

The Mark VI Patrol Boat (PB), manufactured by SAFE Boats International in Bremerton, Washington, is the replacement for the aging Mark V Special Operations Craft (SOC) (see page 219). The new PB is equipped with newer weapons, communications, surveillance, intelligence, and reconnaissance systems. The 85-foot, aluminum-hulled vessel is manned by a crew of ten; powered by twin diesels connected to water jets, it can make speed in excess of 35 knots.

The boat has a covered fly bridge, and the main deck cabin can is reconfigurable, depending on mission parameters. The PB has berthing accommodations, a galley, and head/shower facilities to allow for extended missions. As was the case with its predecessor, crew and passengers ride in the comfort of special seats to lessen the shock of crashing waves beneath them. There is also room for additional personnel and mission-specific equipment. Survivability is increased with the inclusion of armor plating surrounding the engines and fuel tank.

Standard armament for the Mark VI includes two remote-controlled Mark 38 Mod 2 25-millimeter chain guns and six crewed M2 .50-caliber machine guns. Depending on mission needs, various gun mounts can accommodate M240 machine guns, M134 miniguns, and Mark 19 grenade launchers. There are also plans to mount the AGM-176 Griffin guided missiles. The aft deck and stern are capable of launching and recovering Combat Rubber Raiding Craft (CRRCs) as well as Unmanned Aerial Vehicles (UAVs).

Operation Anaconda: Afghanistan

In early March 2002, US conventional forces, Special Operations Forces, and CIA Paramilitary Officers—working with allied Afghan military forces and coalition forces from Australia, Canada, Denmark, France, Germany, and Norway—attempted to destroy al-Qaeda and Taliban forces. Operation Anaconda took place in the Shah-i-Kot Valley and Arma Mountains southeast of Zormat, Afghanistan.

During the operation, the Battle of Takur Ghar was a short and intense military engagement between US SOF and al-Qaeda insurgents atop Takur Ghar Mountain in Afghanistan. For US special ops, the battle proved the deadliest engagement of the operation. Three helicopter landings on the mountaintop were assaulted by al-Qaeda forces. Takur Ghar was eventually taken, but seven US service members were killed and several more wounded. The first casualty was Navy SEAL Neil C. Roberts, who fell from an MH-47 helicopter. The engagement is also known as the Battle of Roberts Ridge.

GMV: Early

In the late 1970s, the US military wanted a general-purpose vehicle that could perform better than the M151 Jeep. In 1979, the branch drafted specifications for a new tactical vehicle, and, in March 1983, AM General was contracted to provide the High Mobility Multipurpose Wheeled Vehicle. The HMMWV, or "Humvee" as it became known, is a lightweight, highly mobile, four-wheel-drive tactical vehicle powered by a diesel engine. Fifteen feet long, it has a low profile of 6 feet and a wide, road-hugging stance.

In the 1990s, Special Forces missions established a need for a more robust version of the HMMWV; during the Gulf War, HMMWVs modified for extended desert missions were deployed by the Special Forces. The modifications included a heavier suspension, a more powerful engine, and an open bed and back for storage of water, fuel, and other mission-essential items. These modified desert HMMWVs were often called "Dumvees," though this was never an official name for the vehicle. They are officially designated as Ground Mobility Vehicles (GMVs).

Pack Mules

After the Korean War, the US Army discontinued the use of pack animals. In their place, the military has relied on air and ground mobility for transporting personnel and equipment. Today, however, SOF operators may still find themselves involved in rural or remote environments where using pack animals is advantageous. Horses and mules allow SOF units to maintain a low profile while lugging heavy equipment through inhospitable terrain. Taking a page from history, military pack animal operations have allowed commanders to transport personnel and equipment into or within a designated Area of Operations (AO). Such operations are ideally suited for, but not limited to, conducting various missions in high mountain terrain, deserts, and dense jungle terrain. SOF units have used such non-traditional means to get in and out of the enemy areas as they battle insurgents covertly. For those units deployed to Afghanistan in support of Operation Enduring Freedom (see page 73), horses were often the only means of transport in the mountains, while pack mules served to carry their equipment.

Paramarines

In May 1940, the commandant of the US Marine Corps, Maj. Gen. Thomas Holcomb, ordered the creation of a marine unit capable of deploying via parachute. This unit, the paramarines, would comprise one battalion of infantry and a platoon of artillery consisting of two 75-millimeter howitzers to act in three tactical roles: (1) as a reconnaissance and raiding force operating under the assumption they may not be able to return to Allied lines; (2) as a spearhead to capture and hold strategic positions or terrain until relieved by larger follow-on forces; and (3) as an independent force functioning in a guerrilla-warfare role behind enemy lines.

A paramarine was armed with an M1911 .45-caliber pistol and a Reising submachine gun. The Reising is an air-cooled, delayed-blowback, shoulder-fired weapon weighing 6.5 pounds with a maximum effective range of 300 yards. It is chambered for .45-caliber Automatic Colt Pistol (ACP) ammunition in either a twelve- or a twenty-round magazine. It has a muzzle velocity of 900 feet per second and cyclic rate of 450 rounds per minute.

Near the end of World War II, the Marine Corps questioned the need for the airborne unit and decided it was not necessary. On December 30, 1943, the unit was disbanded.

Marine Raiders

After the attack on Pearl Harbor, President Franklin D. Roosevelt became interested in creating elite units on par with the British commandos to operate in the Pacific. After some deliberation, Marine Corps Commandant Thomas Holcomb selected the name "Raiders" and created two both activated in February 1942. (Two additional battalions were created and served in the Pacific theater.)

These Marine Raider battalions consisted of lightly armed, intensely trained units tasked with three missions: (1) spearhead larger amphibious landings on beaches thought to be inaccessible; (2) conduct raids requiring surprise and high speed; and (3) operate as guerrilla units for lengthy periods behind enemy lines.

Having been formed by directive from the president, the Raiders enjoyed wide latitude in the acquisition of weapons and equipment. Whether or not it was part of the Corps standard issue, the Raiders got priority, no questions asked. This included manpower, as the battalions sought—and received—the best marine volunteers available. Among some marines, they were viewed as an elite group within an already elite group, leading to some resentment in the Corps, with many believing the majority of operations conducted by the Marine Raiders involved tactics that should be taught to all marine infantry.

The four Marine Raider battalions participated in twenty major campaigns and battles during World War II. They were disbanded in February 1944 in part because their existence was deemed "detrimental to the morale of other troops."

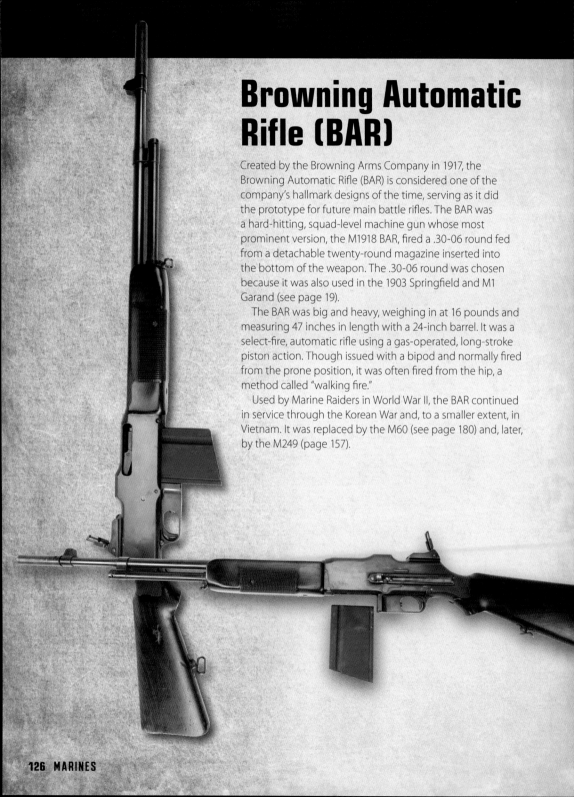

Browning Automatic Rifle (BAR)

Created by the Browning Arms Company in 1917, the Browning Automatic Rifle (BAR) is considered one of the company's hallmark designs of the time, serving as it did the prototype for future main battle rifles. The BAR was a hard-hitting, squad-level machine gun whose most prominent version, the M1918 BAR, fired a .30-06 round fed from a detachable twenty-round magazine inserted into the bottom of the weapon. The .30-06 round was chosen because it was also used in the 1903 Springfield and M1 Garand (see page 19).

The BAR was big and heavy, weighing in at 16 pounds and measuring 47 inches in length with a 24-inch barrel. It was a select-fire, automatic rifle using a gas-operated, long-stroke piston action. Though issued with a bipod and normally fired from the prone position, it was often fired from the hip, a method called "walking fire."

Used by Marine Raiders in World War II, the BAR continued in service through the Korean War and, to a smaller extent, in Vietnam. It was replaced by the M60 (see page 180) and, later, by the M249 (page 157).

Lieutenant Colonel Merritt "Red Mike" Edson

The 1st Marine Raider Battalion was activated on February 16, 1942, followed by the 2nd Marine Raider Battalion on February 19, 1942. Lieutenant Colonel Merritt Edson commanded the 1st Battalion, which earned them the name "Edson's Raiders." Edson retained the traditional eight-man squad, comprising a squad leader, two BAR men, four riflemen armed with M1903 Springfield rifles, and a sniper.

Lieutenant Colonel Edson was awarded the Medal of Honor for extraordinary heroism and conspicuous intrepidity above and beyond the call during action against enemy Japanese forces in the Solomon Islands. On August 8, 1942, the airfield on Guadalcanal had been seized from the Japanese. Commanding a force of eight hundred men comprising Raiders and an attached parachute battalion, Lieutenant Colonel Edson was assigned to the occupation and defense of a ridge dominating the jungle on either side of the airfield. On the night of September 13–14, 1942, these Marines came under attack by a formidable Japanese force. Edson withdrew his forward units to a reserve line. Although continuously exposed to hostile fire, he personally directed defense of the reserve position against a numerically superior force, retaining control of the airfield.

Landing Craft Rubber Small (LCRS)

Today, the F470 Zodiac Combat Rubber Raiding Craft (CRRC) is the special-ops mainstay for over-the-beach infiltration. Back in World War II, however, the craft of choice was the Landing Craft Rubber Small (LCRS), which evolved into the Inflatable Boat Small (IBS).

Marine Raiders used this small inflatable rubber raft for insertion on beach landing sites. Underwater Demolition Teams (UDTs) also used the rafts, securing them to the sides of Landing Craft Personnel Rubber (LCPR) boats for cast and recovery of navy frogmen.

The LCRS was 16 feet long with an 8-foot beam, weighed 210 pounds, and could carry seven men. Note the marine on the bow of the raft seen here providing security with a BAR (see page 126).

Thompson Submachine Gun

Bearing the name of its inventor, John Thompson, the M1928A1 Thompson submachine gun was a selective-fire, semiautomatic or fully automatic weapon adopted by the Marine Corps shortly after its introduction. It was chambered for .45-caliber ammunition loaded into a twenty- or thirty-round stick magazine. In some instances, soldiers welded two magazines together, allowing them to flip it over, thus doubling the ammo capacity. A fifty-round drum magazine was also available—this could be emptied in four seconds when fired on full automatic.

The Thompson (or "Tommy gun," for short) had a velocity of 920 feet per second with an effective range of 55 yards. It was 33.7 inches in length, and, even though it weighed 11 pounds, it still had a tendency to rise as the shooter fired in full automatic. The Thompson was reliable and durable, and it served well for close-in fighting. It was widely used by not only marines (such the one seen here moving up a hill at Guadalcanal), but by paratroopers, Rangers, and the 1st Special Service Force (Devil's Brigade) as well.

Lieutenant Colonel Evans Carlson

Lieutenant Colonel Merritt Edson's counterpart in the 2nd Raider Battalion was Lt. Col. Evans Carlson. Born in 1896 in Sidney, New York, Carlson was the son of the local minister. He dropped out of school in 1912 and enlisted in the US Army. He would serve in the Philippines, Mexico, and France, where he would be commissioned as a captain.

His Marine Corps career began when he enlisted as a private in 1922. His assignments took him to Puerto Rico, Nicaragua, and Shanghai, again rising to the rank of captain. In 1942, he was commissioned as a lieutenant colonel and given command of the 2nd Raider Battalion.

Lieutenant Colonel Carlson departed from the norm by organizing the 2nd, "Carlson's Raiders," into ten-man teams that included a squad leader and three fire teams of three marines apiece. These marines were armed with Thompson submachine guns, BARs, and M1 Garand semiautomatic rifles.

His leadership in the raid on Makin Island, August 17, 1942, earned him a gold star in lieu of a second Navy Cross.

M2 Carbine

Like the M1 carbine (see page 19), the M2 was a lightweight, gas-operated weapon. The primary difference between the two was that the M2 was a select-fire weapon capable of firing on full automatic. The .30-caliber ammunition was fed through a newly introduced thirty-round magazine, often called a "banana mag" due to its shape. The rate of fire for the M2 was 850 to 900 rounds per minute with an effective range of 300 yards. Like the M1, the M2 was used in Korea and with Special Forces in Vietnam. The carbine was phased out when the M16 assault rifle (see page 29) was introduced in the late 1960s.

HRS-1

As the Air Commandos proved in the China-Burma-India theater, helicopters could play a pivotal role in the combat environment. Sikorsky's S-55 helicopter received lift from a single main three-blade rotor assembly above the cockpit with an antitorque rotor on the tail boom. The army and air force model was called the H-19 Chickasaw; the Marine Corps variant was designated the HRS-1 (H for helicopter, R for transport, and S for Sikorsky).

The HRS-1 was powered by a Pratt and Whitney R-1340 Wasp engine and had a range of 330 miles. It had a crew of two and could transport eight fully equipped troops. On September 20, 1951, US Marines of the 1st Marine Division Reconnaissance Company became the first combat troops to deploy via helicopter when they landed on Hill 812 in Korea. Since then, the helicopter has served as a primary insertion platform for the Recon Marines.

Tech Specs

Length: 42 ft. 4 in.
Height: 13 ft. 4 in.
Rotor Diameter: 53 ft.
Weight: 7,300 lb. (loaded)
Maximum Speed: 101 mph

USMC Force Recon

US Marine Corps Force Reconnaissance, as it is known today, was activated on June 19, 1957, with the creation of 1st Amphibious Reconnaissance Company Fleet Marine Force Pacific (FMFPAC) under the command of Maj. Bruce F. Meyers. Located out of Camp Pendleton, California, the newly organized company would be divided into three platoons: Amphibious Reconnaissance Platoon, Parachute Reconnaissance Platoon, and Pathfinder Reconnaissance Platoon.

In 1958, half of the company was transferred from Camp Pendleton to Camp Lejeune in North Carolina to form the 2nd Force Reconnaissance Company Fleet Marine Force Atlantic (FMFLANT) under the command of Capt. Joseph Taylor, supporting the 2nd Marine Division. It would be another four years before the Navy SEALs would come on the scene and another eleven years before the army would designate a counterpart to Force Recon with the creation of Long-Range Recon Patrols (LRRPs). Members of 1st Force Reconnaissance Company were deployed to Vietnam in 1965; during this time, 2nd Force had the assignment of training new Recon Marines to be sent to Southeast Asia. Recon teams usually operate with four marines and carry between 250 and 300 rounds of ammunition per man.

US Marines are taught to fight, to give no quarter, and to defeat the enemy at all costs. Conversely, reconnaissance work requires stealth and patience, at times letting the enemy pass by so you can report on their movements. As a result, marines had to unlearn their aggressiveness in order to be successful at reconnaissance. To enhance these new skills within Force Reconnaissance Companies, many of the marines attended Recondo School, taught by members of the US Army 5th Special Force Group (Airborne).

M3A1 "Grease Gun"

When the marines of Force Recon first deployed to Vietnam, they were armed only with the M3A1 .45-caliber submachine gun. Due to its resemblance to a mechanic's grease tool you might find in the neighborhood service station, it acquired the nickname "Grease Gun." The M3 initially entered service with the US Army in December 1942, as a low-cost replacement for the Thompson submachinegun. The M3A1 had a blowback operating and system and did not have a selective fire switch that operated only in full auto mode. The M3A1 would see service in Vietnam, subsequently giving way to the M14 and, eventually, the M16 assault rifle.

M14 Battle Rifle

The M14 began as the T44, created by the Springfield Armory as the test bed for a heavy battle rifle that would replace the M1 Garand (see page 19), M1 and M2 carbines (pages 19 and 20), M3 "Grease Gun (above)," and Browning Automatic Rifle (page 126). The US Army selected the resulting weapon in 1957 and, two years later, it was in the hands of the soldiers. It soon became the standard-issue riffle of the US military.

The M14 7.62×51-millimeter (NATO) rifle was a gas-operated, rotating-bolt, select-fire gun fed by a twenty-round detachable magazine. It had an effective range out to 500 yards and weighed 10.7 pounds with a loaded magazine. The rifle was 4.3 inches in length with the 22-inch barrel fitted into a wood stock. As the United States entered the war in Southeast Asia, it was determined that the M14 was not suited for jungle warfare; it was eventually replaced by the M16 rifle (see page 29). The weapon continued to be used by Navy SEALs and served as the basis for the M21 and M25 sniper rifles.

Force Recon: Radio Phonetic Alphabet

With communication the central goal of a Force Reconnaissance mission, it is imperative that any information be relayed in a clear and concise form. The phonetic alphabet was designed to allow clarity in communications when speaking over a radio or field phone. Due to vexing radio static and the tremendous background noise that can be found in combat, early communicators found it difficult to distinguish between letters that rhyme or may sound similar, so the phonetic alphabet was established to avoid confusion between, say, a *B* and a *D* when spelling or using letters of the alphabet. This system, known as the NATO phonetic alphabet, has evolved since its inception and has been standardized internationally:

ALPHA
BRAVO
CHARLIE
DELTA
ECHO
FOXTROT
GOLF
HOTEL
INDIA
JULIET
LIMA
KILO
MIKE
NOVEMBER
OSCAR
PAPA
QUEBEC
ROMEO
SIERRA
TANGO
UNIFORM
VICTOR
WHISKEY
X-RAY
YANKEE
ZULU

M40A1 Sniper Rifle

The M40A1 was put into service in the 1970s to meet the need for a long-range sniper rifle. Each M40 is hand-built by specially trained and qualified personnel at the Marine Corps Marksmanship Training Unit (MTU) at Quantico, Virginia. Based on the Remington Model 700, the heavy-barreled, bolt-action rifle uses match-grade 7.62-millimeter ammunition fed from five-round magazines. It is equipped with a special Unertl 10-power sniper scope. With the scope, the rifle weighs approximately 14.5 pounds. The unique characteristics of the M40A1 sniper rifle are its commercial-competition-grade heavy barrel, McMillan fiberglass stock and butt pad, modified Winchester Model 70 floorplate and trigger guard, and modified and lightened trigger. In addition, each stock is epoxy bedded for accuracy, and all weapons must shoot less than 1 minute of angle (MOA).

M79 Grenade Launcher

The M79 is a single-shot, shoulder-fired, break-action grenade launcher that fires a 40-millimeter grenade and whose first use in combat was during the Vietnam War. When fired, the gun makes a distinct thump sound, earning it the nickname "the Thumper." The gun is loaded by opening the breech, which also cocks the hammer, and inserting a single 40-millimeter projectile. Once loaded, the breech is locked back into place; remove the safety and the weapon is ready to fire.

The M79 uses an assortment of 40-millimeter rounds, including M406 HE grenades, which travel at a muzzle velocity of 75 meters per second. The M406 contains enough explosive to produce over three hundred fragments that travel at 1,524 meters per second within a lethal radius of 5 meters. Operators can also fire smoke and illumination rounds as well as antipersonnel rounds, such as the now-defunct "Beehive" round, which contained 45 ten-grain flechettes. In 1966, the Beehive was replaced with a 40-millimeter round loaded with 2-gram metal pellets, which proved more effective.

The M79 was replaced by the M203 40-millimeter grenade launcher (see page 70), yet to this day the Thumper remains in the kit of many SOF units.

Captain John "Rip" Ripley

John Walter Ripley was born on June 29, 1939, in Radford, Virginia, descended from a long line of veterans going back to the Revolutionary War. He enlisted in the Marine Corps prior to his appointment to the US Naval Academy, graduating Annapolis in June 1962 and being commissioned as a second lieutenant in the marines. Attending and successfully completing the US Army Airborne and Ranger schools, the Marine reconnaissance course, and training with the British Royal Marines earned Ripley the "quad body" distinction.

On Easter Sunday, April 2, 1972, Ripley, now a captain, single-handedly stopped the advance of the North Vietnamese Army at Dong Ha, exposing himself to enemy fire for three hours as he prepared to blow up a key twin-span bridge. His actions that day thwarted the advance of an estimated twenty thousand NVA soldiers along with two hundred tanks.

During his tours in Vietnam, he participated in over twenty-five operations. For his extraordinary heroism under fire in destroying the Dong Ha Bridge, he was awarded the Navy Cross, and his actions are now required reading at the Naval Academy. Captain Ripley also holds the honor of being the only marine inducted into the US Army Ranger Hall of Fame.

Tandem Offset Resupply Deliver System (TORDS)

The Tandem Offset Resupply Delivery System (TORDS) was adopted for use by the Marine Corps around 1997. Experienced military freefall (MFF) parachutists, those with a minimum of two hundred jumps, and MFF jumpmasters were chosen for the program. The system was created to give freefall teams the ability to bring non–jump-qualified personnel in on a specified mission, or to jump and land together with large, heavy loads of equipment. The maximum all-up weight for the MC-5 parachute is 360 pounds; with the TORDS, all-up can be 650 pounds for training or 950 pounds for combat situations.

When jumping a passenger, the pair exits the aircraft with all of their equipment on them—rucksacks, weapons, and oxygen—and then lands with all of it. When jumping equipment, the largest container that should be jumped is generally about 3 feet wide by 7 feet tall because of wind resistance. The best thing about jumping tandem with equipment rather than airdropping it is that the tandem master is in control and lands with the equipment. With airdrop, the equipment may land away from the parachutists, requiring them to find and recover it, thereby increasing the time spent linking up and moving out.

M4A1 Carbine

The M4A1 is the carbine version of the full-size M16A2 assault rifle and is the primary weapon for US SOF units. The M4A1 is designed for speed of action and lightweight construction, often the requirements for Critical Skills Operators (CSOs). The barrel is a shortened 14.5 inches, which reduces the weapon's weight while maintaining its effectiveness for quick-handling operation in the field. The issued collapsible buttstock has four intermediate stops that allow adaptability in CQB without compromising shooting capabilities.

The M4A1 has a rifling twist of 1:7, making it compatible with the full range of 5.56-millimeter ammunitions. Its sighting system contains dual apertures, allowing for 0 to 200 meters and a smaller opening for engaging targets at a longer range of 500 to 600 meters. Selective fire controls for the M4A1 have eliminated the three-round burst, replacing it with safe, semiautomatic, and fully automatic fire. The weapon features a detachable carrying handle that, when removed, exposes a Weaver-type rail for mounting Special Operations Peculiar Modification (SOPMOD) accessories.

Insight AN/PEQ-15 Advanced Target Pointer Illuminator Aiming Light (ATPIAL)

The AN/PEQ-15 can be mounted to the M4A1 to make it effective out to 300 meters with standard-issue night-vision goggles (NVG) or a weapon-mounted night-vision device, such as the AN/PVS-14 (see page 293). The infrared illuminator broadens the capabilities of NVGs in buildings, tunnels, jungle, overcast, and other low-light conditions where starlight is insufficient to support night vision; this feature allows visibility in areas normally in shadow. However, it can be used both with and without NVGs.

The PEQ-15 integrates co-aligned visible and IR aiming lasers and combines them with an adjustable and focusable IR illuminator, providing a decisive advantage over an opposing force that has little or no night-vision capability. The AN/PEQ-15 replaces both the AN/PEQ-2 (see page 269) and the AN/PAQ-4C, both of which are twice as large.

Interim Fast Attack Vehicles (IFAV)

The Marine Corp's Interim Fast Attack Vehicle (IFAV) is a DaimlerChrysler model of the Mercedes-Benz 290 GD 1.5-ton diesel-burning off-road truck, built as the Wolf Geländegängig Kleinfahrzeug (small all-terrain vehicle) for Germany's combined armed forces. First deployed to a US Marine unit in November 1999, the IFAV replaces its early-1980s counterpart, the M-151 fast attack vehicle, which previously served as a smaller attack version of the Humvee. Of major importance to marine commanders is the increased offensive power the IFAV offers. Another primary advantage is the IFAV's ability to be transported internally by Marine Corps' workhorse aircraft, including the CH-53 Sea Stallion and V-22 Osprey. Additionally, it can be parachute-dropped behind enemy lines, taking off from forward-deployed navy ships.

Combat Rubber Reconnaissance Craft (CRRC)

The CRRC, or F-470 Zodiac, is used by the SOF teams for insertion, performing various reconnaissance missions and assorted waterborne operations. This small, lightweight, rugged inflatable raft has replaced the inflatable boat, small. With operation configurations of 265 pounds and 15.5 feet in length and 6.3 feet wide, the CRRC can be deployed from the CH-53. It was previously used with the CH-46, which required letting out some of the craft's air in order to fit it.

The CRRC is powered by the Improved Military Amphibious Reconnaissance System (I-MARS) 35-horsepower engine. The I-MARS outboard is a combination of the 35-horsepower Military Amphibious Reconnaissance System (MARS) outboard motor and a pump jet. The pump jet takes the place of the propeller in order to provide the user with a safer outboard motor, allowing marines to insert and extract personnel from the shore with the CRRC more safely, without degrading the overall performance of the old MARS outboard motor or the CRRC. The I-MARS can be operated in any environment in which the MARS outboard motor had been used previously.

Force Recon: Tight 360

Stealth and concealment are among the hallmarks of the Force Recon Marines. Here, a team takes a knee during a security stop as they make their way deep into enemy lines. The men automatically assume a "Tight 360" posture, ensuring every sector around them is being covered. This term denotes a formation in which a small group of armed combatants forms a back-to-back perimeter to afford a 360-degree view of the surrounding area—including any approaching enemy forces or otherwise unknown individuals. A team forms up in a deliberate and fluid motion, and all in complete silence.

Force Recon Creed

Realizing it is my choice and my choice alone to be a Reconnaissance Marine,
I accept all challenges involved with this profession.
Forever shall I strive to maintain the tremendous reputation of those who went before me.
Exceeding beyond the limitations set down by others shall be my goal.
Sacrificing personal comforts and dedicating myself to the completion of the reconnaissance mission
    shall be my life.
Physical fitness, mental attitude, and high ethics—
The title of Recon Marine is my honor.
Conquering all obstacles, both large and small, I shall never quit.
To quit, to surrender, to give up is to fail.
To be a Recon Marine is to surpass failure;
To overcome, to adapt and to do whatever it takes to complete the mission.
On the battlefield, as in all areas of life, I shall stand tall above the competition.
Through professional pride, integrity, and teamwork,
I shall be the example for all Marines to emulate.
Never shall I forget the principles I accepted to become a Recon Marine.
Honor, Perseverance, Spirit and Heart.
A Recon Marine can speak without saying a word and achieve what others can only imagine.

USMC Detachment 1

Marine Corps Special Operations Command Detachment 1 (MCSOCOM Detachment One or Det 1), officially activated at Camp Pendleton on June 20, 2003. The unit was commanded by Col. Robert J. Coates, former commanding officer of the 1st Force Recon Company and the Marine Special Operations Training Group (SOTG), both located at Camp Pendleton, California. Det 1 was headquartered at Camp Del Mar Boat Basin, located at Camp Pendleton. It was disbanded in 2006 and succeeded by the permanent United States Marine Corps Forces Special Operations Command, which is to be a 2,700-person command.

Detachment 1's insignia comes from the World War II Marine Raider's patch, a blue patch with a skull and stars. The scarlet, blue, and gold disk represents the unit's joint navy–Marine Corps origins. The crossed stiletto and lightning bolt represent the unit's special operations mission and its global communications reach. The parachute wings represent airborne-qualified status, and the mask above it represents the combatant diver qualification.

Det 1 in Iraq

Marine Corps Detachment 1 was a "proof of concept" prior to the USMC's official adoption into USSOCOM. Det 1 marines had wide latitude in modifying their weapons with Commercial Off-the-Shelf (COTS) equipment, and this marine has replaced the standard Colt furniture with a Magpul M93 Modular Stock System (MSS) as well as an Ergo pistol grip. On top of the carbine is an Aimpoint "red dot" sight, AN/PEQ-2, and SureFire flashlight. Here, a member of Det 1 waits to move out on a night patrol in Iraq in support of Operation Iraqi Freedom.

Mine-Resistant Ambush-Protected All-Terrain Vehicle (M-ATV)

The M-ATV is a tactical vehicle built by Oshkosh Defense in Wisconsin. SOCOM worked closely with the manufacturer to design a vehicle that would support the needs of Special Operations Forces' missions, requiring it to provide off-road mobility as well as lifesaving protection. What resulted was the "tailor-made" M-ATV, with the protection of the MRAP and the mobility of the GMV.

The heavily armored MRAP vehicles that were fielded successfully in Iraq proved too cumbersome and unstable in the mountainous terrain of Afghanistan. The M-ATV is lighter and has the right combination of agility and armor for the combat and terrain demands of Afghanistan. The M-ATV is well suited to support small-unit combat operations in highly restricted rural, mountainous, and urban environments—mounted patrols, reconnaissance, security, convoy protection, communications, command and control, and combat service support.

The M-ATV, like the MRAPs before it, is still capable of providing protection from IEDs, roadside bombs, and rocket-propelled grenades when using appliqué armor. Its features includes IED jammers; a V-shaped, blast-dispersing monocoque hull; the ability to ford hard-bottom fresh water to depths of up to 5 feet; and a run-flat tire system that enables the vehicle to drive at 30 miles per hour on up to two flat tires. It carries a maximum of five personnel.

Polaris MV 850 All-Terrain Vehicle (ATV)

The ATV has been in the SOF inventory for many years—Combat Control Teams have used them to secure airheads as well as setting up air traffic control (ATC) equipment. As SOCOM units continue to be deployed in support of the Global War on Terrorism, it has become a valuable tool in the arsenal of democracy and the fight for freedom. One of the models currently in use with SOF units is the Polaris MV 850 four-wheel-drive ATV.

This vehicle provides individual all-terrain mobility to deployed units in austere environments and across a myriad of SOF mission types. It is exceptionally flexible and can be air-transported within current SOCOM helicopters and tilt-rotor aircraft. The MV 850 offers no protection from small-arms fire or shrapnel, and the rider depends on its size and speed together with his own skill to maneuver and elude the enemy.

The MV850 is powered by an 850cc four-stroke, twin-cylinder, single-overhead-camshaft gas engine fueled by a 5.25-gallon tank and a 6.5-gallon reserve. The front cargo rack accommodates 200 pounds of gear and the rear rack up to 400 pounds. The ATV also features blackout lighting, allowing the operator to switch off all lights when driving with NVGs. Located in the front of the vehicle is a 3,000-pound Warn winch.

Lightweight Tactical All-Terrain Vehicle (LTATV)

SOF units employ various LTATVs to carry out their missions. Seen here is a Polaris MRZR 2 two-seat LTATV; there is also a four-seat version, the MRZR 4. This vehicle was designed by Polaris Defense from the ground up to handle the types of missions taken on by SOF units, carrying two operators and up to 1,000 pounds of equipment. The MRZR is powered by a Polaris ProStar 900 four-stroke, dual-overhead-camshaft, twin-cylinder 875cc gasoline engine. The vehicle has a 7.25-gallon fuel capacity and can reach a top speed of 88 miles per hour. Its drivetrain features a continuous variable transmission with on-demand all-wheel drive (AWD), providing the SOF units with mobility and maneuverability. The LTATV can easily be transported in an MH-47 helicopter and will even fit in the narrow fuselage of the V-22 Osprey (see page 260). It has run-flat tires, rollover protection via a tool-less collapsing roll cage, and infrared headlamps. It enables combat-equipped SOF operators to traverse the battlefield rapidly in terrain not easily navigated by the larger GMV or M-ATV vehicles.

MARSOC

On February 24, 2006, the Marine Corps officially joined the special-operations community with the creation of the Marine Corps Forces Special Operations Command (MARSOC). MARSOC became a major command within the Corps and SOCOM. At the activation ceremony, an important milestone in the history of the Corps, Secretary of Defense Donald H. Rumsfeld stated, "[MARSOC] pairs two of history's most dedicated groups of warriors—the men and women of the US Special Operations Command and the United States Marine Corps. Special-operations forces and US Marines are legendary for their agility, creativity, and willingness to take on difficult missions, and the marines have played important roles in past US victories. Today in the Global War on Terror, we call on marines again . . . to seek new and innovative ways to take the fight to the enemy. Our country needs agile, highly mobile forces to track down terrorist cells that are dispersed across the globe."

MARSOC Creed

My name is Marine. My title is MARSOC Silent Warrior, and I exemplify both with equal vigor and determination. My judgment, initiative, and professionalism are the hallmarks of my position.

Always Faithful, Always Forward in the fight to defend our Nation and our way of life. I will never surrender, I will never fall back, and I will always remember the Marine Warriors who have gone before me. I will defend, with my life, the honor and legacy of our great fighting spirit.

Realizing that the battlefield is always changing, I will train with fervor and intensity to ensure that I will excel in any environment and in all conditions. I will set the example for all Warrior Marines. My skill and knowledge will inspire them to follow me.

Semper Fidelis will be the guiding principle in my life and chosen profession. I will be faithful to my God, my Corps, my family, and my comrades. I will never fail those who guide me, support me, love me, and fight with me.

Outstanding leadership in combat, training in the field, formation in garrison, and on liberty. I will lead Marines and ensure that they are ready, relevant, courteous, and respectful. By my own example and with concerned leadership, I will forge the next generation of Special Operations Forces warrior leaders.

Committed Special Operations Forces Marine tested by trial and examination. I am a Silent Warrior. I am a Marine by the Grace of our God.

MARSOC Critical Skills Operators

Critical Skills Operators (CSOs) are the marines who conduct the real-world, no-kidding missions. They are the boots on the ground, the door kickers, and the shooters. They make up the Marine Special Operations Teams (MSOTs) that are the tip of the Marine Corps Forces spear. MARSOC marines receive specialized training in accordance with their assigned special operations core tasks. The marines work closely with US Army Special Forces and US Navy Special Warfare Command SEALs to ensure MARSOC marines and sailors have fully integrated and interoperable skills on the battlefield. Those marines who make it as operators possess the essential combination of maturity, mental agility, physical strength, and motivation. CSO marines have a minimum tour requirement of five years within the command. The goal of MARSOC is to grow to 2,500 marines, with over 800 of those slots filled by CSOs.

MARSOC Special Operations Officers

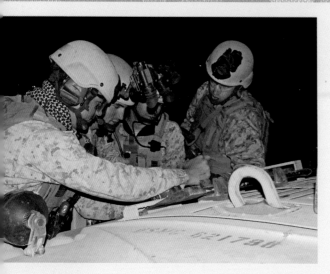

When the Marine Special Operations Command was established, the plan was for Marines to serve a five-year tour in the newly formed command and then be rotated back to the regular Corps. In July 2014, Gen. James Amos, then commandant of the Marine Corps, approved a new Primary Military Occupational Specialty (PMOS), creating the Special Operations Officer. Marine officers graduating the MARSOC Individual Training Course would be assigned this new classification, which created a career path and retention for marine officers serving in MARSOC. The new position provides the Maine Corps with a versatile officer who is skilled in special operations and an asset to the Marine Corps Air-Ground Task Force (MAGTF).

MARSOC GMV-M

The Marines of MARSOC use the GMV-M variant of the Ground Mobility Vehicle. It is designed with an open rear, where the cabin would normally be enclosed. This flatbed area is used to store fuel, ammunition, rations, and other supplies. The GMV has a cruising range of up to 275 miles, which is well suited for Marine Special Operations Battalions, who often need to operate behind enemy lines, on their own, with only occasional resupply from the air. MSOB teams, like other SOF units, undergo extensive training in driving and maintaining the vehicle, with an emphasis on off-road handling and in-field repairs.

Diver Propulsion Device

Many members of the SOF units are qualified as combat divers and are at home in the water, none more so than the SEALs (see page 178). Nevertheless, a long swim through frigid water can be taxing to even the most robust swimmer. For such missions, SOF units can deploy with the Diver Propulsion Device (DPD). Developed by STIDD, the DPD is a rugged submersible device designed to carry two SOF operators, their gear, and an additional 110 pounds of equipment. It is powered by a 26-volt DC electric thruster capable of moving the operators swiftly to their insertion point, whether running just at the water's surface or an operating depth of more than 80 meters. The DPD is equipped with STIDD's Recon Navigation system (RNAV) for onboard mission planning and navigation while submerged. It greatly enhances SOF waterborne infil/exfil capabilities.

TAC-100 Underwater Navigation Board

For times when SOF units have to insert underwater, they will carry a thick piece of high-impact ABS plastic measuring 12 inches by 10 inches. This simple yet versatile device is essential equipment, vital to any SOF waterborne infiltration. The TAC-100 is manufactured by RJE International and is standard issue among elite "frogmen" around the world.

   The board, which weighs 3 pounds when out of the water, has a cutout on each side for the swimmer to grasp. A large compass is central on the board, with luminous markings to maintain heading and internal lubber lines to keep the combat diver on course. It also has a location for a watch and ChemLight glow sticks for night operations.

M27 IAR Infantry Automatic Rifle (IAR)

The Heckler & Koch M27 is a lightweight, magazine-fed 5.56-millimeter weapon used by the US Marine Corps. It is intended to enhance an automatic rifleman's maneuverability and is based on the Heckler & Koch 416. The Marines plan to use the M27 as a replacement for the belt-fed M249 Squad Assault Weapon (SAW), which has been in service with the Corps for almost three decades.

While the manual of arms is similar to the M4/M16 series, the M27 uses HK's proprietary gas-piston system in place of a direct gas-impingement system. The M249 weighs in at 17 pounds empty, while the M27 is a svelte 8 pounds. The IAR is partial to OEM magazines, with Magpul Polymer Magazines (PMAGs) getting officially nixed by the marines. The M27 is also approximately 7 inches shorter than the SAW as well. The issue sight for the IAR is the Trijicon SU-258/PVQ Advanced Combat Optical Gunsight (ACOG) Squad Day Optic (SDO), which was originally created for the M249. While the M27 is the replacement for the SAW, the Corps retains close to ten thousand M249s at the company level for use at their discretion.

M32A1 Multi-Shot Grenade Launcher (MSGL)

Just when you thought "six-shooters" were relics of the Wild West, along comes the M32A1 Multi-Shot Grenade Launcher. The M32 was designed and developed by Milkor (Pty.) Ltd. in South Africa and is now manufactured by Milkor USA in Arizona. The latest force multiplier for SOF units, following the M79 and M203, the MSGL is a semiautomatic, shoulder-fired weapon that can launch up to six 40-millimeter grenades in three seconds (compared to a minute or more with a M203).

The six-round cylinder can accommodate rounds up to 5.5 inches in length, allowing it to fire both low- and medium-velocity rounds; the weapon has a maximum range of 400 meters with low-velocity and 800 meters with medium-velocity. A wide assortment of ordnance is available, including flares, flashbangs, smoke, lethal grenades, and even a round called the "Hellhound"—the latter part of which is defined as High-Order Unbelievably Nasty Destruction—manufactured by Martin Electronics (MEI) of Florida.

The M32A1 will fire as fast as the shooter can pull the trigger. It is fitted with a collapsible stock, pistol grip, and forward grip for stability. The weapon features a holographic-type aiming system that allows the shooter to keep both eyes open while he aims at the target.

Colt 1911 Pistol

When the US military transitioned to the 9-millimeter handgun in the 1980s, there were two organizations who maintained the 1911: the Force Recon Marines and Delta Force. Long-time Recon Marine and commander of USMC Detachment 1 Col. Robert Coates summed up the hard-hitting semiautomatic pistol with the following comment: "The 1911 was the design given by God to us through John M. Browning that represents the epitome of what a killing tool needs to be. It was true in 1911 and is true now."

The Marines had the Rifle Team Equipment (RTE) shop in Quantico, Virginia, modify the M1911A1 .45-caliber pistol to make it more accurate and mission suitable in the M45 Marine Expeditionary Unit (Special Operations Capable), or MEU(SOC), platform. Meanwhile, the operators at Delta would let their armorer tweak them, or use high-performance gun makers, such as Wilson Combat and Les Baer, to make the weapon match the skill of the shooter.

Today, MARSOC marines are issued the M45 Close Quarter Battle Pistol from Colt. The M45 is updated with tritium night sights, dual-recoil springs, Picatinny rail, and lanyard loop; the color is desert tan. Whether it's the new marine M45, or the Delta custom semiautomatic, the 1911 may well be in the hands of our nation's warrior elite for another hundred years.

M249 Squad Automatic Weapon

The M249 Squad Automatic Weapon (SAW) is an individually man-portable, air-cooled, gas-operated light machine gun manufactured by the FN Herstal (FNH) Group. It is chambered for 5.56-millimeter NATO ammunition and is fed by either a thirty-round M16/M4 magazine or disintegrating metallic link-belt feed in a two-hundred-round plastic box; there is also a smaller hundred-round box, which is referred to as the "nut sack." The basic load for the SAW gunner is six hundred rounds of linked ammunition. The M249 can engage targets out to 800 meters and is the base of firepower for a fire team.

The weapon, with bipod, weighs in at 15.1 pounds and is 40.87 inches in length; it has a rate of fire of 725 rounds per minute. Later versions of the M249 have been upgraded with a modified barrel, handguard, stock, pistol grip, buffer, and sights.

M40A3 Rifle

In 1996, the USMC armorers at Quantico began to design the replacement for the M40A1. The result was the M40A3, which, like its predecessor, is based on a Remington 700 short-action and chambered for 7.62-millimeter NATO. The M40A3 has a steel floor-plate assembly and trigger guard built by D. D. Ross and a 24-inch Schneider Match Grade SS No. 7 barrel. The Unertl rings and bases have been replaced with a D. D. Ross base and G&G Machine rings. The rifles also come with a Harris bipod and an accessory rail, also built by G&G Machine. The stock is a new McMillan tactical A4 with adjustable cheek and length of pull. The ergonomics of the A4 stock's adjustable saddle cheek, length of pull (LOP), vertical pistol grip, and butt hook allow the sniper to mold their body to the gun. The sniper's hands, shoulder, and cheek weld all come into place. It is no longer just a rifle, but an extension of the sniper, making them one weapon.

As the older M40A1s rotate in for service and repair, they are replaced by M40A3s. The newer rifles are extremely accurate and rugged, and they are designed from the ground up to be a superb sniper rifle. Combined with the new M118LR ammo, it makes a system that is ranked with the best in the world. The magazine capacity for the rifle is five rounds with an effective range of 1,000 yards.

M40A5 Sniper Rifle

The M40A5 sniper rifle is the latest generation of the M40 sniper rifle. It, too, is a Remington 700 short-action chambered for 7.62×51-millimeter NATO ammunition. It has a 24-inch barrel with a 1:12 twist and is fitted with an adjustable A4 McMillan stock. Using 168-gram or 175-gram, match-grade 7.62-millimeter Boat Tail Hollow Point (BTHP) ammunition, the sniper can repeatedly engage and hit targets out to 800 to 1,000 meters.

The M40A5 is as reliable and durable as it is accurate. Reports have come in from downrange reporting that it has been dropped, lugged across the mountains of Afghanistan, and used for house-to-house fighting in Iraq, and then, when the weapon is shouldered, it performs.

The rifle is also fitted with a Picatinny rail, permitting the sniper to mount lasers and lights. Additionally, the marines issue the weapon with an AN/PVS-27 Magnum Universal Night Sight (MUNS) or forward-looking infrared (FLIR) sight. The barrel is crowned and also capable of mounting a suppressor.

M107A1 Long Range Sniper Rifle (LRSR)

When the mission calls for a Hard Target Interdiction (HTI)—taking out such targets as airplanes, helicopters, or ground vehicles—at ranges of over 1,000 meters, SOF turns to the big guns. The M107A1 LRSR, manufactured by Barrett Firearms Manufacturing, is a semiautomatic, air-cooled, box-magazine-fed rifle chambered for the .50-caliber M2 Browning Machine Gun (BMG) cartridge. The barrel is attached to a double-spring yoke; this unique system provides the large weapon with an additional source of assistance as the barrel slides in and out, spreading the recoil throughout the weapon. It features a 29-inch, free-floating, fluted barrel with a 1:15 right-hand twist.

The M107A1 is no small weapon, coming in at 57 inches in length and weighing 30 pounds empty. A hefty box magazine holding ten rounds of M33 Full Metal Jacket (FMJ) 661-grain, .50-caliber BMG ammunition feeds the large rifle. The effective range of the M33 is 2,000 yards. The standard round has a muzzle velocity of 2,850 feet per second and will fire out to 6,800 yards, equivalent to sixty-eight football fields laid end to end.

Ghillie Suits

The ghillie suit is a camouflage suit covered with irregular patterns of garnish or netting to break up the outline of a sniper. There are many options, the choice often boiling down simply to personal preference. However, the two most common versions are the one-piece, made from a flight suit, and the two-piece BDU version with separate shirt and trousers. Turning the uniform inside out places the pockets inside the suit and protects items in the pockets from damage caused by crawling on the ground. Netting is sewn onto the clothing; various lengths of burlap are tied to the netting and then shredded strip by strip until the outline of the uniform vanishes.

A "boonie hat" is often given the same treatment to break up the silhouette of the sniper's head for concealment once in position. The sniper instructors at Fort Bragg favor a mix of 30 percent burlap strips and 70 percent vegetation, which is stuffed into the netting and held in place by rubber bands. Using local vegetation, the sniper blends in to his surroundings. This also allows him to adjust the foliage in the suit as he moves from one position to the next.

Plastic-Bonded Explosives PBX

Specialty demolitions called PBX are available to covert warriors in an assortment of packages. Plastic-bonded sheet explosives are manufactured with Research Department Explosive (RDX) or pentaerythritol tetranitrate (PETN). They are adaptable, bendable, and, as the name implies, a sheet material. Various types of ribbon PBX are available, including one type of charge for breaching doors and windows and another consisting of pliable tape with metal cladding that forms a linear-shaped charge, which can be used for cutting holes in brick and other masonry walls. Another type of explosive not normally used by conventional forces is an explosive charge that provides instantaneous explosive breaching, capable of blasting through multiple layers of block walls.

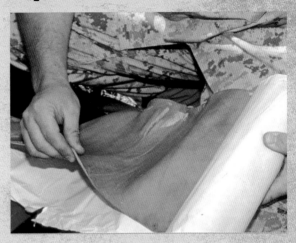

Mark 141 Flashbang

The Mark 141 diversionary grenade, also known as a flashbang grenade, was developed by the US Navy. It is designed to distract hostiles during building- and room-clearing operations when the presence of noncombatants is likely and the assaulting element is attempting to achieve surprise. It looks similar to an M18 smoke grenade in its cylindrical shape, but the color and labeling are different and it is smaller. Unlike a fragmentation grenade, the Mark 141 remains intact and does not disperse shrapnel throughout the area; it creates a loud bang and bright flash when it is deployed in an enclosed area, which serves to disorient any hostile forces. Flashbang grenades are especially useful in hostage-rescue operations.

Australian Rappel

The Australian rappel finds its origins with the Australian Special Air Service Regiment (SASR), hence the name. The method, also called "rap jumping," is a tactical abseiling technique in which the operator lies face down, allowing him to make a controlled descent and have a free hand with which to fire his weapon. Starting from a forward standing position, the operator goes over the precipice face first, as opposed to the standard backward approach. During descent, braking is accomplished by drawing the rappel ropes diagonally across the chest with the ropes running from near the waist to the pocket of the opposite shoulder.

Halligan Tool

The Halligan tool takes its name from the man who created it in 1948, Deputy Fire Chief Hugh Halligan of the New York City Fire Department. This entry tool is employed in mechanical breaching and used for smashing, prying, twisting, punching, or whatever other mayhem is needed to gain egress into a structure. The tool consists of a claw/nail puller on one end and a pick and blade at the other end. The tool can be used as a wedge in conjunction with a sledgehammer to further facilitate entry. The Halligan tool is usually worn in a dynamic-entry tool backpack, ensuring that the necessary tools are within reach as the team makes its assault.

Special Ops K-9s

"The dogs of war" takes on a whole new meaning when you look at the spec ops K-9s and their handlers. The most common breeds of working dog are the German shepherd and the Belgian Malinois. Since the beginning of the Global War on Terrorism, military dogs have been working with SOF units and have proven they are more than worth their weight in kibble. The dogs are trained to endure conditions and situations to which the family pet would never be exposed; unless it comes from a hunting family, the average dog would run and hide in the face of all the gunfire and explosions experienced in combat.

The dogs and their handlers deploy in the same manner—by parachute, helocast, FRIES, and more—and can quickly negotiate terrain, both open ground and urban environments. The K-9s are members of the team, whether that team consists of marines or SEALs. The dogs can sniff out explosives, making them good point men (er, dogs) for identifying enemy IEDs. The most famous of the military dogs is Cairo, a Belgian Malinois who took part in the SEAL Team 6 mission that killed Osama bin Laden.

Power Saw

There are times when you just need more power, and whether they're cutting through rebar, concrete, or a shipping container, SOF units may use a power saw. Similar to those found in fire department rescue rigs, the gas-powered rescue saw can be fitted with a segmented diamond blade to slice through any of the aforementioned materials. These saws are portable and effective in cutting hinges, doorjambs, bars, brick, and chain-link fencing. As most of these tactical breaching saws weigh close to 30 pounds, some feature a backpack harness to provide more mobility for the operator.

AN/PRC-117F Digital Radio

Communications are the lifeline of any SOF team on a mission. For long-range communications, the AN/PRC-117F advanced-software reprogrammable digital radio offers embedded Communications Security (COMSEC) and HAVE QUICK I/II Electronic Counter-Countermeasures (ECCM) capabilities. The AN/PRC-117F supports continuous operation across the 90- to 420-megahertz band, providing 20-watt FM and 10-watt AM transmit power with HAVE QUICK I/II capability (10 watts FM in other frequency ranges), and is fully compatible with the KY-57 TSEC encryption unit in voice and data modes for secure transmissions. The radio supports all common fill devices for HAVE QUICK Word-of-Day (WOD) and encryption-key information. It supports the Department of Defense (DoD) requirement for a lightweight, secure, network-capable, multiband, multimission, anti-jam voice/imagery/data communication capability in a single package.

AN/PRC-148 Multiband Inter/Intra Team Radio (MBITR)

The Thales Communications MBITR is a powerful tactical handheld radio designed for the US Special Operations Command. It more than meets the tough SOCOM requirements and provides a secure voice and digital data radio with exceptional versatility, ruggedness, and reliability.

The immersible unit weighs less than 2 pounds and includes a keypad, graphics display, and built-in speaker-microphone. Typical of the advanced designs of Thales radios, the MBITR uses digital-signal processing and flash memory to support functions traditionally performed by discrete hardware in other manufacturers' equipment. The power output is up to 5 watts over the 30- to 512-megahertz frequency band. The radio has embedded Type 1 COMSEC for both voice and data traffic.

Satellite Communications (SATCOM)

In the old days, American Indians used smoke signals. During World War I, messages were transported by pigeons. Today, SOF units have satellite communications (SATCOM).

SATCOM provides critical communication routing through the Defense Satellite Communications System and the Wideband Global SATCOM constellation, which functions as the primary means for conveying information on the global battlefield. The method involves using satellites to support communication by reflecting or relaying signals into space and back down to Earth; it is the most powerful form of radio and can cover far more distance and wider areas than other radios. The systems provide long-haul capability, as well as backup paths for tactical communications, communications on the move, and beyond-line-of-sight communications. SOCOM provides the latest technology and trained SOF personnel, who in turn provide information to support operations and intel to geographic combatant commanders (GCCs).

Intelligence Surveillance and Reconnaissance (ISR)

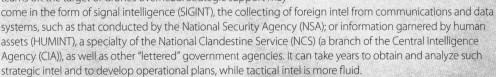

How do the SOF units pull off their daring covert missions? The answer is intelligence. The importance of intel cannot be overstated; without the necessary information, SEAL Team 6 would have just been out for a helicopter ride that evening in May 2011. The dynamic operational tempo (OPTEMPO) of SOF missions requires precise and timely intel in their execution. Tactical ISR may come from recon teams on the target or drones overhead. Strategic support may come in the form of signal intelligence (SIGINT), the collecting of foreign intel from communications and data systems, such as that conducted by the National Security Agency (NSA); or information garnered by human assets (HUMINT), a specialty of the National Clandestine Service (NCS) (a branch of the Central Intelligence Agency (CIA)), as well as other "lettered" government agencies. It can take years to obtain and analyze such strategic intel and to develop operational plans, while tactical intel is more fluid.

An example is the Abu Musab al-Zarqawi mission. The actual airstrike that killed this notorious terrorist was executed within fifteen minutes. The collection of intel to locate, fix, and engage the target took a total of over five hundred hours.

General William "Wild Bill" Donovan, OSS

William Donovan earned his nickname from his exploits on the football field at Columbia University, where he graduated in 1905. He became a lawyer and then a cavalry officer in the New York National Guard, fighting against Pancho Villa. During World War I, Major Donovan was awarded the Medal of Honor for his actions with the 165th Infantry in France and was subsequently promoted to colonel.

On July 11, 1941, President Franklin D. Roosevelt appointed Donovan to the newly created position of Coordinator of Information (COI), tasked with collecting, analyzing, and disseminating foreign intelligence. When the United States entered World War II, the position transitioned into the head of the Office of Strategic Services (OSS). The OSS's covert operatives and paramilitary operational groups executed successful espionage and sabotage missions in Europe and the Pacific during World War II.

The OSS was dissolved in 1945 and succeeded by the Central Intelligence Agency (CIA).

Jedburgh Teams

Operation Jedburgh was a clandestine joint operation conducted during World War II by the OSS, the British Special Operations Executive, the Bureau Central de Renseignements et d'Action, and the Dutch and Belgian armies. The so-called Jedburgh teams featured agents who parachuted into enemy-held territory—Nazi-occupied France, Netherlands, and Belgium—to conduct sabotage and guerrilla warfare and to lead the local resistance in actions against the Germans. Each team included three operators: a commander, an executive officer, and a noncommissioned officer (NCO) who acted as the radio operator. The team's normal makeup included a British or American commander and an officer originating from the country to which the team deployed. The radio operator could be sourced from any of the agencies involved.

Normally, each member of a Jedburgh team was armed with an M1 carbine and a Colt semiautomatic pistol. Along with these personal weapons, team members carried sabotage equipment and a Type B Mark II radio, which was critical for communicating with headquarters in London.

Carpetbaggers

The first "Carpetbagger" missions were carried out by a unit headed by Gen. "Wild Bill" Donovan's OSS, with members of the USAAF's 801st Bombardment Group flying specialized B-24s. The crews of this unit became proficient in flying long-range, low-level, poor-weather, nighttime missions—mostly over mountainous terrain—and were instrumental in the delivery of covert agents, supplies, and psychological leaflets behind enemy lines. One Carpetbagger pilot recalled that flying at 400 feet was not uncommon; on one occasion, upon landing, the crew had to remove tree branches from the bomb bay hatches.

The B-24 Liberator bombers used for the flights were modified with black paint, while the belly and nose turrets and any other unnecessary equipment were removed in order to lighten them and provide more cargo space and speed. The rear guns were kept as protection from night fighters.

From January 1944 to May 1945, Carpetbaggers completed 1,860 sorties and delivered 20,495 containers and 11,174 packages of vital supplies to resistance forces in western and northwestern Europe. The lineage of today's Combat Talon aircraft can be traced to these highly modified B-24s.

FP-45 Liberator Pistol

Manufactured in the United States by Inland Manufacturing division of General Motors, the Liberator pistol was an inexpensive and easily mass-produced single-shot. (The gun's cover name was the Flare Project, hence the designation FP-45.) Made of stamped-steel parts, it was rudimentary to say the least. The simplistic pistol was chambered to fire a .45-caliber round from an unrifled barrel. Accuracy was not paramount, and the maximum effective range was approximately 25 feet.

The idea behind the simple little gun was that the shooter would use it to kill an enemy soldier and then take his weapon. Though this "idea" had some merit, the conventional military did not embrace it as fully practical, and the weapon ended up in the hands of the OSS. Whether the OSS ever used the Liberator against an enemy remains undocumented.

OSS Maritime Unit Swimmer

In addition to the Underwater Demolition Teams (UDTs—see page 174) and the Naval Combat Demolition Unit (NCDU), naval personnel also served with the OSS as Operational Swimmers in the office's maritime unit. Such men, all of them volunteers, were prototypes of the future SEALs, forging new techniques such as combat swimming and limpet mine attacks, and pioneering gear such as swim fins, facemasks, and closed-circuit diving equipment. Members of the OSS maritime unit became part of UDT-10 in July 1944 and, from the USS *Burrfish* in the Caroline Islands, conducted the very first UDT/submarine operation.

In the image seen here, the diver wearing the Lambertsen Amphibious Respiratory Unit (LARU), an early-model closed-circuit rebreather system, designed to give off no telltale bubbles. Such devices were critical for covertly inserting teams into enemy territory.

Central Intelligence Agency

When operating "downrange," SOF units often work with an assortment of operators. Some of these are allied special operations units, some are coalition forces, and some are simply referred to as "OGA," or Other Government Agency. The latter group comes from the CIA, Special Activities Division (SAD), under which are the National Clandestine Service (NCS) and the Special Operations Group (SOG). The mission of the NCS is to strengthen national security and foreign policy objectives through the clandestine collection of human intelligence (HUMINT) and covert actions. SOG is the paramilitary arm of the division, drawing its operatives primarily from the Special Mission Units of the Joint Strategic Operations Command (JSOC). While most missions are conducted entirely on their own, there are times when these operators will work with US SOF units. In the weeks after the 9/11 terrorist attacks, for example, joint CIA and Special Forces teams were inserted by helicopter into Afghanistan as part of Operation Enduring Freedom.

Underwater Demolition Teams (UDTs)

The SEALs of today link their rich heritage to the Underwater Demolition Teams (UDTs) of World War II. These elite "frogmen" were all volunteers who performed their perilous missions armed with only a pencil, a slate, and a Ka-Bar knife, earning the title "naked warriors."

The need for such a unit was addressed on August 15, 1942, when volunteers from the US Army and US Navy were brought together at the Amphibious Training Base at Little Creek in Virginia Beach, Virginia, for Amphibious Scouts and Raiders training. The frogmen's mission was to carry out hydrographic reconnaissance and clear natural or manmade obstacles for amphibious assaults. They also marked enemy mines for minesweepers and attached mines to the hulls of enemy vessels. Frogmen reconnoitered beach landing sites, stayed on position before the landing, and guided the assault unit to the landing site. The resulting UDTs obtained their baptism by fire in Operation Flintlock on the Marshall Islands, January 31, 1944.

Ultimately, thirty-four UDT teams were created and were active throughout the Pacific theater in all major amphibious landing operations, including Eniwetok, Saipan, Guam, Tinian, Angaur, Ulithi, Peleliu, Leyte, Lingayen Gulf, Zambales, Iwo Jima, Okinawa, Labuan, and Brunei Bay.

Though they left no lasting trails in the water, the frogmen of the UDTs made their mark on the world of unconventional warfare and set the benchmark for those who followed.

Scouts and Raiders

The first Scouts and Raiders group was commissioned in October 1942 and saw combat a month later in Operation Torch, the first Allied landings in the European theater, on the North African coast. Scouts and Raiders would also provide support for the Allied landings in Sicily, Salerno, Anzio, Normandy, and southern France. Among this group was Phil H. Bucklew, who came to be referred to as the "Father of Naval Special Warfare."

Special Service Unit No. 1 was the codename for the second Scouts and Raiders group, formed on July 7, 1943. The first mission of this joint Army/Navy unit was on New Guinea in September 1943; subsequent operations took place at Gasmata, Arawe, Cape Gloucester, and the coast of New Britain. All missions were carried out without the loss of any personnel. Special Service Unit No. 1 was summarily separated, with navy personnel assigned to 7th Amphibious Scouts, which participated in more than forty landings in the Pacific.

A third Scout and Raider unit operated in China, carrying out guerilla-type missions against the enemy.

Satchel Charges

One primary mission of UDTs during World War II was preparing beachheads for US forces. This often required eliminating coral reefs or manmade obstacles to provide a clear path for amphibious landings. It must have been a UDT frogman who coined the saying, "There is no problem that can't be solved with the proper amount of explosives." To test this theory, frogmen used the Mark 133 Mod 2 satchel charge. While the Mod 0/1 contained blocks of TNT, the Mod 2 contained Pentolite, which is half PETN (a nitrate similar in composition to nitroglycerin) and half TNT. The satchel charge comprised eight blocks of the explosive connected by primer cord inside a waterproof canvas haversack with a pair of metal hooks that secured it to the target object. The depth placement of the charge could be adjusted by inflating or deflating a flotation bladder inside the bag.

UDT Insignia

The insignia of the Underwater Demolitions Teams was worn on the upper sleeve of the sailor's uniform. During the 1950s, the patch evolved into a badge and was worn on the chest. The UDT badge had a trident and pistol over an anchor; enlisted men wore a silver badge, while the officer's badge was gold. This badge was the basis for later SEAL units, with the addition of the eagle with spread wings. During the Vietnam War, both UDT and SEAL badges were issued, dependent on a sailor's training. The UDT insignia was disapproved for wear in 1975, and those sailors graduating from BUD/S have been awarded the SEAL Trident badge ever since.

UDT: Korean Ops

During the Korean War, Underwater Demolition Teams moved inland from the surf zone. Vice Admiral C. Turner Joy, Commander Naval Forces, Far East, formulated a strategy to harass the North Koreans with small amphibious teams that would infiltrate from the sea and conduct raids against the North's supply routes. The first of these raids conducted by UDT "frogmen" occurred against Yeosu, a vital seaport on the south coast 45 miles behind the enemy lines, consisting of a railhead, three bridges, and a tunnel. Approaching their insertion point in small inflatable rubber boats in the blackness of night, the UDT came under fire and was forced to abort the raid.

SEALs

On January 1, 1962, the navy created the US Navy SEALs and commissioned SEAL Team 1 on the West Coast and SEAL Team 2 on the East coast. The term *SEAL* is an acronym representing each of the environments in which they would fight: SEa, Air, and Land. Shortly after their creation, the SEALs were deployed to the Caribbean in October 1962 during the Cuban Missile Crisis.

During the war in Vietnam, SEALs took the war to the enemy where and when he least expected it.

They had wide latitude in weapons and equipment. The small teams could be attired in a variety of uniforms, from tiger strips to blue jeans; some men wore coral shoes, while others favored going in barefoot. They fought the enemy on his turf, using the same guerilla methods and tactics and earning them the name "the Men in the Green Faces." The SEALs became feared in the delta, rivers, and jungles and continue to serve as an elite fighting force today.

A SEAL platoon consists of sixteen men, usually two officers and fourteen enlisted SEALs. Depending on the mission profile, the platoon can be broken into two squads of eight SEALs each or else into four elements.

Platoons are typically deployed on their missions with a navy lieutenant as the officer in charge (OIC).

SEAL Trident

The SEAL insignia is the largest badge in the US military and is known among the SEALs as "the Budweiser." It is representative of the SEAL acronym: the trident symbolizes the sea, the outstretched wings of the eagle the air, and the flintlock pistol the land. The SEAL Trident badge is awarded to the sailor who has successfully completed Basic Underwater Demolition/SEAL (BUD/S) and SEAL Qualification Training (SQT). Officially, the SEAL is referred to as a Naval Special Warfare Operator.

SEAL Code

The US Navy SEALs' creed and ethos reads, in part: "In times of war or uncertainty there is a special breed of warrior ready to answer our Nation's call. A common man with uncommon desire to succeed. Forged by adversity, he stands alongside America's finest special operations forces to serve his country, the American people, and protect their way of life. I am that man. My Trident is a symbol of honor and heritage. . . . I will not fail."

It embraces the warrior values and the tradition of never leaving a man behind. The essence of the creed is summed up in the SEAL code:

Loyalty to Country, Team and Teammate
Serve with Honor and Integrity On and Off the Battlefield
Ready to Lead, Ready to Follow, Never Quit
Take responsibility for your actions and the actions of your teammates
Excel as Warriors through Discipline and Innovation
Train for War, Fight to Win, Defeat our Nation's Enemies
Earn your Trident every day

M60 Machine Gun

The M60 machine gun was introduced into service in 1957 and has been used each branch of the US military. Weighing 10.5 pounds, it fires 7.62×51-millimeter NATO rounds from linked ammo belts at a rate of fire of 500 to 650 rounds per minute. It is a crew-served weapon, meaning it takes up to three men to operate: a gunner, an assistant gunner, and an ammunition bearer.

During the Vietnam War, the Navy SEALs shortened the barrel of the M60 to reduce the weight and turn it into a one-person weapon. It has an effective range of 1,200 yards and can fire a variety of ammunition, including ball, tracer, and armor-piercing rounds. The M60 has now been replaced by the newer M240 machine gun, but this aging workhorse was used by SOF units in Afghanistan as recently as 2004.

Stoner 63

The weapons of the US Navy SEALs are as unique as their "green faces" and their tactics and techniques. In Vietnam, these waterborne commandos made use of the M16, but they were often armed with a wide assortment of weaponry. It was not unusual to find the SEALs carrying a CAR-15 (see page 32), FN FAL, shotgun, or Stoner 63.

Officially called the Mark 23 Mod 0 machine gun, the Stoner 63 is a modular weapon system with eight different variants: the Rifle, Carbine, Automatic Rifle, Light Machine Gun, Medium Machine Gun, Fixed Machine Gun, Commando, and Survival Rifle. Unique to the Stoner was the use of a drum magazine that carried 100 to 150 rounds of linked 5.56-millimeter ammunition. It weighed less than the M60 and was much more suited to the type of missions conducted by the SEALs.

As versatile and reliable it was, it had to be maintained religiously. Thus, it was deemed too finicky for the average "grunt" and never entered general service. It is still remembered as a hallmark weapon of the SEALs.

MOH: Lieutenant Junior Grade Joseph Kerrey

The first SEAL to be awarded the Medal of Honor was Lt. (j.g.) Joseph Kerrey, for actions on March 14, 1969:

> For conspicuous gallantry and intrepidity at the risk of his life above and beyond the call of duty while serving as a SEAL team leader during action against enemy aggressor (Viet Cong) forces. Acting in response to reliable intelligence, Lt. (J.G.) Kerrey led his SEAL team on a mission to capture important members of the enemy's area political cadre operating on an island in the bay of Nha Trang. In order to surprise the enemy, he and his team scaled a 350-foot sheer cliff to place themselves above the ledge on which the enemy was located. Splitting his team in 2 elements and coordinating both, Lt. (J.G.) Kerrey led his men in the treacherous downward descent to the enemy's camp. Just as they neared the end of their descent, intense enemy fire was directed at them, and Lt. (J.G.) Kerrey received massive injuries from a grenade which exploded at his feet and threw him backward onto the jagged rocks.
>
> Although bleeding profusely he immediately directed his element's fire into the center of the enemy camp. Utilizing his radioman, Lt. (J.G.) Kerrey called in the second element's fire support which caught the confused Viet Cong in a devastating crossfire. After successfully suppressing the enemy's fire, and although immobilized by his multiple wounds, he continued to order his team to secure and defend an extraction site. Lt. (J.G.) Kerrey resolutely directed his men, despite his near unconscious state, until he was eventually evacuated by helicopter.
> —Medal of Honor citation

Patrol Boat, River (PBR)

Today's Special Boat Teams (SBTs) can trace their lineage from the Boat Support Units (BSUs) of the Vietnam War. BSUs operated in what was known as the brown-water navy due to their missions being conducted in the murky waters of the Mekong Delta, the Rung Sat Special Zone, and surrounding areas. One of the crafts that became iconic during the Vietnam War was the Mark II Patrol Boat, River (PBR). The PBR was 32 feet long with a beam of 11.5 feet; it drafted 2 feet, allowing it to navigate in the narrow and shallow waters of the delta. The boat was powered by two Detroit Diesel engines, which drove the Jacuzzi water jets to provide a speed of 25 knots. The PBR had a crew of four—a coxswain and three gunners—and was not only fast but also heavily armed. On the bow was a traversable housing that mounted twin M2 .50-caliber machine guns, aft of the craft was a single .50-caliber M2, and amidships were mounted M60 machine guns or a Mark 19 40-millimeter automatic grenade launcher. During the course of the war, the SBTs would grow to include 250 PBRs, which remained in action until 1971.

SEAL Team Assault Boat (STAB)

Several boats were developed and built specifically for the SEALs' missions in the rivers of Vietnam, including the Light SEAL Support Craft (LSSC) and the SEAL Team Assault Boat (STAB). These boats served as a platform for insertion, extraction, and fire support. SEAL Team 2 developed the first STAB for use in riverine warfare in 1967.

It was a modified version of the PowerCat model 23C fiberglass boat built for the navy. It was just over 21 feet in length and had 0.25 inch of armor plating surrounding the coxswain's position. When loaded with a team of SEALs, the boat would draft 31 inches, and its twin outboard motors provided a range of 120 miles. STABs were sent to Vietnam by SEAL Team 2 in January 1967 and, at first, the SEALs manned them. However, in March 1967, Mobile Support Team 2 personnel (from Boat Support Unit 1, Naval Amphibious Base Coronado) arrived in country and took over the operation and maintenance of the boats.

Although aquatic warriors tried various weapons systems, the normal armament for the STAB was two M60 machine guns and a Mark 18 40-millimeter crank-operated grenade launcher.

Light SEAL Support Craft (LSSC)

The Light SEAL Support Craft (LSSC) was built in 1968 by Grafton Boat Works, Grafton, Illinois, specifically for SEAL operations. The LSSC would replace the Boston Whaler, Landing Craft Personnel Survey (LCPS), and STAB as a SEAL platform. The LSSC were operated and maintained by sailors of Boat Support Unit 1 Mobile Support Teams (MSTs), which would evolve into the Special Boat Teams of the Naval Special Warfare Group. The operator would pilot the boat from a seat in the centerline position, similar to the STAB; unlike the STAB, however, the LSSC was equipped with radar.

The LSSC Mark 1 was 24 feet in length with a beam of 9.5 feet and drafted 1.5 feet. It was powered by two Ford 427-cubic-inch, 350-horsepower gasoline engines through two Jacuzzi water pumps. It had a crew of three and carried six SEALs. Standard armament included two M60 7.62-millimeter machine guns and one .50-caliber M2 Heavy Browning Machine Gun (BMG).

OV-10A Bronco

The North American Rockwell OV-10A was a twin-turboprop, short-takeoff-and-landing aircraft developed in the 1960s as a special aircraft for counter-insurgency (COIN) operations. The navy's Light Attack Squadron 4 (VAL-4), known as the "Black Ponies," adopted the OV-10A and found the aircraft was well suited to support the SEALs in Vietnam.

The OV-10A was powered by two 715-horsepower Garrett T76-G-410/412 turboprop engines, which provided a speed of 281 miles per hour and a ceiling of 28,800 feet. It had a range of 700 nautical miles, which could be extended to 1,200 nautical miles with the addition of a 150-gallon drop tank. With the drop tank equipped, the aircraft had a loiter time of 5.5 hours.

The Bronco was well suited for Close Air Support (CAS), as it could be configured with a wide assortment of armament and ordnance. It could mount four 7.62×51-millimeter M60C machine guns and had five fuselage and two underwing hardpoints for mounting a combination of seven or nineteen tube launchers for 2.75-inch Folding Fin Aerial Rockets (FFARs) or two or four tube launchers for 5-inch FFARs. It was also capable of carrying up to 500 pounds in bombs and could be armed with AIM-9 Sidewinder air-to-air missiles.

Helicopter Attack Squadron: HA(L)-3 "Seawolves"

The "Seawolves" provided close air support (CAS) for the Mobile Riverine Forces and the Navy SEALs during the Vietnam War. The aircraft of the squadron was the Bell UH-1B Iroquois helicopter. The venerable "Huey" was powered by a Lycoming T53-L-11 turboshaft engine, providing 1,100 shaft horsepower, a speed of 125 miles per hour, and a range of 315 miles. The two-blade main rotor assembly had a diameter of 48 feet.

The helicopters were drawn from US Army inventories and were in need of repair and refitting before they would be fit for service. One crucial upgrade was the installation of a radar altimeter, which was essential for operating in adverse weather and at night. The UH-1B could be armed with two 7.62-millimeter M60 machine guns or GAU/17A 7.62-millimeter miniguns, or FFAR pods with either seven or nineteen rounds each. The all-volunteer pilots and aircrews of the "Seawolves" staged their helicopters on Landing Ships, Tank (LSTs) anchored in the Mekong Delta as a base of operations. Two detachments filled a quick-reaction CAS role for the brown-water navy and SEAL teams until the unit was disbanded in 1972.

Helicopter Attack Squadrons: HA(L)-4 and HA(L)-5

As soon as a war is over, units are disbanded and organizations shrink or stand down. This was the case with the navy's armed helicopter gunships. However, in 1976, the navy determined there was still a need for such aircraft, leading to the activation of two new squadrons. The first—Helicopter Attack Squadron (Light) Four, or HA(L)-4, "Blue Hawks"—was activated July 1, 1976, at Naval Air Station Norfolk, Virginia. HA(L)-5, "Red Wolves," was activated June 11, 1977, at Naval Air Station Point Mugu, California.

The mission of these two squadrons was to support the SEALs, Explosive Ordnance Disposal (EOD), and Special Boat Units (SBUs) under the Naval Special Warfare Command. As it had been in Vietnam, their aircraft of choice was a Huey, in this case the HH-1K model. The helicopter had a crew of four: two pilots and two door gunners. Powered by a 1,250-horsepower Pratt & Whitney T400-CP-400 Twin Pac coupled-turboshaft engine, it had a maximum speed of 144 mph and a range of 317 miles. It was armed with 7.62-millimeter machine guns, M-21 GAU-2B/A miniguns and rocket pods.

Commander Richard Marcinko

Richard "Dick" Marcinko began his naval career in 1958. During the Vietnam War, he was awarded the first of four Bronze Stars for his action against the Viet Cong in the Mekong Delta. After a second tour of duty in country, Marcinko was promoted to lieutenant commander. After his return to the United States, he took over as commander of SEAL Team 2.

After the failure of Operation Eagle Claw (see page 39), the navy saw the need for a dedicated counterterrorist unit, and Marcinko commanded the newly formed unit that evolved into what is now known as SEAL Team 6. It is rumored that the navy chose this number even though there were only two SEAL teams at the time, in order to confuse the Soviets; a similar tactic was employed with the first Special Forces group, which was numbered 10. Commander Marcinko handpicked the men he needed for this team from the SEAL community. He commanded Team 6 from August 1980 to July 1983.

His next command in the world of covert operations was the Naval Security Coordination Team OP-06D, unofficially named "Red Cell." The mission of Red Cell, as directed by Vice Adm. James "Ace" Lyons, deputy chief of naval operations, was to test and evaluate the navy's vulnerability to terrorism.

Commander Marcinko retired from the navy on February 1, 1989, after thirty years, three months, and seventeen days of enlisted and commissioned active-duty service.

Naval Special Warfare Development Group (NSWDG)

The NSWDG is still referred to as SEAL Team 6, even though that name was officially discontinued in the 1980s. Based in Dam Neck, Virginia, it is responsible for US counterterrorist operations in maritime environments. Its origin can be traced to the aftermath of Operation Eagle Claw. Prior to this, the SEALs had already begun Counterterrorism (CT) training, including all twelve platoons in SEAL Team 1 on the West Coast. SEAL Team 1, on the East Coast, however, had taken the mission a little more seriously and formed a dedicated two-platoon group known as Mobility 6, or "MOB 6."

Mobility 6 was formed in anticipation of a maritime scenario requiring a CT response. The two platoons training for such an operation developed advanced tactics, such as fast roping. The unit was disbanded in October 1980 with the official formation of SEAL Team 6, which in turn was later disbanded and became the Naval Special Warfare Development Group. Organization and manpower of the group is classified. It is estimated that NSWDG now numbers approximately three hundred operators.

Operation Urgent Fury: Lost at Sea

During the early hours of October 24, 1983, a US Air Force Combat Control Team (CCT) of four combat controllers and a dozen operators from SEAL Team 6 leapt into the night sky over Grenada. Their mission was to perform a Low Altitude Parachute Extraction System (LAPES) insertion and then patrol the Port Salinas airport, placing beacons for the follow-on forces, the 75th Ranger Regiment.

They jumped from the MC-130 Combat Talon, their drop zone some forty "klicks" out from the island. The mission profile called for an over-the-horizon insertion using a pair of Zodiac Combat Rubber Raiding Craft (CRRCs). However, something went terribly wrong: somehow—and to this day, no one knows—four of the SEALs went missing. With time slipping away, the men searched for their comrades, but to no avail: they were gone.

Those who remained continued to carry out their mission, taking evasive actions to avoid a Grenadian patrol boat. The CRRC had gotten swamped and would not start up again. The men drifted out to sea, where they were eventually pulled out by the destroyer USS *Caron*.

The bodies of the missing SEALs were never recovered. Listed as KIA were Machinist's Mate 1st Class Kenneth J. Butcher, Quartermaster 1st Class Kevin E. Lundberg, Hull Technician 1st Class Stephen L. Morris, and Senior Chief Engineman Robert R. Schamberger.

Operation Desert Storm: SEALs

As part of Operation Desert Storm, a unit of six SEALs—five enlisted men led by Lt. j.g. Tom Dietz—successfully undertook Operation Deception, the object of which was to trick Iraqi troops into waiting for an amphibious invasion that would never come. The team planted explosive charges a few hundred yards apart along a length of beach in Kuwait and Iraq, about 25 miles from the Iraqi elite Republican Guards, and set the charges to detonate a few seconds apart. When the charges went off, large portions of two Iraqi divisions were spotted by US recon satellites moving toward the Gulf area and away from the main front of the allied ground forces. Two days after the mission, the SEALs received a message from the operation commander, Gen. Norman Schwarzkopf. It read, "Enemy forces moving to beach. Allied forces going behind them. You have saved the lives of many of our fellow soldiers, sailors, airmen, and Marines. Bravo Zulu." This was high praise coming from "the Bear," who was not a strong proponent of special operations forces—an opinion that was much changed after the war.

SEAL Teams

The SEALs are the navy's contribution to the special operations arena. These waterborne commandos are organized and trained to conduct Direct Action (DA), Unconventional Warfare (UW), Foreign Internal Defense (FID), Special Reconnaissance (SR), and Counterterrorism (CT) operations, primarily in maritime and riverine environments. These operations include sabotage, demolition, intelligence collection, hydrographic reconnaissance, and training and advising friendly military forces in the conduct of naval and joint special operations.

Coronado, California, is the home of the Naval Special Warfare Center, which runs BUD/S (see page 198), as well as Naval Special Warfare Group 1, which oversees SEAL Teams 1, 3, 5, and 7. Naval Special Warfare Group 3 commands NSW undersea forces, which include the SEAL Delivery Vehicle (SDV) teams. Also in Coronado is Naval Special Warfare Group 11, which directs all NSW reservists, and one of its SEAL teams, Reserve SEAL Team 17.

Located at Virginia Beach, Virginia, are Naval Special Warfare Group 2 and its SEAL Teams 2, 4, 10, and 18. SEAL Team 18, a reserve unit, and Naval Special Warfare Group 4 are also located here. Group 4 is responsible for all of NSW's special boat teams.

Pearl Harbor, Hawaii, is the home of the navy's only SEAL Delivery Vehicle Team. The command conducts underwater delivery and insertion of SEALs using flooded minisubmarines.

Operation Just Cause: Paitilla Airport

In December 1989, the United States began Operation Just Cause, the invasion of Panama, one of the primary aims of which was to hunt down and capture Gen. Manuel Noriega, a rogue dictator and drug dealer. One the missions assigned to the SEAL Team 4 was the taking of Paitilla Airport and the destruction Noriega's Learjet, eliminating one of his escape routes. Though SEALs are highly trained and skilled in fighting, Army Rangers normally take down airports, not Navy SEALs. However, this was the mission they were given, and they would carry it out in the finest SEAL tradition.

SEALs typically work in small teams, usually an eight-man squad or sixteen-man platoon; however, for the raid on Paitilla, the plan called for three platoons, or forty-eight SEALs. In the end, the mission was accomplished, but at a very high cost: six SEALs were killed and eight others seriously wounded.

After this Paitilla mission, new operational criteria were established for the employment of SOF units: Is this an appropriate SOF mission? Does it support the theater commander's campaign plan? Is it operationally feasible?

Fast Attack Vehicle (FAV)

FAVs were first introduced into military service in 1980 with the US Army's 9th Light Infantry Division. The program ended in the mid-1980s but had caught the attention of Delta Force and the SEAL teams. As one of the original operators explained, they "began to tinker with them." The vehicle was modified to carry three operators and adapted to SOF's unique missions. Officially called the Desert Patrol Vehicle (DPV), it also carries the moniker of Light Strike Vehicle and is still known as the FAV.

The frame is poly fiber and the cowling can be removed if required by the mission profile. Baskets alongside the frame can hold food, water, ammunition, individuals' gear, or collapsible fuel bladders to give the DPV an extended range. The baskets can also be used for the recovery of downed pilots in the case of Combat Search and Rescue (CSAR) operations.

The DPV has two racks for AT4 antitank weapons and a top mount that would accept an M2 .50-caliber machine gun or Mark 19 40-millimeter grenade launcher. The front mount for the operator riding "shotgun" accepted a 7.62-millimeter light machine gun, while a rear mount would accommodate an M60A3 or other light machine gun. The primary use for this weapon is to break contact with enemy forces. The FAV was deployed from Desert Storm through the Global War on Terrorism.

Operation Red Wings

On the night of June 28, 2005, four SEALs inserted onto a mountaintop in Afghanistan. Their SR mission was to gather intelligence on a local militia commander operating near Asadabad, and they traveled for eight hours to a position 4 kilometers from insertion.

During their observation, however, they were discovered by three goat herders from a nearby village, compromising the mission. The SEALs initially held the three but eventually released them, whereupon they hurried back to their village and reported the Americans' presence to the local Taliban fighters.

Murphy (left) and Axelson (right)

The SEALs headed for their extraction site, but the Taliban surrounded them, firing with small arms, belt-fed machine guns, and then RPGs. The SEALs fought valiantly, but the firepower and sheer numbers of the enemy were overwhelming. When the battle was over, three of the SEALs—Lt. Michael Murphy, Gunner's Mate 2nd Class Danny Dietz, and Sonar Technician 2nd Class Matthew Axelson—were dead. Only Hospital Corpsman 2nd Class Marcus Luttrell would survive.

The last call made by Lieutenant Murphy, which cost him his life, was for help. A Night Stalker MH-47 Chinook, *Turbine 33*, was dispatched with an eight-man SEAL Quick Reaction Force (QRF). As the helicopter arrived, an RPG hit the aircraft, killing all sixteen operators aboard. Luttrell was rescued on July 2, 2005, by US Army Rangers.

MOH: Lieutenant Michael P. Murphy, SDVT-1

Lieutenant Michael Murphy, a member of SEAL Delivery Vehicle Team 1 (SDVT-1), was the leader of the four-man team tasked with reconnaissance near Asadabad, Afghanistan, during Operation Red Wings.

He led his men in engaging the large enemy force, resulting in numerous enemy casualties as well as the wounding of all four members of the team. Comms were shot, and the only way to make contact with headquarters was to gain the high ground. Ignoring his own wounds and braving a deadly fusillade, Lieutenant Murphy managed to make it to an outcropping, where he established contact with HQ. He calmly provided his unit's location and requested immediate support for his element. Lieutenant Murphy returned to his cover position to continue the fight until finally succumbing to his wounds.

SEALs in Operation Iraqi Freedom

During the Iraq War, members of the Navy SEALs were tasked with securing the hydroelectric Mukarayin Dam along with the adjoining power station and facilities. Inserted under the cover of darkness in Air Force Special Operations Command (AFSOC) Pave Low helicopters, a joint SEAL and Polish GROM commando team assaulted the dam, located approximately 60 miles northeast of Baghdad.

Using high-speed Mark V special-warfare craft of the SBUs, the SEALs assaulted two Iraqi offshore oil platforms, Mina al-Bakr and Khawr al-Amaya, in the Persian Gulf. As the waterborne commandos assaulted the platforms, snipers provided cover fire from orbiting helicopters. The seizure of these oil platforms assured that Saddam Hussein's forces could not repeat the ecological assault of the first Gulf War, when raw crude oil was dumped into the Persian Gulf. The SEALs were also instrumental in clearing mines from the waterways that had been impeding naval and humanitarian vessels, as well as other missions.

Basic Underwater Demolition/SEALs (BUD/S)

BUD/S training begins in Coronado, California. A sign found there becomes a mantra for the candidates: *The Only Easy Day Was Yesterday!*

The first phase, basic conditioning, is seven weeks long and develops the class in physical training, water competency, and mental tenacity while building teamwork. In addition to physical training, the class also learns how to conduct hydrographic survey operations. The fourth week of this training is known as "Hell Week"—over five and a half days, each candidate runs more than 200 miles and does physical training for more than twenty hours per day. During this time, trainees get a total of only four hours of sleep.

The second phase is the combat diving phase, which introduces underwater skills unique to US Navy SEALs. Candidates learn open- and closed-circuit diving.

The third phase, the land-warfare phase, is seven weeks long and teaches the class basic weapons, demolitions, land navigation, patrolling, rappelling, marksmanship, and small-unit tactics. Students are also taught to gather and process information that will complete the overall mission. The third phase lays the foundation for the rest of Navy SEALs training—candidates will use these basic moving and shooting skill sets in SEAL Qualification Training (SQT).

Drownproofing

SEALs are at home in the water, and to achieve this level of comfort they go through drownproofing. The purpose of this training is to instill confidence in the water and competence under the most extreme conditions.

With hands tied behind the back and feet bound, the student enters a 9-foot-deep combat-training tank and begins to bob for five minutes. He is then instructed to remain on the surface and float for another five minutes. After floating, he must swim 100 meters and then bob again for two minutes, demonstrating underwater forward and reverse flips. The trainee's last task calls for him to go to the bottom of the tank, retrieve his mask with his teeth, and complete five bobs.

Successful completion of the drownproofing test illustrates to the staff and trainee alike both comfort and competency in the water. This drill is a leading indication of a student's ability to successfully complete the maritime aspect of BUD/S training.

SEAL Qualification Training (SQT)

SQT is a twenty-six-week course that develops the student from the basic level of Naval Special Warfare to advanced tactical training. SQT is designed to provide students with the fundamental tactical knowledge they will need to join a SEAL platoon.

The class learns advanced weapons training, small-unit tactics, land navigation, demolitions, cold-weather skills (with training conducted in Kodiak, Alaska), medical skills, and maritime operations. Before graduating, students also attend Survival, Evasion, Resistance, and Escape (SERE) training and must qualify in both static-line and military-freefall parachute operations.

Upon successfully completing these requirements, trainees are awarded the SEAL Trident, designating them as US Navy SEALs. They are subsequently assigned to a SEAL team to begin preparing for their first deployment.

GMV-N

The GMV-N is a Humvee specifically designed for SEALs. Fitted with numerous mounts for an assortment of weapons, the vehicle can accommodate everything from dual M240 machine guns to the M2 .50-caliber Browning. It is also fitted with a modular armor kit.

The objective of the GMV program is to provide US special operations forces with a mobility platform capable of infiltrating and operating in low- to mid-intensity conflicts over a variety of terrain while significantly improving SOF's capability to travel unassisted over long distances. Depending on the mission, armor can be added or removed to increase either protection or speed and maneuverability. The GMV-N has a suspension upgrade that allows it to carry up to five operators into some of the harshest terrain in the world.

MOH: Petty Officer Second Class Michael A. Monsoor, SEAL

On September 29, 2006, Petty Officer 2nd Class Michael Monsoor, Delta Platoon, SEAL Team 3, was serving as automatic weapons gunner for Naval Special Warfare Task Group Arabian Peninsula in support of Operation Iraqi Freedom (OIF). He was a member of a combined SEAL and Iraqi Army sniper overwatch element tasked with providing early warning and standoff protection from a rooftop in an insurgent-held sector of Ramadi, Iraq.

In the early morning, insurgents prepared to execute a coordinated attack by reconnoitering the area around the allied team's position. Element snipers thwarted the enemy's initial attempt by eliminating two insurgents, but the enemy forces continued their assault, engaging with a rocket-propelled grenade and small-arms fire. As enemy activity increased, Petty Officer 2nd Class Monsoor took position with his machine gun between two teammates on a roof outcropping.

While the SEALs watched vigilantly for enemy activity, an insurgent threw a hand grenade from an unseen location, which bounced off Petty Officer 2nd Class Monsoor's chest and landed in front of him. Although only he could have escaped the blast, he chose instead to protect his teammates. Instantly and without regard for his own safety, he threw himself onto the grenade to absorb the force of the explosion with his body, saving the lives of his two teammates. For his gallant actions he was posthumously awarded the Model of Honor.

Hijacking of the *Maersk Alabama*

The MV *Maersk Alabama* is a container ship that, in April 2009, was operating in the Gulf of Aden with a crew of twenty, en route to Mombasa, Kenya. On April 8, four Somali pirates attacked and boarded the ship. Unable to take full control of the ship, they made the decision to leave the vessel and take the captain, Richard Phillips, with them as a hostage. Their means of escape was in one of the *Maersk Alabama*'s 28-foot lifeboats.

The same day, the frigate USS *Bainbridge* and destroyer USS *Halyburton* were deployed in response to the hostage situation. In addition to the naval vessels, members of SEAL Team 6 were dispatched from their base in Dam Creek, Virginia, to make a parachute insertion and rendezvous with the destroyer. SEAL snipers, armed with Mark 11 Mod 0 sniper rifles, took position on the fantail of the *Bainbridge* and waited. On April 12, the SEALs engaged the pirates in a single, synchronized action—one head shot each, neutralizing the situation.

Recon Corpsman Special Amphibious Reconnaissance Corpsman (SARC)

The Force Recon Company has medical and dive personnel assigned from the navy. While corpsmen have always served with the marines, the Special Amphibious Reconnaissance Corpsmen (SARCs) assigned to Force Recon are unique from their shipboard counterparts. SARCs go through the same as training the marines in Force, but they also complete their own advanced Combat Trauma Training. When assigned to the platoons, they are part of the team, riflemen first blending in with the Recon Marines. They are hybrids, combining the skills of a Recon Marine with the expertise of a corpsman.

Special Operations Forces Combat Assault Rifle, Heavy (SCAR-H Mark 17 Mod 0)

SCAR-H replaces the Mark 11 and the M14/Enhanced Battle Rifle and is chambered for 7.62×51-millimeter NATO ammunition. This hard-hitting round turns cover into mere concealment. Both the SCAR-H and SCAR-L (see page 101) feature three interchangeable, variable-length barrels: for close-quarters combat (CQC), standard, and sniper variant. This allows the SOF operator to fine-tune his weapon based on mission parameters. Also like the SCAR-L, the SCAR-H uses all of the sights, lasers, scopes, and other accessories of the Special Operations Peculiar Modification (SOPMOD) kit. To accommodate this assortment of accessories, the SCAR has multiple Picatinny rails at three, six, nine, and twelve o'clock positions, providing operators with multiple configurations.

SIG Sauer P226 Mark 25

For many years, the US Navy SEALs have been issued the SIG Sauer P226 pistol. Recently, they received an upgraded version of the combat-proven semiautomatic pistol: the Mark 25. Like its predecessor, it is a double-action/single-action pistol and remains chambered in 9×19-millimeter Parabellum, feeding from a fifteen-round magazine. SIG has made a few modifications and upgrades, including a Picatinny rail just fore of the trigger guard for adding a light or laser-aiming device—being able to quickly identify an insurgent is vital when performing close-quarter battle (CQB) operations. The 4.4-inch barrel is now chrome lined, giving the pistol a longer life. To protect the weapon from the harsh environments in which the SEALs operate, the slide is made of Nitron-coated stainless steel, the aluminum frame is hard coated and anodized, and the internal mechanisms are treated with an anticorrosion coating.

M60E3 Machine Gun

The M60E3 is a lightweight version of the Vietnam-era M60 machine gun. Like the M60, it is an air-cooled, belt-fed, portable or tripod-mounted gun. It has an ambidextrous safety, universal sling attachments, a carrying handle on the barrel, and a simplified gas system. Also like its predecessor, it has a fixed headspace, which facilitates the rapid changing of barrels. Its bipod is attached to the receiver; however, most SEALs remove this to lighten the weapon. The M60E3 is 42.2 inches in length and weighs 18.5 pounds. It is chambered for 7.62×51-millimeter NATO ammunition with a maximum effective range of 1,100 meters. As with the stock M60, the M60E3 was replaced in US military service by the M240 machine gun, although the weapon has cropped up here and there during the Global War on Terrorism.

Mark 48 Mod 1 Machine Gun

The FN Herstal Mark 48 Mod 1 is a lightweight version of the M240 and is essentially an M249 scaled up to accept 7.62-millimeter ammunition. This light machine gun features a MIL-STD-913 rail at three, six, and nine o'clock positions to allow for the attachment of SOPMOD accessories: optical sights, night-vision devices, laser designators, IR aiming devices, flashlights, and a forward pistol grip or bipod. Weighing 18.26 pounds empty, it fires the 7.62×51-millimeter NATO standard disintegrating link-belt-fed ammunition with a cyclic rate of 750 rounds per minute.

Ironman Ammo Carrier

The Ironman high-capacity ammunition carriage system was created by the US Army Natick Soldier Systems Center's Quick Reaction Cell and the Rapid Equipping Force to carry and feed up to 500 rounds of linked 7.62-millimeter ammunition. In a case where life imitates art, it is reminiscent of the minigun setup from the movie *Predator*. Soldiers tested different arrangements in the field in their search for an ammo pack that could be worn on patrols in the mountains of Afghanistan. The R&D folks at Natick, Massachusetts, took the idea and developed the Predator Technical Multi Adaptable Carrier (TECMAC) 50, otherwise known as the Ironman. The pack contains an adjustable internal frame that will accommodate various sizes of equipment, and the system enables the individual shooter to carry and fire five hundred rounds of ammunition, self-contained and without reloading.

Mark 11 Rifle System

The Mark 11 Mod 0 Type Rifle System was manufactured by Knight's Armament Company in Florida. Based on Knight's original SR-25 rifle, it was a highly accurate semiautomatic sniper rifle capable of delivering its 7.62-millimeter round well out to 1,000 yards.

The Mark 11 has two main sections, the upper and lower receiver, which allows for cleaning in the same manner with which the troops have been familiar since basic training. Another benefit of the receiver's breakdown is the fact that the rifle may be transported in a smaller package for clandestine activities. Once on target, the rifle is merely reassembled, with no effect on the zero of the optics. The system includes free-floating 20-inch barrel and a free-floating Rail Adapter System (RAS). The RAS is similar to the RIS on the M4A1. Another feature of the SR-25 is the ability to mount a sound suppresser, rendering the muzzle blast negligible—the only sound heard is the sonic crack of the round going downrange.

M14 Enhanced Battle Rifle (EBR)

The M14 was the standard service rifle until it was replaced in the late 1960s by the M16A1. Nevertheless, the M14 has found a new resurgence among US forces. It is a gas-operated, shoulder-fired weapon, firing a 7.62-millimeter round from a ten- or twenty-round magazine, and is capable of semiautomatic and full-automatic fire via a selector on the right side of the weapon. The rifle weighs 11 pounds with full magazine and sling. It has a cyclic rate of fire of 750 rounds per minute and an effective range of 400 meters, offering greater lethality than the M4A1 carbine.

The EBR is equipped with a simple mounting system that will accommodate a day optical sighting scope and other night or low-level target engagement equipment. It also features an operator-attachable flash suppressor.

Mark 13 Mod 5 Sniper Rifle

The Mark 13 was developed as a potential weapon to fill the gap between the M24 Sniper Weapon System (SWS) and the larger M107A1. The M24, chambered in 7.62×51-millimeter NATO, is capable of engaging personnel and soft targets out to 800 meters. The M107A1 is chambered in .50-caliber and is primarily used to engage hard targets out to 1,700 meters. Developed by NSWC Crane, the bolt-action Mark 13 Mod 5 Remington 700 long-action is chambered for the .300 Winchester Magnum (Win Mag) and fitted with a Lilja precision barrel, which can accept a Knight's Armament Mark 11 suppressor. The stock is an Accuracy International Chassis System (AICS) and has a three-sided, Picatinny-compatible Remington Modular Accessory Rail System for the mounting of scopes, optics, lasers, and other accessories. The rifle weighs 11.2 pounds and uses a five-round box magazine.

M18 Smoke Grenades

While SOF units do have the latest technology at their disposal, there are times when it's best to KISS—keep it simple, stupid. When a fast mover is coming for CAS, or the extraction HELO needs to know exactly where to land, the team on the ground will "blow smoke." The M18 Colored Smoke Grenade is used as a ground-to-ground or ground-to-air signaling device, a target or landing-zone marking device, or a screening device for unit maneuvering. It has an olive drab body with a light gray band and markings; the top is painted yellow, green, red, or violet (*not* purple) to indicate the smoke color, which is also marked on the side. The body of the grenade is a sheet-steel cylinder with four emission holes at the top and one at the bottom to allow the smoke to release when the grenade is ignited. Pulling the M201A1 ring initiates a 1.2- to 2-second delay, after which the filler is ignited and expelled from the grenade body. The grenade produces a cloud of colored smoke for fifty to ninety seconds.

Ka-Bar Knife

As they do with sidearms, SOF operators have wide latitude in what fighting knife they affix to their kit. A wide assortment of edge weapons can be found among SOF units, from specially made Randalls to the legendary Ka-Bars. From the beaches of World War II to the desert wasteland of Iraq during Operation Iraqi Freedom, the Ka-Bar fighting knife has accompanied special operations warriors as they carry out their missions. Manufactured by Ka-Bar Knives of Olean, New York, this traditional fighting knife has an overall length of 12 inches, with 7 of those being the blade. Whether used as a probe, a tool for opening an ammo crate, or a weapon to dispatch a sentry, it has earned it place in history as the gold standard of fighting knives.

Buckmaster Knife

After the release of the first *Rambo* movie, every kid on the block (like every operator in the field) wanted to have a "survival" knife. Not any ordinary knife, but a knife that, if you were dropped in the middle of a tropical island, you could use to survive, thrive, and build a condo. Enter the Buck 184 Buckmaster Survival Knife, made by Buck Knives. It is purported the knife was developed especially for the SEALs; understandable, because it was so heavy (24 ounces) it could also function as a small anchor. However, it was the quintessential survival knife of its time. The 12.5-inch Buck 184 had a large, 7.5-inch Bowie-style blade, which was 0.290 inches thick and rated between 57 and 59 on the Rockwell hardness scale. On the top of the blade were 3 inches of saw teeth capable of tearing through logs or blocks of ice. Keeping with the survival theme, the handle was hollow and sealed with an O-ring, permitting the storage of survival items du jour. There were also two anchor pins, which could be used as grappling hooks. The knife came in a black thermoplastic sheath with two pouches attached, one for a sharpening stone and the other with a Silva compass.

SOG SEAL 2000 Knife

SEALs are constantly looking for the perfect blade. One that passed exhaustive testing and evaluation by the US government—which included the breaking strength of the tip of the blade, the toughness of the blade and whether it would retain a sharp edge after use, and a two-week saltwater immersion test—was the SOG Specialty Knives SEAL 2000 Knife. It had to chomp, hammer, pry, and cut six varieties of rope and nylon lines. The SEAL 2000 was the vanguard of SOG knives for the SEALs. It was 12.25 inches overall, with a 7-inch blade and a weight of 12.8 ounces. A smaller version of the knife, called the SEAL Pup, featured a 4.85-inch serrated fixed blade and was 9.5 inches overall. These proven weapons were the beginning of the SEAL Team series of knives, which are still in use today.

Folders and Multitools

If you checked the pockets on a plate carrier, chest rig, or operator's "go bag," it is likely you would find a folding knife, a multitool, or both. Whether it is used to engage the enemy, crimp a blasting cap, or slice open an MRE bag, these implements provide operators with the appropriate tool for the task.

Shown here are the Emerson CQC-7 and Leatherman Super Tool 300 EOD. The CQC-7 has been a favorite of Delta Force for some time, and its latest claim to fame is that it was one of the knives carried on the bin Laden raid by the SEALs. The 3.3-inch *tanto* blade is razor sharp, with an overall length of 8 inches.

The Leatherman multitool is a toolkit in the palm of your hand. There are a variety of models, but the Super Tool 300 EOD includes nineteen different tools: combination straight/serrated 3.2-inch knife blade, needle-nose pliers with Mil-Spec blasting-cap crimpers, replaceable fuse-wire cutters, stranded-wire cutters, fixed regular saw, replaceable T-shank metal saw, replaceable C-4 punch, electrical crimper, four screwdrivers, bottle opener, can opener, 9-inch ruler, wire stripper, cleaning rod/ brush adapters, and an awl with a thread loop—all in a package that is less than 5 inches long when closed, weighing 9.6 ounces.

Operation Neptune Spear

On the night of May 1, 2011, a pair of highly modified MH-60 Black Hawk helicopters lifted off from the US airbase in Jalalabad, Afghanistan. Less than an hour later, the Night Stalker pilots (see pages 79-80) crossed the border in to Pakistan; dropping into the valley, they flew nap-of-the-earth (NOE) to elude Pakistani radar. Aboard the helicopters were members of DEVGRU, better known as SEAL Team 6. Their mission? To capture or kill the most wanted terrorist in the world, Osama bin Laden. Following the Black Hawks was a flight of MH-47 Chinook helicopters, which would serve as backup and Quick Reaction Force (QRF) should the SEALs run into any trouble. In total, there were seventy-nine commandos and one dog.

As the Black Hawks arrived on site, the SEALs got their first real view of the compound: the high walls, the outbuildings, and the three-story structure where bin Laden was hiding. They hit the ground, literally, as their helicopter lost lift and crashed in the compound. Undaunted, the men simply went to plan B and continued their mission. Breaching walls and locked doors, they engaged and neutralized any combatants along the way. They ultimately reached the third floor of the large structure, where they located bin Laden and killed him. Mission accomplished—"Geronimo, E-KIA."

SWCC Insignia

The men of the Special Boat Teams can trace their lineage back to the PT boat crews of World War II, as well as the Patrol Boat (PBR) and Light Seal Support Craft (LSSC) sailors of the Vietnam War. Today's Special Warfare Combatant-Craft Crewmen (SWCCs) operate and maintain the surface craft of the Special Boat Teams, conducting coastal patrol and interdiction and supporting special-operations missions. Focusing on infiltration and exfiltration of SEALs and other SOF units, they provide dedicated rapid mobility in shallow water areas where larger ships cannot operate. They are also trained in an SOF capability called the Maritime Combatant Craft Aerial Delivery System (MCADS), which is the ability to deliver combat craft via parachute drop. Their insignia badge depicts a boat cresting across the waves with a flintlock and saber just aft of the vessel.

Special Operations Craft-Riverine (SOC-R)

The SOC-R, which drafts a mere 2 feet and is operated by SWCCs of the navy's Special Boat Teams, performs short-range insertion and extraction of special-operations forces in riverine and littoral environments. The SOC-R is a high-performance craft powered by twin 440-horsepower Yanmar 6LY2M-STE diesel engines and Hamilton HJ292 waterjets, which propel the craft at 40-plus knots. The overall length of the SOC-R is 33 feet, permitting it to be air-transported aboard C-130 or larger military aircraft, or air-lifted by MH-47 helicopter. Each craft is manned by a crew of four SWCCs, one helmsman and three gunners; it can also transport eight SOF personnel. With a fuel capacity of 190 gallons, it has a range of 195 nautical miles. The SOC-R has mounts fore and aft to accommodate a variety of weapons, providing a 360-degree field of fire.

M134 Minigun

The M134 minigun is a six-barreled, Gatling-style, electrically driven machine gun chambered in 7.62×51-millimeter NATO. It is normally used for soft targets and troop suppression, which requires a high rate of fire; the M134 has an adjustable rate of fire of 3,000 or 4,000 rounds per minute. It is air cooled and link fed and has a maximum effective range of 1,500 meters with tracer burnout at 900 meters. Crewmembers currently fire ball Saboted Light Armor Penetrator (SLAP) ammunition with a mix of four balls to one tracer, or a nine-to-one mix to prevent Night Vision Device (NVD) shutdown on low-illumination nights.

M2 .50-Caliber Machine Gun

Another legendary weapon provided to the military by John Browning (see the Browning Automatic Rifle, page 124) is the venerable Browning M2 .50-caliber machine gun. Referred to as the "Ma Deuce" or simply the "fifty-cal," the M2 has been serving American soldiers since the late 1920s and will put the fear of God into any enemy. It was designed as a crew-served, automatic, recoil-operated, air-cooled machine gun. A disintegrating metallic link-belt is used to feed the ammunition into the weapon, and it may be fed from either side by reconfiguring some of the component parts.

This gun is has a back plate with spade grips, trigger, and bolt latch release. It may be mounted on ground mounts and most vehicles as an antipersonnel and antiaircraft weapon and is equipped with a leaf-type rear sight, a flash suppressor, and a spare barrel assembly. Associated components are the M63 antiaircraft mount and the M3 tripod. The weapon is rather large, with a length of 62 inches and weighing in at 84 pounds. It has an effective range of 2,000 meters and a maximum range of over 4 miles.

M240B Tandem Mount Machine Gun

Manufactured by Fabrique Nationale (FN), the 24.2-pound M240B medium machine gun is a gas-operated, air-cooled, linked-belt-fed weapon. It is a replacement for the aging M60 machine gun (see page 180) and fires at an extended range with greater dependability and accuracy than its predecessor.

The M240B is chambered for the 7.62×51-millimeter NATO round, which is belt-fed into the open-bolt operation of the weapon. It has an effective range of 1,800 meters with a cyclic rate of fire of 650 to 950 rounds per minute, controlled by three different regulator settings. While the weapon does possess some of the basic characteristics of the M60, the M240 series is an improvement on the older weapon in reliability and maintainability. The M240B is fitted with improvements for ground mounting, such as a forward heat shield, ammunition adapter, and a hydraulic buffer, and can be tandem-mounted on the SOC-R for double its firepower.

Rigid-Hull Inflatable Boat (RHIB)

The RHIB is a high-speed, high-buoyancy, extreme-weather craft with the primary mission of insertion and extraction of SOF tactical elements from enemy-occupied beaches. It is constructed of glass-reinforced plastic with an inflatable tube gunwale made of a new Hypalon neoprene/nylon reinforced fabric. The RHIB has demonstrated the ability to operate in light-loaded conditions in sea state 6 (wave height of 4 to 6 meters) and winds of 45 knots. Outside of heavy-weather coxswain training, however, operations are limited to sea state 5 (wave height of 2.5 to 4) and winds of 34 knots or less. The craft is air-transportable by C-5 Galaxy, C-17 Globemaster III, and C-130 Hercules aircraft and can be air-dropped from C-130 or larger military aircraft. It is crewed by three Special Warfare Combatant-Craft Crewmen and can transport a SEAL or other SOF element.

Mark V Special Operations Craft (SOC)

The Mark V SOC is manufactured by VT Halter Marine in Gulfport, Mississippi, and began to deliver in the mid-1990s to SOCOM, which uses it mainly for the infiltration and exfiltration of special operations forces, primarily SEALs. SOCs also support limited coastal patrol and interruption of enemy activities.

Featuring special seats that mitigate the shock of cruising across the waves at top speed, the Mark V can carry up to sixteen fully equipped SEALs or other SOF personnel. It has a beam of 17.5 feet, which can accommodate four Combat Rubber Raiding Crafts (Zodiacs) equipped with outboard motors and fuel. This allows the operators to use the SOC as a standoff platform to insert using the CRRC. The Mark V also has an aft ramp, allowing the CRRC to skim right up the rear of the vessel. It is fitted with five gun mounts, which can support multiple weapons: the M2 or M240 machine gun or the Mark 19 40-millimeter automatic grenade launcher. Later modifications to the craft have included Mark 95 twin .50-calibers, a Mark 38 chain gun, and Mark 48 25-millimeter guns.

Tech Specs
Length: 82 ft.
Beam: 17 ft. 6 in.
Displacement: 57 tons
Speed: 50 kn
Crew: 5

M80 Stiletto

The M80 Stiletto is a prototype naval ship manufactured by M Ship Company, San Diego, California. Designed and developed for high-speed military missions in shallow, littoral, and near-shore environments, it is 88 feet long with a breadth of 41 feet and draft of a mere 2.5 feet. It is powered by four Caterpillar C32 1,232-kilowatt (1,652-horsepower) diesel engines and Arneson ASD 14 drives, making speeds in excess of 50 knots. The cargo bay will accommodate an 11-foot RHIB, four UAVs, and a SEAL platoon. The M80 has a range of 500 nautical miles and can be outfitted with jet drives for shallow-water operations and beaching. The unique M-hull is made of carbon fiber, which not only reduces weight and increases strength but also creates a cushion of air, recapturing the energy of the bow wave. This provides a much smoother ride at high speeds, significantly reducing the hammering the crew and SOF team take from waves in rough waters. The faceted shape of the Stiletto is crucial to "stealth" designs.

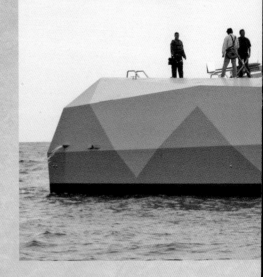

SEAL Insertion, Observation, and

The SEALION program began in 2000 as a test bed and proof of concept as the Naval Warfare Command explored advanced technologies for transporting SOF teams into combat. Manufactured by Oregon Iron Works, Clackamas, Oregon, the SEALION evolved from the smaller Alligator, a semi-submersible high-speed vessel that could travel right at the water's surface, resulting in a very low radar signature. The SEALION II program now comes under Naval Special Warfare Group 4 at Naval Amphibious Base Little Creek in Virginia and is operated by SWWCs. The SEALION II rides a little higher than the Alligator and has a much larger cabin to accommodate a pair of CRRCs and SEALs. The craft is 71 feet long; the draft remains classified. It is propelled by two Kamewa waterjets powered by a pair of MTU diesel engines, providing a speed of 40 knots. The all-aluminum SEALION is not armed, but it can be fitted with the same weapons as the Mark V SOC: 40-millimeter, 25-millimeter, .50-caliber, and 7.62-millimeter automatic weapons. For air transport, the SEALION easily fits into a C-17 Globemaster.

Neutralization (SEALION II)

SEAL Delivery Vehicle (SDV)

The Mark VIII Mod 1 SDV is a wet submersible designed for the covert insertion and extraction of SEALs into enemy or denied territory. It is piloted by two SEALs who are also part of the squad; in addition to the pilot and copilot, the SDV can carry up to four additional SEALs and their equipment. The vehicle can also be used by hydrographic reconnaissance missions. The term *wet* means the occupants are exposed to the underwater environment and must breathe using individual scuba gear. The standard method of inserting an SDV is via a Dry Dock Shelter (DDS) attached to a submarine, but it can also be delivered by surface ship or air-dropped. The SDV holds compressed air to extend the range of a swimmer's own air supply. The vehicle is propelled by a lithium-ion battery and equipped with propulsion, navigation, communication, and life-support equipment. A digital Doppler navigation sonar displays speed, distance, heading, and other piloting functions.

Dry Deck Shelter

The Dry Deck Shelter (DDS) is fitted aft of a submarine's sail and is connected to the vessel's after hatch to create a passageway between the two while the submarine is underwater and traveling toward an objective area. The DDS is 9 feet wide, 9 feet high, and 40 feet long, and it displaces 30 tons. It provides a dry working environment for mission preparations; in a typical operation, the DDS hangar module will be flooded and pressurized to the surrounding sea pressure, at which point a large door is opened to allow for launch and recovery of the vehicle. The DDS can be used to launch and recover an SDV or platoon of SEALs and their CRRCs.

Advanced SEAL Delivery System (ASDS)

The ASDS was a combatant submersible developed by Northrop Grumman Corporation for the USSOCOM for use in the clandestine insertion and extraction of SOF units, primarily SEALs. The program was cancelled at the prototype stage, and the vessel never saw service.

Classified as a submersible, the ASDS was in reality a minisub designed to be piloted by a submariner and copiloted by a SEAL. The pilot would be responsible for controlling and navigating the ASDS, while the copilot would be responsible for life support, lock-in/lockout systems, communications, and mission planning. Whereas the SDV is a "wet" submersible, meaning the SEALs are exposed to the undersea elements, the ASDS was a "dry," pressurized environment, and its occupants would have traveled in comfort inside the vessel. Advanced sonar systems and electro-optical sensors were installed to provide undersea situational awareness for the team of SEALs and allow them to conduct shore surveillance prior to landing. The ASDS would have provided improved range of 125 miles and speed 9 knots faster than the SDV.

Host submarines were modified with latching pylons and hatches in order to host the ASDS for transport to mission areas. The ASDS had a lockout chamber controlled by operators for lockout from an anchored position. In 2008, the only existing prototype ASDS was extensively damaged in an accidental fire. On July 24, 2009, US Special Operations Command announced that the program had been officially cancelled.

General Henry "Hap" Arnold

General Henry H. "Hap" Arnold, West Point class of 1907, was the commander of the US Army Air Forces (USAAF) during World War II. Having learned how to fly under the tutelage of Wilbur and Orville Wright, he became one of the earliest military aviators. During World War II, General Arnold was instrumental in the creation of a new breed of airmen—the Air Commandos, who used the sky as their home, covert actions as their techniques, and unconventional warfare as their tactics.

Lieutenant Colonel Philip Cochran

In the spring of 1943, USAAF commander General Arnold selected Lt. Col. Philip Cochran and Lt. Col. John Alison to serve as co-commanders of the new, "secret" 1st USAAF Air Commando Group. (Reportedly, an informal agreement had Cochran as commander and Alison as his deputy.)

In the China-Burma-India theater, Cochran and Alison developed and implemented a variety of innovative techniques and procedures for tactical air combat, transport, and air assault against the Japanese in the mountainous and jungle-covered terrain of Burma. Their inventory included fighters, gliders, bombers, transports, and even a strange new aircraft called a helicopter. One British officer provided an observation of the Air Commandos that evolved into their motto: "Anytime, Anywhere, Anyplace."

YR-4B

Pilots of the US Army Air Forces became the first to fly helicopters in combat when the 1st Air Commando Group introduced the Sikorsky YR-4B to the China-Burma-India theater. The aircraft carried one pilot and one passenger, had a range of 153 miles, and was powered by a 200-horsepower Warner Super Scarab R550-3 engine, providing a cruising speed of 65 miles per hour. The cockpit was encased in Plexiglas with doors on both sides. Four YR-4Bs arrived in theater in April 1944; within thirty days, only one remained operational due to crashes and mechanical difficulties.

When an L-1 light observation aircraft went down behind enemy lines, Air Commandos conducted the first helicopter CSAR (combat search and rescue) mission. Lieutenant Carter Harman flew behind Japanese lines to rescue the American pilot and three British soldiers who had been traveling in the airplane. Because the YR-4B could seat only one passenger, Harman had to make four sorties between the Allied base and the crash site. Colonel Phillip Cochran, commander of the Air Commandos, knew it was risky, but, as with all special ops, the benefits outweighed the risks.

Tech Specs

Length: 33 ft. 8 in.
Height: 12 ft. 5 in.
Rotor Diameter: 38 ft.
Weight: 2,581 lb. (loaded)
Maximum Speed: 75 mph

9-565 CG-4A

WACO CG-4 Glider

The CG-4, designed by the WACO Aircraft Company, was the most widely used US troop/cargo glider of World War II, with more than fourteen thousand seeing service during the conflict. Constructed of fabric-covered wood and metal, the CG-4 had a crew of two—a pilot and copilot. It could transport thirteen fully equipped soldiers, one Jeep, a quarter-ton truck, or a 75-millimeter howitzer. Loading the aircraft was accomplished through a hinged nose section that swung upward.

The C-47 Skytrain normally served as a tug to get the CG-4 in the air. The glider's most familiar use was during the D-Day invasion, though it was also a strategic asset of the Air Commandos in the Chinese-Burma-India theater. The aircraft was considered expendable, and most were abandoned or destroyed after delivery of the soldiers or cargo.

Tech Specs

Length: 48 ft. 4 in.
Height: 12 ft. 7 in.
Wingspan: 83 ft. 8 in.
Weight: 7,500 lb. (loaded)
Maximum Towed Speed: 150 mph

MOH: Major Bernard Fisher

On March 10, 1966, the Special Forces camp in the A Shau Valley, Vietnam, was attacked by two thousand North Vietnamese Army regulars. Hostile troops positioned themselves between the airstrip and the camp. The tops of the 1,500-foot hills were obscured by an 800-foot ceiling, limiting aircraft maneuverability and forcing pilots to operate within range of hostile gun positions.

   During the battle, Maj. Bernard Fisher observed a fellow airman crash-land on the battle-torn airstrip and announced his intention to land on the airstrip in an attempt to rescue the downed pilot. Directing his own air cover, he landed his aircraft and taxied almost the full length of the runway, which was littered with battle debris and parts of an exploded aircraft. Fisher effected a successful rescue of the downed pilot under heavy ground fire, with nineteen bullets striking his aircraft. In the face of the withering fire, he applied power and gained enough speed to lift off at the overrun of the airstrip. Major Fisher's profound concern for his fellow airman, at the risk of his life and above and beyond the call of duty, made him the first Air Commando of the Vietnam War to be awarded the Medal of Honor.

Smith and Wesson Model 15 Revolver

During the Vietnam War, pistols for pilots and aircrews were often at a premium. For this reason, air-force pilots would scrounge up whatever they could find. It was not out of the ordinary to see one with a Colt 1911, Smith and Wesson Snub Nose .38, or the like—anything that would add to their lethality should they find themselves down in enemy territory. Many would even bring weapons from home, such as a personal Colt .357 Python.

While the USAF pilots had several options for personal protection, the standard sidearm issued was the Smith and Wesson K-38 Combat Masterpiece Model 15. A six-shot, .38-caliber, double-action revolver with a 4-inch barrel, the Model 15 was built on the medium K-frame and featured adjustable sights. Loaded, it weighed in at 34 ounces and was often carried in a holster on a cartridge belt just below the SRU-21/P survival vest.

HH-53 "Super Jolly Green Giant"

The "Super Jolly Green Giant" entered service with the Aerospace Rescue and Recovery Service (ARRS) in 1968. Based on the Sikorsky CH-65 Sea Stallion, which was used by the US Marines as a heavy-lift assault chopper, the Super Jolly was a formidable aircraft and weapons system and became the air force's premier combat rescue aircraft. Two General Electric T64-GE 413 turboshaft engines rated at 3,925 shaft horsepower each gave the HH-53 a maximum speed of 170 knots. Internally, it carried 450 gallons of aviation fuel, with the option of mounting external fuel tanks on the sponsons that would carry 650 gallons of fuel. It was equipped with fully retractable landing gear, even though it had a watertight hull due to its seagoing CH-65 origins. The pilots sat in titanium-armored bat-wing seats, and metal plate armor was installed in the floor of the nose. Its powerful rescue hoist was mounted in the starboard cabin door, equipped with 250 feet of cable, and fitted with a "jungle penetrator." The rear-loading ramp could be opened in flight, allowing the insertion of SF teams or engaging one of the GAU-2A six-barreled 7.62-millimeter miniguns; the other was mounted near the forward winch. Normal crew for the Super Jolly was pilot, copilot, flight engineer (who could act as winch operator), gunner, and two pararescue specialists (PJs).

AC-47 Spooky

In 1965, the 1st Air Commando Squadron at Bien Hoa Air Base, Vietnam, began working on the conversion of the C-47 Dakota transport into the AC-47 gunship. Due to its impressive nighttime fire-breathing capabilities, it was nicknamed "Puff the Magic Dragon," though its official name was Spooky. Its emblem is still in use today with the current gunship crews of the Air Force Special Operations Command.

Aptly named, the aircraft indisputably brought a ghostly display to the enemy who would come under its massive firepower. The AC-47 was equipped with three General Electric SUU-11A/A Gatling miniguns capable of firing 6,000 7.62-millimeter rounds per minute on its port side. It carried twenty-four rounds of conventional ammunition along with forty-five flares that, when dropped, would hang suspended by parachutes for up to three minutes. The AC-47 had a crew of six: pilot, copilot, navigator, and three gunners. In combat, the pilot banked the plane into a pylon turn and ran a "racetrack" around the ground position to be attacked. Flying at 120 knots in a 3,000-foot circle, the gunship was capable of placing a 7.62-millimeter round in every square inch of a football-field-sized target in three seconds.

AC-119 Stinger

The next progression in gunship modification was the conversion of the C-119 "Flying Boxcar." The 71st Special Operations Squadron took delivery of the first AC-119G model gunships in January 1969, call sign Shadow. The AC-119Gs carried four 7.62-millimeter miniguns, which delivered rounds with deadly accuracy. By the end of 1969, the 14th Air Commando Wing had sixteen AC-119G Shadows and twelve AC-119K Stingers operating throughout Vietnam. The K model had the addition of two 20-millimeter chain cannons, along with a large radar dome to guide the firepower to the target.

During the seven-week siege of US Army Special Forces camps at Dak Pek and Dak Seang, the AC-119 proved indispensable as the Air Commandos flew 147 sorties in support of the SF camps. More than two million rounds of 7.62-millimeter and twenty-two thousand rounds of 20-millimeter ammunition were expended in support of the camp.

AC-130A Spectre

AC-130A Spectre gunships carried more than the four 7.62-millimeter miniguns of other AC-130 variants, upgrading to include four 20-millimeter M61 Vulcan chain cannons. Along with this rather impressive array of firepower, the Spectres were packed to the gills with advanced electronic devices. The Night Observation Device (NOD) was an image light intensifier that magnified the moon and starlight to provide the NOD operator with a clear view of ground activity. A Forward-Looking Infrared (FLIR) system was installed to pick up heat signatures from both humans and vehicles, regardless of the lighting conditions. A fire-control computer was installed, linking the gunsight, sensors, and guns into a coordinated weapons system. A steerable illuminator was mounted on the port side, which consisted of two 20-kilowatt xenon arc lamps capable of giving off visible, infrared, or ultraviolet light. These early AC-130 gunships were operated by the newly formed 16th Special Operations Squadron, attached to the 6th Tactical Fighter Wing at Ubon Royal Thai Air Force Base. In Vietnam, gunships destroyed more than ten thousand trucks and were credited with many lifesaving close-air-support missions.

AC-130H Spectre

The primary missions of AC-130 gunships are Close Air Support of troops in contact, convoy escort, and urban operations. They also conduct air interdiction against preplanned targets or targets of opportunity, and coordinate strikes, recon, and armed overwatch mission sets. Additionally, the aircraft can be used for force-protection missions, including air base and facilities defense.

Heavily armed, the AC-130H variant incorporates side-firing weapons integrated with sophisticated sensor, navigation, and fire-control systems to provide surgical firepower or area saturation during extended periods, primarily at night as well as in inclement weather.

Included in the sensor array are Low-Light Television (LLTV) and infrared (IR) sensors, and the H model is also equipped with radar and electronic devices that give the gunship a positive Identify Friend/Foe (IFF) to distinguish between the support of friendly ground forces and the efficient delivery of ordnance on hostiles during all weather conditions. Navigation devices include an inertial navigation system and GPS.

Tech Specs

Length: 97 ft. 9 in.
Height: 38 ft. 6 in.
Wingspan: 132 ft. 7 in.
Speed: 300 mph
Unrefueled Range: 1,496 mi.
Crew: 13
Armament: 40mm Bofors gun, 105mm howitzer

AC-130J Ghostrider

The AC-130J Ghostrider, set for delivery in 2017, encompasses all of the gunship's missions. It adds to previous AC-130 variants the capability to provide ground forces with a direct-fire platform ideally suited for urban operations and delivers precision low-yield munitions against ground targets.

The Ghostrider contains an advanced two-pilot flight station with fully integrated digital avionics and is capable of extremely accurate navigation thanks to integrated systems and GPS. Aircraft defensive systems, countermeasures, and color weather radar are also integrated.

Additionally, the AC-130J is modified with a Precision Strike Package (PSP), which includes a mission-management console, robust communications suite, two electro-optical/infrared sensors, advanced fire-control equipment, precision guided munitions delivery capability, and trainable 30- and 105-millimeter weapons. The mission-management system fuses sensor, communication, environment, order of battle, and threat information into a common operating picture.

Tech Specs

Length: 97 ft. 9 in.
Height: 38 ft. 9 in.
Wingspan: 132 ft. 7 in.
Speed: 385 mph
Unrefueled Range: 3,200 mi.
Powerplant: 4 Rolls-Royce AE 2100D3 turboprops
Crew: 7 (2 pilots, 2 combat systems officers, 3 enlisted gunners)
Armament: Precision Strike Package (PSP): 30mm GAU-23/A cannon; 105mm cannon; Standoff Precision Guided Munitions (SOPGM), e.g., GBU-39 Small Diameter Bombs; AGM-176 Griffin missiles

AC-130U Spooky II

The Spooky II is the third generation of C-130 gunships, all of which evolved from the first operational gunship, the AC-47 (see page 230). The primary functions of the AC-130U are CAS, force protection, and air interdiction. It is powered by four Allison T56-A-15 turboprop engines, providing an air speed of 300 miles per hour. It employs a synthetic aperture strike radar for long-range and adverse-weather target detection and identification. The AC-130U's navigational devices include inertial navigation systems and global positioning systems. The gunship employs the latest technologies and can attack two targets simultaneously.

Tech Specs

Length 97 ft. 9 in.
Height: 38 ft. 6 in.
Wingspan: 132 ft. 7 in.
Speed: 300 mph
Unrefueled Range: 1,496 mi.
Crew: 13 (pilot, copilot, navigator, fire-control officer, electronic-warfare officer, flight engineer, TV operator, infrared detection set operator, loadmaster, 4 aerial gunners)
Armament: 25mm Gatling gun, 40mm Bofors gun, 105mm howitzer

AC-130W Stinger II

As AC-130 gunship squadrons continue to age, AFSOC is engaged in upgrading their fleet of aircraft to maintain the lethality they are expected to provide. The AC-130W Stinger II is one of these new aircraft. Though similar to the AC-130's missions, the primary mission of the Stinger II is the armed overwatch of friendly SOF units. It may also be used for reconnaissance and is capable of delivering ordnance to precise targets to provide CAS in open and urban environments.

Stinger II modifications include improved navigation, threat detection, countermeasures, and communication suites; two electro-optical/infrared sensors; fire-control equipment; precision-guided munitions-delivery capability; and one side-firing, trainable 30-millimeter gun. The AC-130W is also modified with a Precision Strike Package (PSP) to perform the gunship mission.

Tech Specs

Length: 97 ft. 9 in.
Height: 38 ft. 6 in.
Wingspan: 132 ft. 7 in.
Speed: 300 mph
Unrefueled Range: 1,496 mi.
Crew: 7 (2 pilots, 2 combat system officers, flight engineer, 2 special-mission aviators)
Armament: Precision Strike Package (PSP) includes: 30mm GAU-23/A cannon; GBU-39 Small Diameter Bombs; AGM-176 Griffin missiles

EC-130J Commando Solo

The 193rd Special Operations Wing (SOW), located at Harrisburg International Airport, Middletown, Pennsylvania, is home to the only airborne psychological-operations broadcasting platform in the US military. A unique subordinate command of AFSOC, the 193rd is an Air National Guard unit. Another unique aspect is the aircraft the 139rd flies: the EC-130J Commando Solo. Like the AC-130 variants, the EC-130J is based on the Lockheed C-130 Hercules transport aircraft; unlike the AC-130, however, it is not a gunship. The Commando Solo is used for Military Information Support Operations (MISO) and information operations—in layman's terms, psychological warfare and civil affairs.

The aircraft is capable of broadcasting in AM, FM, HF, TC, and military communications bands. Its crew of pilot, copilot, flight-systems officer, mission-systems officer, loadmaster, and five electronic communications systems operators can carry out PSYWAR operations targeted at either military or civilian personnel. The EC-130SJ Super J is an upgraded slick 130 for Special Operations Flexible (SOF-FLEX) missions, including airlift, Military Freefall (MFF), Maximum Effort, Joint Precision Air Drop System (JPADS), and Psychological Operations (PSYOP) leaflet drops.

In 2001, the Commando Solo aircraft broadcasted messages to the local Afghan population and Taliban soldiers during Operation Enduring Freedom. In 2003, the aircraft was deployed to the Middle East in support of Operation Iraqi Freedom.

MC-130 Combat Talon

The MC-130E Combat Talon I and the MC-130H Combat Talon II are designed for long-range clandestine or covert delivery of Special Operations Forces and equipment and for providing global day, night, and adverse-weather capability to air-drop and air-land personnel and equipment in support of US and allied special-operation forces. They are equipped with FLIR, terrain-following/avoidance radars, and specialized aerial delivery equipment. Incorporated into the Talons are a fully integrated Inertial Navigation System (INS), GPS, and a high-speed aerial delivery system. These special systems are used to locate small drop zones and deliver personnel or equipment with greater accuracy and at higher speeds than is possible with a "vanilla" C-130.

MC-130E/H Combat Talons are able to penetrate hostile airspace at low altitudes to carry out these missions, and crews are specially trained in night and adverse-weather operations. Instrument flight rules (IFR) govern ordinary aircraft flying through clouds. However, the Talons use their own version of IFR, called infrared flight rules, which basically ignores all the rules and allows them to fly at high speeds and low levels in heavy ground fog or low cloud cover.

Tech Specs

Length: 100 ft. 10 in. (MC-130E)/99 ft. 9 in. (MC-130H)
Height: 38 ft. 6 in.
Wingspan: 132 ft. 7 in.
Speed: 300 mph
Unrefueled Range: 2,700 mi.
Crew: 7

MC-130J Commando II

The MC-130J replaces the aging fleet of MC-130E and P tankers. It flies covert or low visibility, single or multiship, low-level air-refueling missions for special operations helicopters and the CV-22 Osprey (see page 260). It also provides infiltration, exfiltration, and resupply of special-operations forces by air drop or landings on remote airfields in enemy territory. The Commando II primarily flies missions at night.

Tech Specs

Length: 97 ft. 9 in.
Wingspan: 132 ft. 7 in.
Speed: 362 mph
Range: 3,000 mi.
Ceiling: 28,000 ft.
Powerplant: 4 Rolls-Royce AE 2100D3 turboprops
Horsepower: 4,591 shaft
Crew: 5 (2 pilots, 1 combat systems officer, 2 loadmasters)

MC-130P Combat Shadow

The Combat Shadow extended the range of special-operations helicopters by providing air refueling. Operations were conducted primarily in formation, at night, and at low altitudes to reduce the probability of visual acquisition and intercept by airborne threats during clandestine, low-level missions into politically sensitive or hostile territory. The Shadow was a Visual Flight Rule (VFR) aircraft, used only when pilots could see the ground, although penetrations were often aided by radar. The MC-130P flew in a multiship or single-ship mission to reduce detection.

The secondary mission of the Combat Shadow was the delivery of special-operation forces. Small teams, assorted gear, equipment, Zodiacs, and Combat Rubber Raiding Craft (CRRCs) were a few of the specialized items that are conveyed by the aircraft and its crew.

Tech Specs

Length: 98 ft. 9 in.
Height: 38 ft. 6 in.
Wingspan: 132 ft. 7 in.
Speed: 289 mph
Unrefueled Range: 4,000 mi.
Crew: 8

MC-130W Dragon Spear

Conceived in 2009 as interim gunships to replace old AC-130s until the new AC-130J could come online, the MC-130W Dragon Spear was a gunship version of the MC-130W Combat Spear special-mission aircraft fitted "precision strike packages" developed by L-3 Communications. In addition to an optional Bushmaster II GAU-23/A 30mm auto cannon, the Dragon Spears feature and electronic complement of sensors and communications systems, including day/night video cameras, and a precision-guided munitions system capable of firing ten Viper Strike or Griffin small standoff munitions. The package proved so successful, the Dragon Spear became the model for the AC-130J program. The first Dragon Spear proved its worth one month after arriving in Afghanistan in 2010 when one of its Hellfire missiles took out five Taliban.

Tech Specs

Speed: 300 mph
Range: 2,500 nm
Ceiling: 28,000 ft.
Powerplant: 4 Allison T56-A-15 turboprops
Crew: 7 (2 pilots, 2 combat system officers, 1 flight engineer, 2 special-mission aviators)

MC-130 Fulton Skyhook

The Fulton Surface-to-Air Recovery System (STARS)—simply called "Skyhook"—was developed for the CIA to extract operatives from behind the lines; for this reason, it would be fitting for other SOF units as well.

The operator on the ground would be dropped the recovery kit, which included an exposure suit with an integral harness, nylon lift lines, a balloon, and tank of helium. Once inflated, the balloon ascended skyward; trailing behind would be the nylon lines, which were attached to the wearer's harness. For daylight missions, the line would have orange Mylar flags, for night recoveries, there would be lights on the line. An approaching MC-130 Combat Talon would deploy the hydraulically operated yokes, called "whiskers," and the pilot lined up the Talon straight toward the vivid orange flags. The flags indicated the exact position the pilot needed to aim for on the lift line, closer and closer until the yoke would capture the line.

The operator waiting on the ground was suddenly snatched upward and, once stabilized, would trail the aircraft at 125 knots. His journey from the ground to inside the aircraft all accomplished within five minutes.

A-1E "Sandy"

In May 1963, the 1st Air Commando Group was redesignated the 1st Air Commando Wing. Operational strength rose from 2,665 to 3,000, and the squadrons increased to six. In the tradition of their predecessors, the Vietnam-era Air Commandos developed tactics and techniques that earned their exploits an honored place in Air Force Special Operations heritage.

In 1964, the Air Commando Squadron traded its T-28 Trojans for the A-1E Skyraider. Often referred to as the "flying dump truck," it had a range of more than 1,100 miles and could loiter over a target for hours. The Skyraider was 40 feet long with a wingspan of 50 feet. Power was generated by a 2,700-horsepower Wright R-3350-26WA engine. The A-1E could carry an ordnance load of 12,000 pounds of bombs, rockets, or napalm canisters and mounted four 20-millimeter cannons.

Missions began to change for the squadrons, from training South Vietnamese pilots to the direct combat action of air support for US ground forces throughout Vietnam. The Air Commandos and their Skyraiders became a common sight for many a downed pilot, as the "Sandys" or "Spads" (nicknames for the A-1E) were called upon to assist with Search-and-Rescue (SAR) operations.

Operation Desert Storm: 20th SOS

The Pave Lows of the 20th Special Operations Squadron, the Green Hornets, began the Gulf War. General Schwarzkopf had studied the many maps and intelligence reports and pondered his next plan to action.

Near the end of October 1990, Col. Gary Gray of the 20th SOS met with General Schwarzkopf. Colonel Gray had a plan called "Eager Anvil," which called for a flight of four MH-53 Pave Lows and an assault force of army AH-64 Apache attack helicopters. The Pave Lows were equipped with FLIR, terrain-avoidance radar, GPS, and other sophisticated electronics and navigational aids. They would cross into Iraq, leading the Apaches through the dark and over the featureless desert terrain to the target areas. Once on site, the army pilots in their Apaches would take out two enemy radar installations, simultaneously, with AGM-114 Hellfire laser-guided missiles. With these radar sites destroyed, a corridor would be opened for US and Coalition aircraft to begin the air campaign.

General Schwarzkopf asked Colonel Gray whether he could guarantee 100 percent success on the mission; Gray looked at the general and replied that he could. General Schwarzkopf responded, "Then you get to start the war."

Kawasaki KLR250 D8 Motorcycle

Motorcycles have been used in the military since Gen. John J. "Blackjack" Pershing fought Pancho Villa in the "Border War," 1910–1919. During the same era, in World War I, these mechanical horses served as machine-gun platforms, for reconnaissance, and, when equipped with a sidecar, for medical evacuation. The D8 has an aluminum frame and is powered by a liquid-cooled, four-stroke single with dual overhead camshafts and a four-valve, cylinder-head 249cc engine and five-speed transmission. Ground clearance is 13 inches.

Today, the motorcycle is again being used by the military to provide reconnaissance and increased mobility of SOF units through rugged terrain. A pair of AFSOC combat controllers is seen here on D8 motorcycles. They survey the airfield and ensure that the tarmac is accessible and free of debris for follow-on aircraft to land.

Kawasaki KLX110 Minibike

The motorcycle continues to be a valuable means of transportation for SOF units. The capability to rapidly traverse rugged terrain makes it indispensable for recon and scouting missions. Motorcycles can navigate landscape that would not be accessible to larger vehicles, such as HMMWVs, or even ATVs. Using them in support of convoys, operators can rush up a hill for overwatch or race ahead to survey the route. The motorcycle can navigate through soft soil and narrow and steep trails while maintaining fast speeds. These vehicles are often modified with infrared headlights for night operations and brackets for holding the riders' weapons.

Here, an AFSOC combat rescue officer speeds across the field on a Kawasaki KLX110 minibike. The bike is powered by a four-stroke, single-overhead-camshaft, two-valve single engine with a four-speed transmission and automatic clutch. When a mission requires the use of such bikes, they can be transported on special mounts affixed to MH-6 Little Bird helicopters.

Rescue All Terrain Transport (RATT)

When the Special Tactics Teams needed a versatile rescue and evacuation vehicle, they turned to Raceco. This manufacturer of off-road racing vehicles built a prototype of the Rescue All Terrain Transport (RATT) in 1991.

The RATT is manned by a driver and two pararescuemen (PJs) and can carry up to six ambulatory patients on litters. The RATT has many features to maximize its utility and mobility, including an "instant kill" switch that turns off all white lights and engages infrared headlights for night travel. The overall structure of the RATT is light but strong. Its 110-horsepower Porsche engine is air cooled, thereby eliminating the weight of the radiator and cooling fluid used in a water-cooled engine. The vehicle can be transported in a C-130 aircraft and in some helicopters.

During Operation Just Cause in 1989, PJs could be seen speeding up and down the runway in their RATTs; they collected casualties and brought them to a collection point until medevac could be arranged. Throughout, firefights were going on around them while they cared for their wounded.

Non-Standard Tactical Vehicle (NSTV)

NSTVs are civilian four-wheel-drive (FWD) vehicles, mostly trucks or SUVs, adapted for use by special operations forces. Favorite among units in Afghanistan are Toyotas, both the Hilux and Tacoma. Some units acquire the vehicles in theater, while others are purchased and modified in the States and shipped to the unit.

The Hilux is used by both the Afghan Northern Alliance and the Taliban, helping SOF blend in and source spare parts when needed.

As the Global War on Terrorism progressed, SOCOM procured numerous Toyota Tacoma trucks, which were then modified by 5th Special Forces Group (Airborne) at Fort Campbell, Kentucky. Modifications have included specially made machine-gun mounts; antenna mounts for VHF, UHF, and SATCOM radios; winches; and brush guards. The Tacomas' V-6 engines remain stock. It is worth noting that lights inside and out are disconnected, as are the safety alarms, while headlights are switched to infrared for night operations.

HK Mark 23

The Mark 23 Mod 0 SOCOM pistol was developed by Heckler and Koch for SOCOM Offensive Handgun program in the early 1990s. Chambered for the .45-caliber Automatic Colt Pistol (ACP) round, it is a match-grade, double-/single-action semiautomatic pistol that holds a twelve-round magazine. The HK Mark 23 pistol has an effective recoil-reduction system, which reduces recoil forces to the components and shooter by 40 percent. The barrel is threaded to accept attachments such as the Knight's sound suppressor, and the frame is grooved to accept the Integrated Technology Inc. Laser Aiming Module (LAM).

One innovative design feature is a high-temperature rubber O-ring on the barrel, which seals the barrel in the slide until unlocking. To meet operational environmental requirements, the pistol was tested at +160 and −60 degrees Fahrenheit, and exposed to two hours of seawater at 66 feet, as well as to surf, sand, mud, and icing—unlubricated. A special maritime surface coating protects the pistol from corrosion in all of these environments. At the time of its introduction, some argued the Mark 23 was too large and ungainly for real-world ops; it is perhaps evidence they were right that it is no longer the weapon of choice among operators today.

HK MP5SD Submachine Gun

For missions where the interests of stealth and secrecy require fully integrated sound and flash suppression, operators may turn to the Heckler and Koch MP5SD. The model type, SD, comes from *Schalldämpfer*, the German term for sound dampener. The sound suppressor is integrated into the MP5's design and measures up to the normal length and profile of a standard, unsuppressed submachine gun. The gun uses an integral aluminum or optional wet-technology stainless-steel sound suppressor. It does not require use of subsonic ammunition for effective sound reduction as do most conventional sound-suppressed submachine guns, instead firing a 9-millimeter Parabellum pistol round that is carried in a 30-round magazine. The integrated silencer also suppresses the muzzle flash. When firing the weapon, the only noise you hear is that of the bolt going back and forth, making the MP5SD an excellent choice for operators operating in a nighttime environment.

MS-2000 Strobe

Signaling has evolved immensely over the ages, from biblical times when armies used torches to the angle-head flashlight, often referred to as the "moon beam," that has been in use since 1942. In the 1980s, chemical light sticks became popular and can still be seen in use on today's battlefield. One of the most critical uses of signaling is for the purpose of Identification, Friend or Foe (IFF). Installed in aircraft and combat vehicles, IFF devices emit a signal positively identifying it as friendly.

As SOF units hit the battlefield today, they have numerous methods for signaling, both visible and infrared, but the MS-2000 (M2) strobe is the most common among the US military. Powered by two AA batteries, this strobe can be configured in white light, with IR filter (making it visible only with night-vision goggles), and with a blue filter that acts as a directional shield so the strobe will not be mistaken for ground fire.

VIPIR Lights

To identify themselves to other soldiers during the Normandy invasion in World War II, paratroopers of the 101st Airborne were issued "crickets." These small devices, manufactured of brass and other metals, were officially called the Acme No. 470 clicker. Paratroopers would click them and, if they did not receive the proper response, they knew to come up shooting. In later conflicts, soldiers sewed pieces of material from a VS17 signal panel inside their boonie hats. Another technique was the application of glint tape, which was often helpful in identifying a soldier to orbiting AC-130 gunships with IR imaging.

Today, when the US military goes to war, a new generation of signaling devices is available to Special Operations Forces. Manufactured by Adventure Lights in Quebec, Canada, they have been modified to include interactive IFF capabilities. This series of Light Emitting Diode (LED) lights can be used for everything from personal identification to landing-zone lighting. An epoxy resin is used to encapsulate the semiconductor while producing a lens to further focus the light. Depending on the particular model, the light may have from one to five of these LED lights.

Phoenix Jr.

The smallest of the IR transmitters is the Phoenix IR beacon transmitter. It weighs a mere 2 ounces and is powered by a 9-volt battery; a newer version uses a CR123 lithium battery. The Phoenix can be programmed to various lighting patterns, while the Phoenix Jr. simply has an on/off switch. A combat controller can carry enough of these miniature beacons in the pocket of his BDU to set up an ad hoc landing zone. The diode is encased in epoxy, making the beacon waterproof, and it has a visibility of roughly five miles. The Phoenix beacon makes a perfect addition to an operators escape and evade (E&E) kit.

Air Force Special Operations Command (AFSOC)

AFSOC was established May 22, 1990, with headquarters at Hurlburt Field, Florida. AFSOC is the air force component of the unified US Special Operations Command. AFSOC is committed to continual improvement in providing US Air Force Special Operations Forces for worldwide deployment and assignment to regional linked commands; its mission is to provide mobility, surgical firepower, covert tanker support, and Special Tactics Teams. These units will normally operate in concert with US Army and US Navy special-operation forces, including Special Forces, Rangers, Special Operations Aviation Regiment, SEAL teams, Psychological Operations (PSYOP) forces, and civil affairs units. AFSOC supports a wide range of activities, from combat operations of a limited duration to longer term conflicts. It also provides support to foreign governments and their military forces. Dependent on shifting priorities, AFSOC maintains a flexible profile that allows it to respond to numerous missions.

Combat Control Training (CCT)

Combat controllers are part of the AFSOC's Special Tactics Teams and are FAA-certified air-traffic controllers. Combat Control Teams are responsible for ground-based fire control of AC-130 gunships and all air assets, including army and navy aircraft. They also provide vital command and control capabilities in the forward Area of Operations (AO) and are area qualified in demolition to remove obstructions and obstacles to the landing or drop zone.

The CCT pipeline includes the Combat Control Selection Course (called "Indoc") at Lackland Air Force Base, Texas (two weeks); Combat Control Operator Course at Keesler Air Force Base, Mississippi (fourteen and a half weeks); Basic Jump School at Fort Benning, Georgia (three weeks); Combat Survival Training (SERE) at Fairchild Air Force Base, Washington (two and a half weeks); Combat Control School at Pope Air Force Base, North Carolina (thirteen weeks); Advanced Skills Training (twelve months) at Hurlbut Field, Florida; Military Freefall School (HALO) at Yuma Proving Grounds, Arizona; Combat Diver School (Scuba) in Panama City, Florida; and Core/Operational Skills, locations undisclosed (three months).

It takes about two and a half years to produce a combat controller—a ground troop embedded with Special Forces teams and charged with providing Close Air Support. While CAS is an important tool for the battlefield, CCTs are also trained in infiltration, exfiltration, drop zones, resupply, helicopter landing zones, and other various specialized skills. Its members wear scarlet berets.

Combat Controller, Kabul, Afghanistan

Combat controllers are AFOSC operators who operate with other SOF units. They are trained in CAS and are certified air-traffic controllers. Their motto, "First There," indicates the CCT commitment to be the first deployed into restricted environments by air, land, or sea to the airhead for follow-on special operations forces.

The first AFSOC combat controller officially with boots on the ground in Afghanistan in support of Operation Enduring Freedom was Master Sgt. Calvin Markham. A member of the 720th Special Tactics Group, Markham was also the first combat controller to enter the American Embassy in Kabul, joining up with another combat controller from the 21st Special Tactics Squadron working with a Special Forces ODA. Attached to the team was an Air Force K-9 specialist, who went in and cleared the building of any booby traps or any types of explosives. The US operators entered the embassy, clearing it and the grounds. On December 13, 2001, the marines and the State Department officially opened up the embassy.

Pararescue Jumpers (PJs)

The AFSOC Pararescuemen—commonly known as PJs, from the term Pararescue Jumpers—serve as the surface-to-air link during personnel recovery in both friendly and hostile areas. Their primary mission, as personnel-recovery specialists with emergency trauma medical capabilities in combat environments, is to rescue, recover, and return American or allied forces from enemy territory. Pararescuemen are the only Department of Defense (DoD) personnel specifically trained and equipped to conduct conventional and unconventional recovery operations.

While PJs are proficient in trauma medical techniques, they are also combatants capable of laying down suppressive fire with an M4 with as much aplomb as they insert an IV line. Their motto, "That Others May Live," confirms the pararescuemen's commitment to lifesaving and self-sacrifice. Since the attacks on September 11, 2001, AFSCO pararescuemen have conducted over twelve thousand lifesaving combat-rescue missions.

PJ Training

PJs are the ones who establish overall combat search-and-rescue operations, planning, and procedures. They are instructed in the latest medical procedures in combat and trauma medicine. Their pipeline consists of the Pararescue Indoctrination Course ("Indoc") at Lackland Air Force Base, Texas (nine weeks); Army Airborne School at Fort Benning, Georgia (three weeks); Air Force Combat Diver Course at the Navy Diving and Salvage Training Center, Naval Support Activity Panama City, Florida (six weeks); Navy Underwater Egress Training at Naval Air Station Pensacola, Florida (one day); Air Force Basic Survival School at Fairchild Air Force Base, Washington (two and a half weeks); Army Military Free Fall Parachutist School at Fort Bragg, North Carolina; and Yuma Proving Ground, Arizona (five weeks); Pararescue EMT-Paramedic training at Kirtland Air Force Base, New Mexico (twenty-two weeks); and Pararescue Recovery Specialist Course at Kirtland Air Force Base, New Mexico (twenty-four weeks).

Once a pararescueman has completed the pipeline, he is assigned to a Rescue or Special Tactics Team, where he will receive informal on-the-job training. Pararescuemen assigned to a Special Tactics Teams receive additional training along with air force combat controllers in what is known as Advanced Skills Training. Pararescuemen wear the maroon beret.

Special Tactics Officer (STO)

AFSOC STOs manage the training and equipping of ground special operations and deploy as team leaders or mission commanders, as direct combatants, or as operations planners in combat. These personnel seize and control airstrips, conduct combat search and rescue, guide airstrikes and fire support using air assets for special operations, and provide tactical weather observations and forecasting.

STOs receive the same initial training as enlisted combat controllers, a process that takes approximately eight to ten months (see page 251), followed by a year of Advanced Skills Training (AST). The entire training program includes eight schools: Combat Control Orientation Course, Combat Control Operator/Air Traffic Control Officer Course, Air Force Basic Combat Survival School, US Army Airborne School, Combat Control School, Advanced Skills Training, Combat Diver Course, and Military Freefall Parachutist Qualification Course.

Combat Rescue Officer (CRO)

AFSOC CROs are the DoD's premier ground combat force specifically organized, trained, equipped, and postured to conduct full-range Personnel Recovery (PR) in both conventional and unconventional combat-rescue operations. The CRO specialty includes direct combatant command and control of Combat Search and Rescue (CSAR) operations. CROs are qualified in weapons and small-unit tactics, airborne and MFF parachute operations, combat-dive and subsurface search-and-recovery operations, technical rescue operations, small-boat operations, rescue swimming, and command and control. They are trained to fast-rope, rappel, or hoist from any vertical lift aircraft to both land and open ocean rescue objectives.

Combat Rescue Officers oversee organization and training, deploy as direct combat commanders or operations planners, and lead the Guardian Angel (GA) weapon system. Guardian Angel is a non-aircraft, equipment-based weapon system employed by combat rescue officers (CROs), PJs, and SERE specialists. Its mission is to rescue, recover, and return American or allied personnel in times of danger or extreme threat, whether in war or in peace. Although the GA Rescue Squadrons (RQSs) report to Air Combat Command as their lead major command and conduct conventional operations, a large portion of GA manning is in AFSOC, and they conduct special operations.

Special Operations Weather Team (SOWT)

SOWTs are composed of air force weather technicians who are trained as meteorologists and receive additional training that allows them to operate with other SOF units in hostile or denied territory. These special ops weathermen accumulate weather, ocean, river, snow, and terrain intelligence to assist in mission planning and generate mission-tailored target and route forecasts in support of worldwide special operations.

Special operations weathermen go through sixty-one weeks of training: Special Operations Weather Selection Course, Lackland, Air Force Base, Texas; Special Operations Weather Initial Skills Course, Keesler AFB, Mississippi; US Army Airborne School, Fort Benning, Georgia; US Air Force Basic Survival School, Fairchild AFB, Washington; US Air Force Water Survival Training, Fairchild AFB, Washington; US Air Force Underwater Egress Training, Fairchild AFB, Washington; Special Operations Weather Apprentice Course, Pope AFB, North Carolina; Special Tactics Advanced Skills Training, Hurlburt Field, Florida. Upon successful completion of training, airmen are awarded the gray beret.

Tactical Air Control Party (TACP)

Air Force Special Operations Command TACP members deploy with US SOF units and special mission units of the Joint Special Operation Command (JSOC) as joint terminal attack controllers (JTACs), operating and supervising communication nets to support army ground-maneuver units. TACP personnel provide expertise in planning and executing airpower in support of the land to advise ground commanders on airspace, to integrate air combat power, and to direct airstrikes. They act primarily as precision airstrike controllers, bringing lethal firepower to the battlefield.

TACPs know US and coalition aircraft and their weapons systems capabilities in detail. They also ensure potential targets are valid to prevent unnecessary casualties. Combat-related skills include land navigation, SERE techniques, small-unit tactics, camouflage techniques and hostile environment operations, and mastery of a variety of weapons.

One tool of the TACP is the AN/PEQ-4. Officially designated as Medium Power Laser Illuminator (MPLI), it is unofficially known as the "lightsaber." The PEQ-4 is handheld IR laser pointer, designed to illuminate and mark targets for night-vision-capable aircraft and supporting arms out to 10 kilometers. Powered by six AA batteries, it is waterproof to 2 atmospheres of pressure.

25mm Gatling Gun

As you enter the AC-130U by way of the front crew hatch and turn to your right, you'll find the first weapons system, the GAU-12/U 25-millimeter Gatling gun, a fully traversable weapon capable of firing 1,800 rounds per minute from altitudes of up to 12,000 feet. The weapons system automatically ejects the spent brass into a holding area, where it is emptied at a later time; there is no longer a need for the crew to shovel out the shell casings after a mission. This feature provides a safer environment for the crew, as they will not trip over loose 25-millimeter shells on the fuselage floor. Munitions available for the GAU-12 include the PGU-25 and PGU-38 high-explosive incendiary (HEI) and PGU-23 target practice (TP) rounds. The PGU-25 and PGU-38 HEIs are effective against exposed personnel and light materials with both fragmentation and incendiary effects. The PGU-23 TP is primarily used for target practice, although it does provide some penetration capability.

40mm Bofors Gun

The 40-millimeter Bofors has been associated with gunships since 1969. Once used on naval vessels as anti-aircraft guns, the weapons were stripped down from pedestal mounts and placed in the AC-130s.

Ammunition for the 40-millimeter Bofors includes a variety of projectiles. The primary ordnance types are the PGU-9B/B and PGU-9C/B HEI Zirconium liner cartridges, but the gun may also be loaded with the PGU-9B HEI-P Misch metal liner, the Mark 2 series HE-P and HEI-P cartridges (primarily used for training), and the M81

series Armor Piercing (AP) projectile, some of which contain 12-second-burn-time tracer elements (approximately 10,000 feet). The PGU-9B/B and PGU-9C/B HEI rounds are effective against personnel and light vehicles and as an incendiary for open flammables. The PGU-9B is a little less effective against the same target, as it contains less HE filler, resulting in a less effective fragmentation. The 40-millimeter is preferred for CAS in "danger close" support to friendly forces due to its small fragmentation pattern.

105mm Cannon

The other veteran on board most AC-130 variants, just aft of the Bofors, is the M102 105-millimeter howitzer, derived from the US Army field artillery M1A1 howitzer. It has been modified to fire from an aircraft and is placed in a special mounting, positioned in the port side of the gunship. The M102 fires both the M1 32.5-pound high explosive (HE) and the M60 34.2-pound white phosphorous (WP) projectile at a range of 11,500 meters. The fuse options for the HE rounds are the super-quick M557, selectable to point detonation or a 0.05-second time delay; the hard-end FMU-153B, with point detonation or 0.004- to 0.009-second delay; and the M732 proximity fuse, which detonates approximately 7 meters above the ground or point detonates if not set for delay. The M1 HE projectiles with fast-fuse point detonation are effective against personnel and light vehicles. While the HE round with fuse delay is effective against light structures and personnel under heavy cover or foliage, the HE FMU-153B is used for hardened target penetration capability. The M60 WP round, used only with the M557 fuse, is an effective smoke round with limited incendiary effect.

30mm Bushmaster

The weapons systems on the AC-130 gunships of AFSOC are receiving an upgrade to the 30-millimeter Bushmaster cannon. The rearmed AC-130U Spooky will keep its 105-millimeter cannon, but the 25-millimeter Gatling and 40-millimeter Bofors guns will be replaced with the new Bushmasters. These 25-millimeter cannons were originally installed in gunships as a suppression weapon to keep enemy troops pinned down; one of the reasons for the update is that it has no airburst capability, which is preferable for suppression fire. The Bushmaster is the same system used on USMC Amphibious Assault Vehicle (AAVs) as well as some navy ships.

The Bushmaster has a cyclic rate of 200 rounds per minute, which is faster than the 40-millimeter and a bit slower than the 25-millimeter it replaces. According to Lt. Col. Mike Gottstine, AFSOC's chief of strike/intelligence, surveillance, and reconnaissance requirements, "The twenty-five-millimeter throws a lot of lead down, but it scatters it more than the thirty-millimeter will. We're expecting increased lethality and increased accuracy with this weapon. Hits are what counts."

CV-22 Osprey

The Osprey is a tilt-rotor, vertical-lift aircraft that takes off like a helicopter and flies like an airplane. Initially developed for the marines as the MV-22, the program began in 1981. On March 20, 2006, AFSOC took delivery of the first operational CV-22, the special-operations variant.

The CV-22 differs from the MV-22 in the addition of a third seat in the cockpit for a flight engineer and an optional refueling probe to facilitate midair refueling. The CV-22 has a modern suite of electronics, such as a terrain-avoidance (TA) and terrain-following (TF) radar. To deal with the nature of special operations, it also has enhanced electronic warfare equipment for increased battlefield awareness, with more than two and a half times the volume of flares and chaff of the MV-22, radar-jamming gear, and improved integration of defensive countermeasures.

For Combat Search and Rescue (CSAR), the aircraft is fitted with an internally mounted rescue hoist and a crew door located on the starboard side of the aircraft. Another significant difference between the AFSOC and marine version is the amount of fuel it will carry: the CV-22 can hold approximately twice as much as the MV-22.

Tech Specs

Length: 57 ft. 4 in.
Height: 22 ft. 1 in.
Wingspan: 84 ft. 7 in.
Speed: 277 mph
Rotary Diameter: 38 ft.
Range: 2,100 mi. with 1 refueling
Crew: 4 (pilot, copilot, 2 flight engineers)

U-28A Utility Aircraft

The U-28A is a modified single-engine Pilatus PC-12 operated by the 34th, 319th, and 318th Special Operations squadrons. Deployed during Operation Enduring Freedom, among other conflicts, the U-28A provides a fixed-wing, on-call/surge-capable platform for improved tactical airborne intelligence, surveillance, and reconnaissance (ISR) in support of Special Operations Forces.

To create the U-28A, the civilian PC-12 was modified with communications gear, aircraft-survivability equipment, electro-optical sensors, and advanced navigation systems. The advanced radio communications suite is capable of establishing DoD/NATO datalinks, full-motion video, data, and voice communications. The aircraft is powered by a Pratt and Whitney PT6A-67B 1,200-horsepower turboprop engine providing a speed of 220 knots and range of 1,500 nautical miles. It is crewed by two pilots, a combat systems officer, and a tactical systems officer. Akin to the old Helio Courier of the Vietnam era, the U-28 is well suited for landing and takeoff in short, unprepared air strips. This allows up to nine SOF operators with equipment a platform to insert and extract in areas not suited for the larger MC-130, with more expediency than a helicopter.

MH-53J Pave Low

The mission of the MH-53J was to carry out low-level, long-range, undetected ingress into denied or hostile areas. This was accomplished day or night, even under the worst weather conditions, for infiltration, exfiltration, and resupply of Special Operations Forces.

The MH-53J Pave Low III Enhanced was the main helicopter in service with the Air Force Special Operations Command for nearly a decade; it was the largest and most powerful helicopter in the US Air Force inventory and the most technologically advanced helicopter in the world. It was equipped with forward-looking infrared, inertial GPS, Doppler navigation systems, a terrain-following/avoidance radar, an on-board computer, and integrated advanced avionics. On September 27, 2008, in Iraq, the Pave Low conducted its last combat mission as six MH-53 helicopters, call signs Cowboy 21 through 26, headed home.

MQ-1B Predator UAV

The MQ-1 Predator Unmanned Aerial Vehicle (UAV) is a medium-altitude, long-endurance, remotely piloted aircraft. Its primary mission is interdiction and conducting armed reconnaissance against critical, perishable targets. The MQ-1 acquires real-time target data and transmits it back and forth with Command and Control, the SOF team on the ground, and close air support (CAS) platforms.

The Predator brings persistent surveillance and strike capabilities without risking a manned aircraft to an SOF area of operations. It is operated from a control van, officially called the Mobile Ground Control Station and affectionately known as "the dumpster." All members of the Predator control and support team are assigned to AFSOC. The pilots who operate the Predators include both men and women. The basic crew consists of one pilot and two sensor operators.

Tech Specs
Length: 27 ft.
Height: 6 ft. 9 in.
Wingspan: 48 ft. 7 in.
Maximum Speed: 135 mph
Cruise Speed: 84 mph
Range: 454 mi.
Armament: AGM-114 Hellfire missiles

MQ-9 Reaper

The MQ-1 Predator is a "killer scout," whereas the MQ-9 Reaper is a "hunter-killer." Designed to hunt down and destroy high-value targets and time-sensitive targets with persistence and precision, the Reaper is a completely different aircraft, able to fly three times as fast and twice as high and to carry fifteen times the external payload. The primary mission of the Reaper is armed reconnaissance. Though its full combat load varies depending on the munitions selected, it can carry up to fourteen AGM-114 missiles as well as laser guide bombs such as the GBU-12 and GBU-39 Joint Direct Attack Munition (JDAM).

Tech Specs
Length: 36 ft.
Height: 12.5 ft.
Wingspan: 66 ft.
Speed: 230 mph
Range: 3,682 mi.
Ceiling: 25,000 ft.
Powerplant: Honeywell TPE-331-10T turboprop
Horsepower: 900 shaft

RQ-20A Puma AE

The Puma AE (All Environment) by AeroVironment, is a small, unmanned aircraft system (UAS) developed as an ISR platform. Fully waterproof, the drone is designed for ground or waterborne operations and can land in the water or on land. Weighing thirteen pounds, the Puma is hand-launched by the operator, after which it can stay aloft over three hours at 500 feet.

The RQ-20 is fitted with an EO and IR camera plus an illuminator allowing the operator to maintain "eyes on target." Equipped with AeroVironment's ground control station (GCS), the drone can fly autonomously via GPS navigation or can be flown manually by the operator.

Tech Specs
Length: 4.6 ft.
Wingspan: 9.2 ft.
Speed: 20-46 kn.

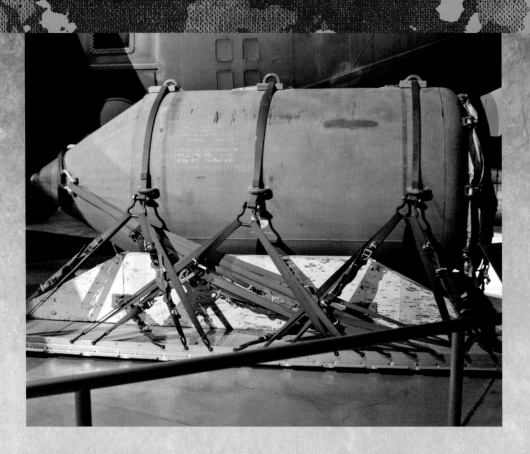

Bomb Live Unit 82 (BLU-82)

The BLU-82 (Bomb Live Unit 82) was the largest non-nuclear conventional ordnance in US inventory. Originally developed to clear the jungles of Vietnam, this 15,000-pound bomb creates an instant Landing Zone (LZ) for helicopters. In Vietnam, it was nicknamed "Commando Vault" and, later, the "Daisy Cutter."

Due to its large size, the BLU-82 was deployed by parachute from a Combat Talon. During Operation Desert Storm, eleven of these bombs were dropped from AFSOC MC-130E aircraft. The bomb produces an overpressure of 1,000 pounds per square inch, and the explosion and resulting dust cloud billowed so high into the sky, a British SAS team that witnessed it radioed back to their headquarters, "The Yanks are using nukes!"

AFSOC again dropped a number of BLU-82 bombs during Operation Enduring Freedom to destroy Taliban and al-Qaeda bases in the mountains of Tora Bora, Afghanistan. On July 15, 2008, an MC-130E Combat Talon I of the 711th Special Operations Squadron dropped the last operational BLU-82 at the Utah Test and Training Range.

6th Special Operations Squadron

The mission of the 6th Special Operations Squadron (6th SOS) Combat Aviation Advisory unit is to assess, train, advise, and assist foreign aviation forces in airpower employment, sustainment, and force integration. Squadron advisors help friendly and allied forces employ and sustain their own airpower resources and, when necessary, integrate those resources into joint and combined (i.e., multinational) operations.

The Combat Aviation Advisors of the 6th SOS possess specialized capabilities for foreign internal defense, unconventional warfare, and coalition support—integrating foreign airpower into the theater campaign, promoting safety and interoperability, facilitating air-traffic control, and upgrading host-nation aviation capabilities. Such capabilities imparted to the host nation forces are particularly applicable in the Global War on Terrorism and are especially important when it is necessary for the host nation's forces to fight along with the US forces as coalition partners or when allied forces have to carry the tactical initiative with US training and advisory assistance. Unique to the 6th SOS are the vintage and foreign aircraft in their inventory.

Special Operations Command (SOCOM)

SOCOM is responsible for all Special Operations Forces in the US military: the army's Special Forces, Rangers, and 160th Special Operations Aviation Regiment; the air force's Special Operations Wings and Squadrons; and the navy's SEALs, Special Warfare Combat Crewmen, and Marine Special Operations. Its primary mission is to provide combat-ready forces for rapid reinforcement of the other unified commands around the world. To carry out this mission, SOCOM develops doctrine, tactics, techniques, and procedure for all special-operations forces; conducts specialized training for all SOF units; trains assigned units and ensures interoperability of equipment and forces; monitors the preparedness of its forces assigned to other unified commands; and develops and acquires unique SOF equipment, material suppliers, and services.

The subordinate units under SOCOM are the Army Special Operations Command (ARSOC), Air Force Special Operations Command (AFSOC), Marine Corps Special Operations Command (MARSOC), Naval Special Warfare Command (NSWCOM), and Joint Special Operations Command (JSOC).

Joint Special Operations Command (JSOC)

JSOC was created in 1980 and is a joint headquarters designated specifically to analyze special operations requirements and techniques and to ensure interoperability and equipment standardization for US SOF units. JSOC plans and conducts joint special operations exercises and training and develops joint special operations tactics. Under the command are two units that are so secret their existence is not even acknowledged by the DoD: the US Army Delta Force and US Navy DEVGRU.

Although each unit has an expansive capability, all have the primary mission of Counterterrorism (CT). JSOC is located at Pope Field, Fort Bragg, North Carolina.

Special Operations Peculiar Modification (SOPMOD) Block I

The SOPMOD accessory kit allows operators to modify their weapons depending on mission parameters. Using the Rail Interface System (RIS), numerous components of the kit may be secured to the weapon. The kit includes a 4×32mm Trijicon Day Optical Scope, allowing soldiers to judge range and deliver more accurate fire out to 300 meters; a Trijicon Reflex sight, designed for close-in engagement; and an AN/PEQ-2 infrared target pointer (see page 269), which places a red aiming dot on the target, a useful tool in building and close-quarter battle (CQB). It is also equipped with a high-intensity flashlight mounted on the rail system; a backup iron sight; and a forward hand grip, stabilizing the weapon and keeping the user's hands away from the hand guards and barrel, which tends to heat up in combat. (As one soldier commented, "With all the extra stuff on the rifle, there's no room to hold the hand guard, anyway.") Finally, the kit includes a sound suppressor, which significantly reduces the noise and muzzle blast.

Rail Interface System (RIS)

The Knight's Armament Company RIS is a notched quad-rail system that replaces the front hand guards on the M4A1 receiver. This rail system is located on the top, bottom, and sides of the barrel and allows the attachment of SOPMOD kit components on any of the four sides. The notches are numbered, making it possible to attach various components in the same position each time they are mounted. Optical sights and NVDs can be mounted on the top, while top and side rails can be selected for positioning laser-aiming devices or lights. The bottom of the RIS normally accommodates a vertical grip and/or lights. When no accessories are mounted to the RIS, plastic hand guards are emplaced to cover and protect the unused portions of the rail.

Advanced Combat Optical Gunsight (ACOG)

The ACOG Model TA01NSN 4–32-millimeter was manufactured by Trijicon as the Day Optical Scope for the Block I SOPMOD kit. It is a four-power telescopic sight that includes a ballistic compensating reticle, which increases the capability of directing, identifying, and hitting targets to the maximum effective range of the M4A1 carbine (600 meters). With both eyes open, an operator can use the sight in a CQB situation; closing one eye, he can then acquire a target farther out. As a backup, the ACOG is equipped with an iron sight for rapid Close Range Engagement (CRE). Both the front iron sight and the scope reticle provide target recognition and standoff attack advantage while retaining a close-quarter capability equivalent to standard iron sights.

AN/PEQ-2 Infrared Target Pointer/Illuminator/Aiming Laser (ITPIAL)

The Insight Technology AN/PEQ-2 allows the M4A1 carbine to be effectively employed to 300 meters with standard-issue Night Vision Goggles (NVGs), such as PVS-7s, or a weapon-mounted Night Vision Device, such as an AN/PVS-14. The IR illuminator broadens the capabilities of the NVGs in buildings, tunnels, jungle, overcast, and other low-light conditions, where starlight is not sufficient to support night vision; it also allows visibility in areas normally in shadow. At close range, a neutral-density filter is used to eliminate glare around the aiming laser and improve the view of the target for identification as well as precision aiming. This combination allows for a decisive advantage over an opposing force with little or no night-vision capability. One captain commented, "When using a PEQ-2 on an M4 and PVS-7s, it is like the Hand of God reaching out and taking out an individual."

Trijicon Reflex II Sight

Another sight in the Block I kit is the Trijicon Reflex, a reflex collimator sight designed for CQB. The Reflex sight, which features a tritium-illuminated dot usable for low-light and nighttime use, provides a fast method of acquiring and hitting close targets as well as engaging targets while moving. Effective out to 300 meters, it is optimized for speed and accuracy in close-range engagements (less than 50 meters) and close combat (less than 200 meters), providing the operator with heads-up fire control during both day and night, with the aid of night-vision equipment. The Reflex sight can be used either with NVGs or in combination with a night-vision monocular, such as the AN/PVS-14; this arrangement provides lightweight day/night capability without having to re-zero during the transition between day and night sights.

KAC Quick-Detach Sound Suppressor (QDSS)

The QDSS can quickly be attached to or removed from the M4A1 carbine. With the suppressor in place, the report of the weapon is reduced by a minimum of 28 decibels. As the weapon's 5.56-millimeter round is supersonic, you will hear the bang, but it sounds more like a .22-caliber pistol than a rifle. This can buy some time while the enemy tries to figure out the nature of the sound and the location from which it came. By the time they realize what is going on, the assault team should be in control of the situation. The suppressor also keeps muzzle blast to a minimum.

Using the suppressor is effective as a deceptive measure to interfere with the enemy's ability to locate the shooter and take immediate action. Additionally, it reduces the need for hearing protection during CQB/CRE engagements, thus improving interteam voice communication.

SureFire M600 Ultra Scout Light

In the world of tactical flashlights, you get what you pay for; if you want the best, you pay for SureFire. There are a lot of good Commercial Off-the-Shelf (COTS) flashlights out there, but when your life depends on blinding white light where and when you need it, you don't want good—you want the best. This Special Forces soldier has attached an M600 flashlight to the Geissele rail-mounted to his M4A1.

The M600's recoil-proof LED is powered by two CR123 batteries and provides 500 lumens of blinding white light for 1.5 hours. At 5.6 ounces and just over 5 inches in length, the flashlight minimizes added weight and frees up rail space for other accessories. Its case is made of high-strength aluminum, with anodizing for superior toughness and corrosion resistance, and it is also fitted with an O-ring to keep out the elements.

AN/PEQ-5 Visible Laser

Insight Technology's AN/PEQ-5, as the name implies, is a visible laser that attaches to the RIS and provides a close-range visible laser-aiming beam. The VL can be used at close range in a lighted building, in darkness with the Visible Light Illuminator, or at night with night-vision equipment. It is used primarily in CQB/CRE situations, providing a fast and accurate means of aiming a weapon. It is especially valuable when the operator is wearing a protective mask, firing from an awkward position, or firing from behind cover and around corners; it permits the shooter to focus all his  attention on the target while being able to accurately direct the point of impact. Since it is visible, it also provides a non-lethal show of force that can intimidate hostile personnel: letting the "bad guys" know you quite literally have them in your sights.

AN/PVS-17A Miniature Night Sight

The M955 AN/PVS-17 MNS is a lightweight, compact night-vision sight that enables the operator to locate, identify, and engage targets at distances of 20 to 300 meters. The MNS features a wide 20×17 field of view, magnified 2.25-power night-vision image, and illuminated reticle. It is adjustable for windage/elevation, with an internally projected red-dot aiming point, and a remote trigger pad for momentary on/off control. It is fitted with a mount for a Picatinny rail and can be used handheld or mounted on a weapon. The sight weighs 2 pounds and is powered by a single AA battery.

Aimpoint CompM Sight

Though not officially part of the SOPMOD kit, the Aimpoint CompM sight is used for CQB activities by SOF operators. Shooting with both eyes open and head up, a shooter is able to acquire the target with excellent speed and accuracy. The CompM superimposes a red dot on the target, which allows the soldier to adjust his weapon accordingly when required in the fast-paced shooting environment of CQB. The CompM is parallax free, which means the shooter does not have to compensate for the distance between their eyes when aiming. The sight may be mounted on the carrying handle or RIS of the M4A1.

SU-231/PEQ Holographic Display Sight (HDS)

The EoTech SU-231/PEQ displays holographic patterns, providing instant target acquisition under any lighting situation without obscuring the point of aim. The holographic reticle can be seen through the sight, providing the operator with a large view of the target or zone of engagement. The SU-231/PEQ is passive and gives off no telltale signature. Its heads-up, rectangular full view eliminates any blind spots, constricted vision, or tunnel vision normally associated with cylindrical sights. Keeping both eyes open, the operator sights in on the target for a true two-eye operation.

The wide field of view of the SU-231/PEQ allows the operator to sight in on the target while maintaining peripheral viewing through the sight if needed. A unique feature of the HDS is that it works even if the heads-up display window is obstructed by mud, snow, or other material. Even if the laminated window is shattered, the sight remains fully operational, and the point of aim/impact is maintained. Since many SOF missions take place at night, the HDS can be used in conjunction with NVGs or other NVDs. The sight's hallmarks are speed and ease of use, translating to incredible accuracy and instant sight on target operations.

EXPS3 and G33 Magnifier

The EOTech EXPS3 is part of the SOPMOD program and continues to be SOCOM's optic of choice for CQB. This HDS is extremely fast in reticle-to-target acquisition in multiple-target situations and in conditions where either the operator or the threat is moving rapidly. The rectangular, full view, heads-up sight eliminates the tunnel vision that occurs with other sights. As quickly as the eyes acquire the target, the holographic reticle can be locked on to the threat (or threats). Whether engaging a target straight on or offset due to physical obstacles or awkward shooting positions, the EXPS3 makes it easy for the operator to achieve rapid reticle-to-target lock-on. The EXPS3 operates with a CR123 battery in a transverse housing.

With the addition of the G33 3-power magnifier, the operator can engage targets farther out. The latest G33 is shorter and lighter than previous models and has an improved mount for faster transitioning from 3× to 1× magnification. The magnifier offers tool-free azimuth adjustment, a large field of view, and an adjustable diopter for improved, precise focusing; the swing mount has a distinct tactile feel, ensuring that it is secure. The magnifier is currently a COTS item, and SOF units obtain them as needed.

ELCAN SU-230 PVS Sight

The Raytheon ELCAN Spectre DR's official nomenclature is the SU-230 PVS, but most SOF operators simply call it the ELCAN. The SU-230 is a dual-role optical sight—it combines both 1× and 4× magnifications into a Dual Field of View (DFOV) in one combat optic. This switchable sight allows the operator to transition from CQB to longer range by simply throwing a lever. This changes the optic from a 1-power to a magnified 4-power sight. The sight is designed to optimize the optical path and identical eye relief in either 1× or 4× mode. The ELCAN may be used with an illuminated reticle or merely as a red-dot sight. In addition to day operation, the SU-230 allows the operator to easily clip on an NVD in front of the optic.

Christini AWD Motorcycle

One of the benefits of the motorcycle is that it can be ridden off the ramp of a MC-130 Combat Talon, CV-22 Osprey, MH-47 Chinook, or any other large cargo transport in the SOCOM inventory. While the teams are getting their GMVs ready, motorcycle riders can be out scouting the area of operations (AO). The Christini All-Wheel Drive (AWD) Military Edition is in use by the Special Forces and SEALs.

This motorcycle is based on the Christini AWD 450 series, which has been modified for protection and durability. It is powered by a liquid-cooled 450cc four-stroke engine with a five-speed transmission. Fuel capacity is 2.3 gallons, plus a 1.5-gallon axillary tank. A finely tuned suspension system and AWD afford the motorcycle superb traction and stability, providing exceptional handling. With a ground clearance of 13 inches, it is capable of traversing the most rugged terrain even with an operator carrying his weapon and field gear.

Land Navigation

One of the most essential skills for any SOF operator is the ability to navigate, whether it is in the desert, mountains, or jungle. It doesn't matter how skilled you are in warfare if you're not in the right place at the right time. For this reason, land navigation is a requirement for all SOF units. While SOCOM ensures its spec ops warriors are outfitted with the latest and greatest technology, there are times when batteries die, satellites go offline, or a dreaded electromagnetic pulse (EMP) knocks out all electronics. GPS is taught, but it is used as a secondary method. Each operator is required to be proficient in both daylight and nighttime navigation. He must know the basics of geography, how to read a map and navigate from one, and how to use a lensatic compass, a pace counter, and an altimeter to determine his exact location. The most rudimentary method of navigation uses the stars, a magnetic compass, and a map. SOF operators are expected to apply these skills in the darkest of night with and without the aid of NVGs.

LAR V Rebreather

LAR stands for Lung Automatic Rebreather. A closed-circuit system, it does not give off any telltale bubbles to compromise the swimmer. The LAR V Mark 25 provides a special operations combat diver with enough oxygen to stay underwater for up to four hours. The exact time will depend on the individual diver's rate of breathing and their depth in the water.

The term *closed-circuit oxygen rebreather* describes a specialized type of underwater breathing apparatus (UBA) in which all exhaled gas is kept within the rig. As it is exhaled, the gas is carried via the exhalation hose to an absorbent canister and through a bed that removes the carbon dioxide produced as the diver breathes by means of a chemical reaction. After the unused oxygen passes through the canister, the gas travels to the breathing bag, where it is available to be inhaled again by the diver.

The gas supply used in the LAR V is pure oxygen, which prevents inert gas buildup in the diver and allows all the gas carried by the diver to be used for metabolic needs. Closed-circuit oxygen UBAs offer advantages valuable to SOF units, including stealth infiltration, extended operating duration, and a lighter weight than open-circuit scuba.

FN40GL Grenade Launcher

The FN40GL is a single-shot 40-millimeter grenade launcher developed and manufactured by FN Herstal as an accessory. It is fully ambidextrous and integrates seamlessly with the SCAR rifles; the FN40GL-L model attaches to the SCAR-L (see page 101), the FN40GL-H to the SCAR-H (page 203). With the addition of a buttstock assembly, the FN40GL can also be used as a standalone weapon. It is pump action, rotary locking, and attaches to the lower rail of the SCAR securely and rapidly via two throw levers. Once a round has been fired, the shooter slides open the barrel assembly, which then automatically ejects the grenade case. The side-opening option allows the operator to inspect the barrel or to load longer, specialized grenades.

HK MP5 Rifle

There was a time when you could not spell CQB without H&K. Heckler & Koch's MP5 series has become the hallmark of counterterrorism operators worldwide, and Delta Force is no exception. While "the Force" has moved to the M4A1 carbine as its primary weapon, there are those who believe the MP5 still has a viable place in CT and CQB operations. Compact, durable, hard-hitting, and just plain cool-looking, this series of weapons still remains a favorite of some shooters. For the times when you don't want or need a cartridge capable of penetrating 0.75 inch of steel plate (like the 5.56-millimeter) and instead want a more compact, concealable, and maneuverable weapon, the MP5 remains a practical option. It makes sense in scenarios involving extremely close quarters or thin walls, though, even then, you probably want a few guys on the team with M4A1s. The MP5 fires a 9-millimeter Parabellum pistol round usually carried in a thirty-round magazine and is often equipped with dual magazine holder. An operator with an MP5 can be effective when encountering a terrorist in a hostage situation or when engaging other mission-critical targets.

HK416 Assault Rifle

In the early 1990s, Delta Force was looking for a new carbine. The quest brought together a collaborative effort between this Tier 1 unit and Heckler & Koch, and the result was the HK416 assault rifle. The HK416, like the M4A1 it was designed to replace, is chambered in 5.56×45mm NATO caliber; the dynamic change came in the modification of the operating system. Instead of the direct-impingement gas system of the M4A1, the 416 uses a short-stroke gas piston system. After extensive testing, it was determined that this new system allowed the weapon to operate cooler, more cleanly, and with fewer malfunctions. The HK416 has several barrel variants—11, 14.5, 16.5, and 20 inches—and is also compatible with the HK 40-millimeter grenade launcher. In 2004, Delta replaced its M4A1 carbines with the HK416. The new weapon would also find its way into the armory of SEAL Team 6, where its claim to fame was being the weapon they used to take down Osama bin Laden in 2011.

HK417 Rifle

The Heckler and Koch 417 is a 416 on steroids. There are times when the 5.56-millimeter cartridge is the right ammunition for the mission; for those other times, when size really matters, you choose the 7.62×51-millimeter NATO. The heavier-caliber round turns cover into concealment, reaches out farther, and knocks down what it hits. The HK417 battle rifle was developed for the designated marksman for whom penetration, distance, and accuracy were required. It is available in 13-, 16.5-, and 20-inch barrel lengths and shares the same short-stroke gas piston system as the HK416. For added firepower, a 40-millimeter grenade launcher can be mounted beneath the rail system.

HK M320 40mm Grenade Launcher

The Heckler & Koch M320 40-millimeter grenade launcher is being fielded by the US Army as a replacement for the M203 (see page 70). Like the M203, the M320 attaches to the M4A1 carbine as well as the HK416. The single-shot launcher has a side-pivoting barrel that swings to the side, resulting in a smaller design and allowing the shooter to utilize longer, medium-velocity rounds. With the M203 attached to the weapon, the shooter would use the M4's magazine as a grip. The M320 has an integral pistol grip built in, as well as a forward grip under its 11-inch barrel; it also features a manual safety selector. The detachable buttstock can be affixed to the M320, and the HK grenade launcher can also be used as a standalone weapon.

HK USP45CT Pistol

The USP45CT Compact Tactical is a double-/single-action semiautomatic pistol handgun developed by Heckler & Koch for US SOF units. The extended barrel of this .45-caliber Universal Self-Loading Pistol (USP) has an O-ring and is threaded to facilitate using a suppressor. The purpose of the 45CT is to replace the larger Heckler & Koch Mark 23, providing the same features in a more compact and easily concealable size. The pistol utilizes a mechanically locked breech with a short recoil system. It weighs less than 2 pounds and can carry ten rounds of .45-caliber Automatic Colt Pistol (ACP) ammunition in a removable magazine.

HK45 Joint SOF Pistol

While the US military may have officially switched to the M9 Beretta, it was never accepted or adopted by the door kickers as a serious weapon, especially for counterterrorism and hostage-rescue missions. Now, the Joint SOF Combat Pistol program is being conducted by USSOCOM to evaluate the next handgun of choice for US SOF units—caliber .45! Currently in the preliminary stages of development, the program will examine the offerings of several manufactures, among them the HK45 manufactured by Heckler and Koch.

The HK45 is based on the manufacturer's Universal Self-Loading Pistol. Following the USP design, the HK45 has ambidextrous slide and magazine releases. Its polygonal barrel and linkless operating system are housed in a steel slide, which is mated to a polymer frame. Depending on the operator's preference, the weapon can be configured for single action (SA), double action (DA), or double action only (DAO). Additionally, the hand grip features interchangeable back straps to accommodate a variety of users. Molded into the frame is a Picatinny rail, permitting the attachment of lasers, lights, and other accessories. The HK45 comes in two models, the full-size HK45 and the compact HK45C, both of which can be fitted with threaded barrels to facilitate the attachment of a suppressor.

HK MP7 Personal Defense Weapon (PDW)

Heckler and Koch's MP7 PDW was designed to fill the gap between the assault rifle and the submachine gun, providing the operator with a compact weapon suitable for covert operations as well as personnel security details (PSD). The action of the MP7 is a gas-operated, short-stroke piston with rotating bolt. The 4.6×30-millimeter round greatly enhances shooters' ability to penetrate body armor over standard 9-millimeter ammunition. The 4.6-millimeter round will penetrate twenty layers of Kevlar out to 200 meters.

The MP7 is lightweight (4.188 pounds) and extremely compact (25 inches, or 16 inches with the stock retracted); as a result, it can be used in very confined spaces. The weapon features a rail system to accommodate the addition of mission-specific optics, lasers, and lights, and there is also a flip-down forward hand grip to provide greater stabilization for the shooter. The MP7 fires 950 rounds per minute and is fed by a twenty-, thirty-, or forty-round magazine.

M24 Sniper Weapon System (SWS)

The M24 Sniper Weapon System is the military version of the Remington 700 rifle, M24 being the model name assigned by the US Army after it adopted the weapon as its standard bolt-action sniper rifle in 1988. The M24 SWS consists of the rifle, a detachable Leupold Mark 4 LR/T M3 10×40-millimeter fixed-power scope, and a detachable Harris 1A2-LM or 1A2-L 9-to-13-inch bipod. The M24A1 is chambered for the 7.62×51-millimeter NATO cartridge, which feeds from a five-round feed system. The M24A2 is chambered for the .300 Winchester Magnum and the M24A3 for the .338 Lapua Magnum. The stock is an H-S Precision PST024 model with fixed cheek piece, adjustable length of pull (LOP), and hinged floorplate. It is made of Kevlar and fiberglass bound in aluminum bedding. The free-floating barrel is made of 416 Rockwell stainless steel with a right-hand twist of 1:11. The rifle weighs 12 pounds; the barrel is 24 inches, and the weapon's overall length is 43 inches.

Task Force 121

America's overt military response to the heinous attack on September 11, 2001, was Operation Enduring Freedom (see page 73). This was the "Super Bowl" for SOCOM's Special Operations Forces—while no one wants war, especially soldiers, as they bear the burden, there was still a sense among special ops forces that *this* was the mission for which they had trained. The task force deployed was a veritable "who's who" of SOF, a multiservice force from Joint Special Operations Command comprising operators from Delta Force, the 75th Ranger Regiment, the 160th Special Operations Aviation Regiment, SEAL Team 6, the 24th Special Tactics Squadron, combat controllers, pararescuemen, tactical air-control party operators, special operations weather technicians, and the CIA's Special Activities Division. TF121 was also augmented by Australian Special Air Service Regiment (SASR), British Special Air Service (SAS), Canadian Task Force 2, and Polish GROM units. The primary mission of the task force was to capture or kill what the United States referred to as High Value Targets (HVTs).

Operation Red Dawn

When the US military launched Operation Iraqi Freedom in April of 2003, the Iraqi dictator who had launched the "mother of all wars" over a decade earlier went into hiding. Intelligence gathered would lead members of TF121 to the town of ad-Dawr, Iraq, near Tikrit, and Operation Red Dawn was launched with the objective of capturing or killing Saddam Hussein. The operation was spearheaded by US SOF and supported by the 1st Brigade

Combat Team of the 4th Infantry Division. On December 13, 2003, the force focused its attention on a remote farmhouse; after searching the area, soldiers discovered the entrance to a "spider hole." Removing the bricks and debris that had covered the hole revealed a space approximately 8 feet deep; lying at the bottom was a disheveled, shaggy-bearded Hussein. The former president of Iraqi surrendered without a fight and was taken into custody. No longer filled with bravado, he was now a simple prisoner of war (PW or POW).

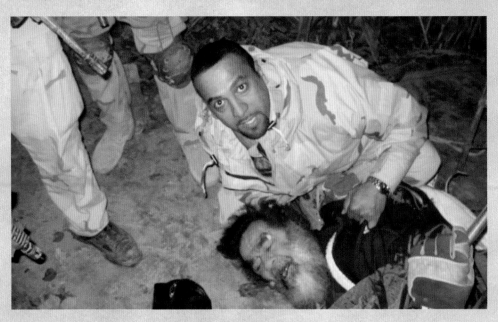

Individual Load Bearing Equipment (ILBE)

During the Vietnam War, web gear consisted of an equipment belt, suspenders, a butt pack, ammo pouches, a canteen with cover, and a first aid/compass pouch. As the years went by and carrying methods as well as missions evolved, shooters placed extra magazines into battle-dress uniform (BDU) pockets, pouches, and vests. Today's Improved Load Bearing Equipment (ILBE) is a load-carrying system designed to provide operators with a durable and lightweight method to transport individual equipment.

The gear is fitted with a grid of webbing called the Pouch Attachment Ladder System (PALS), allowing each operator to configure the kit to his specific needs. These systems provide easy access to ammunition and other items during the ever-changing mission profile of an SOF unit. From fast-paced CQB missions to lengthy Special Reconnaissance (SR) operations, the configurable pouches may hold magazines for M4A1 5.56-millimeter, MP5 9-millimeter, or 7.62-millimeter ammunition, depending on the weapon of choice. Other small pockets and pouches are readily available to accommodate .45-caliber or 9-millimeter pistol magazines, shotgun shells, Individual First Aid Kits (IFAKs), flex cuffs, strobes, ChemLights, or various types of grenades.

Chest Harness/Plate Carrier

As the name implies, the plate carrier is a load-bearing vest with specially designed compartments in which ballistic armor is placed. The carrier is laced with PALS webbing so the operator can modify the kit as needed based on mission parameters, adding assorted holsters, magazine pouches, or radio pockets. Internal pockets allow operators to stow maps or other gear. Additionally, these vests may have variously sized back pouches to accommodate such items as gas masks, helmets, demolition equipment, and other items essential for the mission.

Recently, as seen in Operation Enduring Freedom and Operation Iraqi Freedom, many SOF units have gravitated toward the chest harness/ armor plate carrier. A number of manufactures feature COTS harnesses, including Blackhawk, Eagle Industries, High Speed Gear, and Tactical Tailor. Larger pouches can accommodate two to three M4 thirty-round magazines, depending on the manufacturer, while some operators use what is called a shingle, with one magazine per insert. The other pouches accommodate such items as hydration systems, radios, MREs, compasses, and laser pointers.

Chest Rigs

Chest rigs, which can be attached to a plate carrier or used as a standalone system, have been gaining in popularity with SOF operators. The D3 Disruptive Environment Chest Rig by Haley Strategic seen here is designed to carry four M4 type magazines as well as other gear. In front of the magazines is the multimission pouch system, which features two general purpose pouches, one on each side of the rig, and three additional pouches in between. Two of these are designed for pistol ammo and will accommodate double- or single-stacked magazines; they are designed to contour to the magazine and also incorporate rare-earth magnets to keep them secure. A third is what Haley Strategic calls the "StuffIt" pouch, which will accommodate a wide assortment of gear, from ChemLights to fighting knives. The two general-purpose pouches on the ends are larger and can each fit a handgun holster or small Individual First Aid Kit (IFAK). There is also a drop-down pouch that affixes to the rear of the rig to provide extra storage. The D3 chest rig offers the operator a low-profile method for carrying his ammunition and other gear. A D3 Heavy version is also available, designed for larger SCAR or SR-25 magazines.

MICH Helmet

The Modular Integrated Communications Helmet (MICH) was originally developed for the US Army Special Forces and Rangers as a replacement for the issued Kevlar PASGT ballistic helmet. The Personnel Armor System for Ground Troops had been introduced to the military in the early 1980s and saw use for two decades, nicknamed the "K-pot" by some soldiers. The MICH is slightly smaller than the PASGT helmet and features a padding system and four-point retention system, similar to the cushions and straps found on bicycle helmets. It also replaces the nylon cord suspension system, sweatband, and chinstrap found on the PASGT.

These changes provide greater impact protection and comfort for the wearer. The MICH can be fitted with a mounting bracket for an AN/PVS-14 Monocular Night Vision Device (MNVD) on the front as well as straps on the rear to keep protective goggles in place. The smaller size helmet compared to its predecessor reduces weight and obstruction of the user's view and hearing, providing improved situational awareness while still offering ballistic protection. Further modifications were made after the MICH's introduction as operators had the helmet cut down to accommodate comm headsets.

Ops-Core Helmet

While the MICH was an improvement over the K-pot, it was still not a perfect brain bucket for SOF missions. It interfered with snipers as they attempted to get the proper cheek weld, and fitting headsets required modifying the helmets. The solution for spec ops units was the Ops-Core FAST Ballistic High Cut Helmet. Made of carbon and ultra-high-molecular-weight polyethylene, it provides a 20 percent reduction in weight over the MICH while maintaining ballistic protection. The helmet is rated as Level IIIA body armor, which provides protection up to a .44 Magnum Semi-Jacketed Hollow Point (SJHP) bullet. The high cut allows the operator more comfort when wearing headsets and allows him to put on and take off the helmet more easily. The exterior has Velcro pads for attachment of flag, team, or morale patches and a bungee arrangement for attaching a strobe and mounting rail for IR and white LED lights. The addition of the low-profile Visual Augmentation Systems (VAS) shroud facilitates the attachment of further mounts for NVDs, lights, and, when called for, a camera.

Tactical Headsets

SOF door kickers are armed with the latest weaponry and skilled in the most lethal tactics, techniques, and procedures. However, the one item that is key to any successful special operations mission is communication. When SOF units hit a target, they are often equipped with Peltor ComTac communications headsets, powered by two AAA batteries and designed for use with ballistic helmets; the ComTac III is specifically configured for use with the Ops-Core FAST helmet. These headsets allow operators to communicate with each other, maintain ambient hearing for situational awareness, and at the same time reduce any harmful noise levels inherent to the combat environment. The system also features a noise-cancelling boom microphone, which the operator can mount on either side for his convenience.

AN/PVS-14 Night Vision Device (NVD)

The AN/PVS-14D NVD is the optimal night-vision monocular ensemble, or pocket-scope, for special operations. It can be handheld, placed on a facemask, helmet mounted, or attached to a weapon. The PVS-14D offers the state-of-the-art technology in a package meeting the rigorous demands of SOF units. The monocular configuration is important to shooters, who want to operate with night vision while maintaining dark adaptation in the opposite eye. The head-mount assembly, a standard in the kit, facilitates hands-free operation when helmet wear is not required; the weapon mount allows for use in a variety of applications, from using your iron sights to coupling with a red-dot or tritium sighting system, such as Trijicon ACOG system (see page 269) or EOTech HDS (page 273). A compass is available to allow the user to view the bearing in the night-vision image.

Recently introduced and being evaluated is a modified PVS-14 called the AN/PSQ-20 Enhanced Night Vision Goggle (ENVG), which incorporates a thermal imager into the device. Operators will be able not only to see the enemy in the dark but, with the thermal capability, to identify the heat signatures of individuals and vehicles in all weather conditions as well as degraded battlefield environments.

AN/PVS-7 Night Vision Goggles (NVG)

In the late 1980s, SOF units transitioned from the AN/PVS-5 to the third-generation AN/PVS-7 Night Vision Goggles (NVGs). The PVS-7 differs from the PVS-5 in that it uses a single image-intensifier tube with a binocular eyepiece, and it has an integral infrared LED to assist in extreme low-light environments. The PVS-7B model incorporates a high light-level protection circuit in a passive, self-contained image-intensifier device, which amplifies existing ambient light to provide the operator a means of conducting night operations. NVGs can be worn in a special head harness or attached to the helmet using an accessory mount.

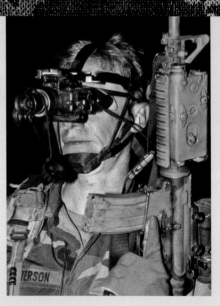

AN/PVS-15 Night Vision Device (NVD)

There is a saying that "everything old is new again," and the military is not exempt from the truth in that adage. While the PVS-7 had its advantages, there were still limitations, and an NVG with better depth perception and a system more compatible with aviation operations was needed. For this reason, the AN/PVS-15 by L-3 Communications—the current NVG issued by SOCOM to the SOF units in the field—is designed with a dual tube. This makes it particularly suited to tasks for which depth perception is critical for mission performance, such as controlling land vehicles and boats at high speeds. In addition, it more easily accommodates operating a vehicle while also providing hands-free operation. The PVS-15 is powered by a single AA battery, is submersible down to 66 feet, and, like its predecessor, incorporates an infrared LED for short-range illumination.

Ground Panoramic Night Vision Goggle 18 (GPNVG-18)

If two image-intensifier tubes are better than one, how about four? The GPNVG-18, manufactured by L-3 Warrior Systems, yields an operationally enhanced, wide-angle panoramic view of their environment. With four separate tubes, the operator now has depth perception, peripheral view, and situational awareness at a level that was previously unattainable. The center two tubes focus forward while the left and right are offset, affording a 97-degree field of view. The 27-ounce goggles mount to the front of a helmet, with the weight offset by a remote battery pack tethered to the unit. The unit is powered by four CR123A batteries, which provide approximate thirty hours of use. Used by SEAL Team 6 during Operation Neptune Spear, the raid on bin Laden (see page 214), these goggles punctuate the statement that when it comes to special operations: the US Special Operations Forces own the night!

Admiral William McRaven

Admiral William McRaven was the ninth commander of the United States Special Operations Command (USSOCOM), headquartered at MacDill Air Force Base, Florida. USSOCOM ensures the readiness of joint special-operations forces and, as directed, conducts operations worldwide.

Admiral McRaven has commanded at every level within the special operations community, including assignments as the deputy commanding general for operations at JSOC, commodore of Naval Special Warfare Group 1, commander of SEAL Team 3, task group commander in the US Central Command area of responsibility, task unit commander during Operations Desert Storm and Desert Shield, squadron commander at the Naval Special Warfare Development Group, and SEAL platoon commander for Underwater Demolition Team 21/SEAL Team 4. With this experienced leader as the commander of SOCOM, overseeing JSOC and organizing mission parameters, few would doubt why the SEALs received the mission to take out bin Laden.

Unconventional Warfare (UW)

Unconventional warfare is the direct support of a resistance movement against a hostile nation. It encompasses guerrilla warfare; the use of irregular forces, normally indigenous personnel operating in enemy-held territory; and other direct-offensive, low-visibility, covert and clandestine operations. Also incorporated in the UW mission are the indirect activities of subversion, sabotage, intelligence gathering, and evasion and escape nets. Armed rebellion against an established force or occupying power is often within its scope. In wartime, Special Operations Forces may be tasked with directly supporting a resistance or guerrilla force. This is most often accomplished by infiltrating Special Forces operational detachments, or A-Teams (see page 24), into denied or sensitive areas for the purpose of training, equipping, and advising or directing indigenous forces.

Direct Action (DA)

Under the category of direct action are small-scale offensive actions, normally of short-term duration, conducted by SOF teams. Such actions include airfield seizure, capture of enemy personnel, and any action that would inflict damage on enemy personnel or destroy their warfighting materiel. Direct-action missions may also include the recovery of sensitive items or isolated personnel, such as POWs. SOF units may employ raids, ambushes, and other small-unit tactics; use mines and other demolitions; or deploy fire support from air, ground, or sea assets in the pursuit of these mission goals. Direct action may also involve standoff weapons, such as a sniper team or a SOF team with a Special Operation Force Laser Acquisition Marker (SOFLAM) "lasing" a target for Terminal Guidance Ordinance (TGO) with precision-guided "smart bombs." SOF units performing a DA mission will normally withdraw from the objective area as rapidly as possible to limit the operation's scope and duration.

Special Reconnaissance (SR)

Special reconnaissance is defined as the reconnaissance and surveillance activity conducted by Special Operation Forces. Special reconnaissance provides strategic intelligence required by national decision-makers in formulating national or foreign defense policies, details and reports to theater level commanders to plan and conduct campaigns, and tactical information that commanders need for fighting battles. This covers the area of HUMINT (HUMan INTelligence), placing US "eyes on target" in hostile, denied, or politically sensitive territory to accomplish what no satellite can do. A small operations team (ODA— see page 24), Force Recon team, or similar unit performing a SR mission will be infiltrated into enemy area to report back to their commanders information needed to carry out ongoing attacks. These highly skilled operators may be tasked with acquiring or verifying, by visual observation or other methods available, information concerning the capabilities, intentions, and activities of an enemy force. SR includes meteorological, hydrographic, and geographic characteristics of the objective area. Additionally, SR comprises target acquisition, the placement of remote sensor equipment in enemy territory, bomb-damage assessment (BDA), and post-strike reconnaissance.

Foreign Internal Defense (FID)

FID is a primary means of providing the expertise of US military Special Operations Forces to other governments in support of their internal defense and developmental efforts. By providing such training to the host nation, Special Operations Forces may preclude the deployment or combat involving conventional forces in a particular region of the world. FID was developed to teach the military of a host nation to protect and defend against subversion, insurgency terrorism, and other threats to their internal security. Employing SOF units in such missions keeps the teams prepared for their role as combat advisors in the event of war. FID missions have included basic static-line parachute training, MFF, jumpmaster training, light infantry tactics, counterinsurgency operations, advance patrolling, urban combat, advance marksmanship/sniper training, water operations (including riverine ops, small-boat ops, and scout swimming), engineering, and communications training. Medical and veterinary training are also included.

Visit, Board, Search, and Seizure (VBSS)

VBSS is the term used by the US military to describe maritime boarding actions and tactics designed to capture enemy vessels as part of efforts to combat terrorism, piracy, and smuggling. Conducting maritime interdiction is a crucial part of the US Navy's larger maritime strategy, and the VBSS teams serve as a vital asset in executing that mission. Depending on the mission or proximity to the threat, the SEALs and Marines are both well suited for this operation.

There are several levels of VBSS tactics employed. Level 1 is used when the target vessel is compliant with the boarding team; Level 2 when the target vessel is noncompliant and has a freeboard (height from deck to waterline) of 25 feet or less; Level 3 when the target vessel is noncompliant and has a freeboard over 25 feet high and/or is actively opposing the boarding; and Level 4 when there is active armed resistance. Level 3 and 4 VBSS operations are typically carried out by teams of Special Operations Forces, who may be inserted by helicopter (fast-rope) and/or Rigid-Hull Inflatable Boats (RHIBs).

Counterterrorism (CT)

Counterterrorism consists of the offensive actions taken to prevent, deter, and respond to terrorism; this includes intelligence gathering and threat analysis. SOF troops are ideal for engaging in antiterrorism and counterterrorism missions, and the deployment of Special Operation Forces personnel can greatly enhance the flexibility in meeting the critical demands of such an undertaking. CT missions may include training of host nation counterterrorist forces, hostage rescues, recovery of sensitive material from terrorists, or performing DA on the terrorist infrastructure to reduce the effects of international or state-sponsored terrorist activities.

Combating Weapons of Mass Destruction (CWMD)

Since the attacks on the United States on September 11, 2001, the possibility of another attack has prompted the question, "What if the terrorists get a nuclear weapon?" Combating Weapons of Mass Destruction (CWMD) is one of SOCOM's core missions. WMDs include Chemical, Biological, Radiological, and Nuclear (CBRN) weapons or devices that are capable of inflicting a high level of destruction along with mass causalities. CWMD covers a wide range of players, from law enforcement to the military, and SOF units may be deployed to intercept, divert, seize, and secure CBRN materials, devices, or personnel supporting WMD operations. To accomplish this mission, SOF units may incorporate multiple core missions, such as DA (see page 298) or UW (see page 297).

Sensitive Site Exploitation (SSE)

SSE is the process of collecting intelligence, material, and persons from designated locations and analyzing them to answer information requirements, which may facilitate subsequent operations. *Exploitation* is defined as taking full advantage of any information that has come to hand for tactical, operational, or strategic purposes.

Examples of locations where SSE operations may take place include but are not limited to chemical, biological, radiological, nuclear, and high-yield explosives (CBRNE) facilities; locations containing evidence of war crimes, such as mass graves, illegal detainment facilities, and clandestine command-and-control facilities; terrorist training camps; prisoner-of-war locations; research and production facilities; government buildings and infrastructure of strategic value; official government residences; and sites suspected of harboring enemy leaders or other HVTs.

Blood Chit

A blood chit is a notice carried by military personnel of the United States, as well as those of other countries, that is addressed to any civilian who may come across an operator in trouble—for example, one who is injured or down behind enemy lines. It identifies the bearer as friendly and displays a message requesting the service member be rendered assistance. Blood chits, when presented and properly validated, represent an obligation of the US government to provide compensation for services rendered to isolated personnel.

Commonly used by American pilots during World War II, the chits are still in use today. In addition to aircrews, other SOF teams are issued them by the Joint Personnel Recovery Agency (JPRA). Each chit carried by an American soldier has a US flag along with instructions in English as well as several languages used in the region of operation. It indicates that the United States will reward anyone who assists the bearer of the chit and brings him back to safety.

Morale Patches

There are many official patches worn by military personnel. These include patches for units or squadrons (such as the Special Forces, Rangers, AFSOC, and Raiders); qualification tabs (Airborne, Ranger, and the like); US flag (sometimes seen in reverse, as the stars are always to face forward); and patches representing individual or unit call signs or a soldier's blood type. Common among SOF units is an infrared flag, which is visible in darkened environments when observed though NVGs.

Morale patches fall in the realm of unofficial and unsanctioned, yet they serve a valuable purpose among troops. From unit cohesion to identification, these patches provide esprit de corps and identify the wearer as a member of a certain unit or team. Some units have them specially made, while others will obtain generic patches. Morale patches in general are meant to lighten the mood—they are humorous, irreverent, and some even insulting toward the enemy. Since they are not authorized by the services, depending on the command and the nature of specific patches, they may or may not be tolerated in an official capacity. From "FUBAR" to "Hadji Don't Surf," these patches are meant to lighten the mood and lift the spirits during day-to-day operations as operators place themselves in harm's way.

Land

A Special Forces team may move stealthily through the woods, carrying 100-plus-pound rucksacks as they infiltrate into hostile territory to set up a guerrilla force. To meet with coalition fighters, it may be necessary for combat controllers to traverse narrow, ancient mountain paths on horseback. A Ranger direct-action mission may plunge the team into the night, jammed into an equipment-laden Ground Mobility Vehicle, while Delta operators head off to an undisclosed location in a nondescript  Non-Standard Tactical Vehicle (NSTV). A Special Tactic Team riding on ATVs under a moonless sky may move to establish an airhead for follow-on forces. Whatever the route may be, SOF units will travel the distance by horsepower, horse power, or foot.

Sea

Seventy percent of the earth is covered by water. There are seven continents, and 80 percent of all people live near the water surrounding them. From large amphibious operations to covert missions, SOF teams are experienced in using this environment to their advantage. They may helocast from helicopters moving low and slow, jumping into the water and surface swimming to the beach; for a more clandestine approach, teams may infiltrate by submarine, and subsequently via CRRC or SDV. For surface runs, operators can insert using RHIBs and Mark VI Patrol Boats or, for shallow waters, the SWCC will support them with the SOC-R.

Air

The most expedient method of inserting any SOF unit is by air. Mass tactical parachute jumps (mass tac jumps for short) are normally performed by the Rangers when they have to get a large number of soldiers on an objective. For combat operations, drop altitudes may be less than 500 feet above ground level (AGL), as was the case during Operation Urgent Fury. Once on the ground, the unit assembles and proceeds to the target.

Other SOF insertions may require jumping from very high altitudes, using HALO or HAHO techniques (see page 49). Fixed-wing aircraft, such as MC-130 Combat Talons, are well suited for such insertions, though other airplanes as well as helicopters can be used. Landing a large MH-47G Chinook can bring LTATVs or GMVs to the battle, while fast-roping can get an entire ODA on the ground in fifteen seconds. On the ground, the team can depend on CAS from an AC-130 gunship on station orbiting overhead. Additionally, the helicopter gunships of the 160th SOAC (A) are capable of delivering lethality up close and personal should the team call for support.

Desert

Close to one third of the world's land surface is desert, which can be mountainous, rocky, sandy, or covered in dunes. When temperatures can go from 112 degrees Fahrenheit during the day to a chilly 43 degrees at night and where a dust storm can bring 30-mile visibility down to 30 feet or less, operating in an arid environment brings unique challenges and limitations for the SOF fighter. GMVs and helicopter insertions are the norm for units working in desert environments. Hide sites and lighting strikes are hallmarks of missions in these areas.

Arctic

The distance between Russia and Alaska across the Bering Strait at its narrowest point is approximately 53 miles. During the Cold War, this was referred to as the Ice Curtain. In this area, where the average temperature in the winter is −40 degrees, a Russian *Zubr*-class hovercraft with a range of 300 miles and a speed of 55 knots per hour could easily cover that distance within an hour, transporting a complement of over two dozen Spetsnaz troops.

  With the current geopolitical landscape as inhospitable and challenging as the region, SOCOM must be prepared for any contingency, anywhere in the world, including the frigid arctic, subarctic, and mountainous regions where the environment is as unforgiving as the adversary they may face. For this reason, US SOF units are trained in arctic warfare. Units fighting in these regions must know how to snowshoe, ski, use snowmobiles, and mountaineer. They must also be well acquainted with survival skills for cold environments, where hypothermia can be as deadly as a bullet.

Jungle

The jungle environment wraps around the globe like a belt centered on the equator. As with each of the other environments in which SOF teams operate, this landscape presents its own set of rules for survival and can dictate the tactics, techniques, and procedures employed by the units. Jungle regions have high temperatures with humidity upwards of 90 percent. In addition to the enemy, a plethora of poisonous snakes and vicious animals can threaten operators' lives. Whether they are performing a hostage rescue from pirates in Somalia, destroying drug labs in South America, or hunting terrorists in Indonesia, SOF units are ready to carry out their missions with precision and proficiency.

SOF Truths

Humans are more important than Hardware.
Quality is better than Quantity.
Special Operations Forces cannot be mass produced.
Competent Special Operations Forces cannot be created after emergencies occur.
Most Special Operations require non-SOF assistance.

List of All SOF Medal of Honor Recipients

The Medal of Honor is the highest award for valor that can be awarded to a soldier, sailor, airman, or marine for combat action against the enemy. This medal is traditionally presented to the recipient or family member (if the award is posthumous) by the president of the United States in the name of Congress. While some of the recipients have been profiled in this book, the following list encompasses all special operations warriors who have received the Medal of Honor for acting with conspicuous gallantry and intrepidity at the risk of their life, above and beyond the call of duty—some making the ultimate sacrifice.

Korea
Army Master Sgt. Ola L. Mize

Vietnam
Army Sgt. 1st Class Eugene Ashley Jr.*
Army Sgt. Gary B. Beikirch
Army Master Sgt. Roy P. Benavidez
Army Sgt. 1st Class William M. Bryant*
Army Sgt. Brian L. Buker*

Army Staff Sgt. Jon R. Cavaiani
Army Staff Sgt. Drew D. Dix
Army Capt. Roger H. C. Donlon
Air Force Maj. Bernard F. Fisher
Air Force Capt. James P. Fleming
Army 1st Lt. Loren D. Hagen*
Army Master Sgt. Charles E. Hosking Jr.*
Army 1st Lt. Robert L. Howard
Air Force Lt. Col. Joe M. Jackson
Air Force Col. William A. Jones III
Army Spc. 5th Class John J. Kedenburg*
Navy Lt. j.g. (SEAL) Joseph R. Kerrey
Army Spc. 4th Class Robert D. Law*
Air Force Airman 1st Class John L. Levitow
Army Sgt. 1st Class Gary L. Littrell
Army Staff Sgt. Franklin D. Miller
Navy Lt. (SEAL) Thomas R. Norris
Navy Seaman David G. Ouellet*
Army Staff Sgt. Robert J. Pruden*
Army Staff Sgt. Laszlo Rabel*
Army Capt. Ronald E. Ray
Army 1st Lt. George K. Sisler*
Navy Petty Officer (SEAL) Michael E. Thornton
Army Capt. Humbert R. Versace*
Army 1st Lt. Charles Q. Williams
Navy Boatswain's Mate 1st Class James E. Williams
Army Sgt. Gordon D. Yntema*
Army Sgt. 1st Class Fred W. Zabitosky

Somalia
Army Master Sgt. Gary I. Gordon*
Army Sgt. 1st Class Randall D. Shughart*

Afghanistan
Army Staff Sgt. Robert J. Miller*
Navy Lt. (SEAL) Michael P. Murphy*
Army Sgt. 1st Class Leroy A. Petry

Iraq
Petty Officer 2nd Class (SEAL) Michael A. Monsoor*

* Awarded posthumously

Glossary of Acronyms, Initialisms, and Abbreviations

AAF	Army Air Forces	DOS	Department of State
AFSOB	Air Force Special Operations Base	DZ	Drop Zone
		E&E	Evasion and Escape
AFSOC	Air Force Special Operations Component	ELINT	Electronic Intelligence
		FARP	Forward Arming and Refueling Point
ARSOF	Army Special Operations Forces	FID	Foreign Internal Defense
C2	Command and Control	FOB	Forward Operations Base
C3	Command, Control, and Communications	FRIES	Fast Rope Insertion/ Extraction System
C4	Command, Control, Communications, and Computers	GPS	Global Positioning System
		GW	Guerrilla Warfare
		HA	Humanitarian Assistance
C4I	Command, Control, Communications, Computers, and Intelligence	HAHO	High-Altitude High-Opening
		HALO	High-Altitude Low-Opening
CA	Civil Affairs	HE	High Explosive
CAS	Close Air Support	HQ	Headquarters
CCT	Combat Control Team	HUMIT	Human Intelligence
CD	Counter Drug	JSOC	Joint Special Operations Command
CHOP	Change of Operational Control	JSOF	Joint Special Operations Forces
CIA	Central Intelligence Agency		
CinC	Commander in Chief	JSOTF	Joint Special Operations Task Force
CD	Counter Drug		
COMSEC	Communications Security	JTF	Joint Task Force
CONUS	Continental United States	K-9	Spec Op Dogs
COTS	Commercial Off-the-Shelf	LBE	Load Bearing Equipment
CQB	Close Quarter Battle	LIC	Low-Intensity Conflict
CSAR	Combat Search and Rescue	LOC	Lines of Communications
CT	Counterterrorism	LZ	Landing Zone
CWMD	Combating Weapons of Mass Destruction	MAGTF	Marine Air-Ground Task Force
DA	Direct Action	MEU(SOC)	Marine Expeditionary Unit (Special Operations Capable)
DDS	Dry Deck Shelter		
DIA	Defense Intelligence Agency	MISO	Military Information Support Operations
DOD	Department of Defense		

MOLLE	Modular Lightweight Load-Carrying Equipment	PSYOP	Psychological Operations
MOUT	Military Operation Urban Terrain	PSYWAR	Psychological Warfare
		ROE	Rules of Engagement
MSPF	Maritime Special Purpose Force	SAR	Search and Rescue
		SAS	Special Air Service (UK)
MSS	Mission Support Site	SASR	Special Air Service Regiment (Australian)
MTT	Mobile Training Team	SBT	Special Boat Teams
NAVFOR	Navy Forces	SBU	Special Boat Unit
NAVSOC Component	Naval Special Operations	SDV	SEAL Delivery Vehicle
		SEAL	Sea-Air-Land
NAVSOF	USN Special Operations Forces	SF	Special Forces
		SFG	Special Forces Group
NAVSPECWARCOM	Naval Special Warfare Command	SFOB	Special Forces Operations Base
NCA	National Command Authority	SIGINT	Signals Intelligence
		SMU	Special Mission Unit
NCS	National Clandestine Service	SO	Special Operations
		SOAR	Special Operations Aviation Regiment
NOD	Night Optic Device		
NSA	National Security Agency	SOC	Special Operations Command
NSW	Naval Special Warfare		
NSWG	Naval Special Warfare Group	SOF	Special Operations Forces
		SOS	Special Operations Squadron
NSWTG	Naval Special Warfare Task Group	SOSB	Special Operations Support Battalion
NSWTU	Naval Special Warfare Task Unit	SOWT	Special Operations Weather Team
NSWU	Naval Special Warfare Unit		
NVG	Night Vision Goggle	SWCC	Special Warfare Combatant-Craft Crewman
OCONUS	Outside Continental United States	SR	Special Reconnaissance
ODA	Operational Detachment-Alpha	STS	Special Tactics Squadron
		STT	Special Tactics Team
OGA	Other Government Agency	TACON	Tactical Control
OOTW	Operations Other Than War	TTP	Tactics, Techniques, and Procedures
OPCON	Operational Control		
OPCOM	Operational Command	USASOC	United States Army Special Operations Command
OPLAN	Operation Plan		
OPSEC	Operations Security	USSOCOM	United States Special Operations Command
PALS	Pouch Attachment Ladder System	UW	Unconventional Warfare
PJ	Para Jumper—Pararescueman	WMD	Weapon of Mass Destruction

Glossary of Terms

Antiterrorism (AT): Defensive measures taken to reduce the vulnerability of individuals and property to terrorism.

Clandestine Operation: Activities sponsored or conducted by governmental departments or agencies in such a way as to assure secrecy or concealment. Clandestine operations differ from covert operations (see below) in that the emphasis is placed on concealment of the operation rather than on concealment of the identity of sponsor. In special operations, an activity may be both covert and clandestine and may focus equally on operational considerations and intelligence-related activities.

Close Air Support (CAS): Air action against hostile targets in close proximity to friendly forces, requiring detailed integration of each air mission with the fire and movement of those forces.

Counterproliferation: Activities taken to counter the spread of dangerous military capabilities, allied technologies, and/or know-how, especially weapons of mass destruction and ballistic missile delivery systems.

Counterterrorism (CT): Offensive measures taken to prevent, deter, and respond to terrorism.

Covert Operations: Operations planned and executed so as to conceal the identity of or permit plausible denial by the sponsor.

Direct Action (DA) Mission: In special operations, a specified act involving operations of an overt, covert, clandestine, or low-visibility nature conducted primarily by a sponsoring power's special operations forces in hostile or denied areas.

Door Kicker: See Shooter.

Exfiltration (Exfil): The removal of personnel or units from areas under enemy control.

Humanitarian Assistance: Assistance provided by Department of Defense forces, as directed by appropriate authority, in the aftermath of natural or manmade disasters to help reduce conditions that present a serious threat to life and property. Assistance provided by Untied States forces is limited in scope and duration and is designed to supplement efforts of civilian authorities that have primary responsibility for providing such assistance.

Infiltration (Infil): The movement through or into an area or territory occupied by either friendly or enemy troops or organizations. The movement is made, either by small groups or by individuals, at extended or irregular intervals. When used in connection with the enemy, contact is avoided.

Insurgency: An organized movement aimed at the overthrow of a constituted government through the use of subversion and armed conflict.

Internal Defense: The full range of measures taken by a government to free and protect its society from subversion, lawlessness, and insurgency.

Interoperability: The ability of systems, units, or forces to provide services to and accept services from other systems, units, or forces and/or use the services so exchanged to enable them to operate effectively together.

Low-Intensity Conflict: Political-military confrontation between contending states or groups below conventional war and above routine, peaceful competition among states, frequently involving protracted struggles of competing principles and ideologies. Low-intensity conflict ranges from subversion to the use of armed force and is waged using a combination of political, economic, informational, and military instruments. Low-intensity conflicts are often localized, generally in the developing countries, but contain regional and global security implications.

Mission: An organization's statement of reason for being and what it aims to accomplish.

National Command Authorities (NCA): The president and the secretary of defense or their duly deputized alternates or successors. The term signifies constitutional authority to direct the US Armed Forces in their execution of military action.

Objectives: Specific actions to be achieved in a specified time period. Accomplishment will indicate progress toward achieving the goals.

Operator: See Shooter.

Psychological Operations (PSYOP): Planned operations to convey selected information and indicators to foreign audiences to influence their emotions, motives, and objective reasoning—and, ultimately, the behavior of foreign governments, organizations, groups, and individuals. The purpose of psychological operations is to induce or reinforce foreign attitudes and behavior favorable to the originator's objectives.

Shooter: Special Operations Forces trooper, e.g., Army Special Forces, Navy SEAL, Army Ranger, MARSOC, Delta, SAS.

Special Reconnaissance (SR): Reconnaissance and surveillance actions conducted by Special Operations Forces to obtain or verify, by visual observation or other collection methods, information concerning the capabilities, intentions, and activities of an actual or potential enemy or to secure data concerning the meteorological, hydrographic, or geographic characteristics of a particular area. SR includes target acquisition, area assessment, and post-strike reconnaissance.

Strategy: Methods, approaches, or specific moves taken to implement and attain an objective.

Credits

Index